Melvin Watson

ACTS
an exposition

ACTS
an exposition
Volume I Chapters 1-8

W.A. Criswell

ZONDERVAN
PUBLISHING HOUSE OF THE ZONDERVAN CORPORATION
GRAND RAPIDS, MICHIGAN 49506

ACTS: AN EXPOSITION, VOLUME 1
Copyright © 1978 by W.A. Criswell
Grand Rapids, Michigan

Library of Congress Cataloging in Publication Data

Criswell, Wallie A
    Acts, and exposition.

    1. Bible. N.T. Acts—Criticism, interpretation, etc.   I. Title.
BS2625.2.C74   226'.6'06   78-13525
ISBN 0-310-22880-8 (v. 1)

Printed in the United States of America

To

PASTOR JOE JOHNSON AND OUR SILENT FRIENDS MINISTRY,

*who uplift our hearts by their
devotion and love for the Savior,
and who make untold contribution
to the life of our dear church.*

Contents

Foreword

With this volume the outstanding pastor of Dallas's First Baptist Church begins an exposition based upon Luke's history, the Acts of the Apostles. This series of messages elucidating the exciting story of the rapidly growing number of those who acknowledged the faith of the Christ will appear in a number of volumes, of which this is the first. Physicians, attorneys, educators, a host of other professionals and businessmen, and an amazing mixture of common people concentrate their attention on the Scriptures and alternately laugh and weep as the eternal verities of the text are explicated.

Among those who evidence the most profound interest in the expository messages of Dr. Criswell are the young theologues who attend the Criswell Center for Biblical Studies, the Bible college and graduate school sponsored by the First Baptist Church. More than five-hundred of these men and women enroll in this school annually. Many serve as pastors and staff members of other local congregations. However, a multitude of these young prophets take advantage of sitting at the feet of a man who believes that the Scriptures are a sure word from God, an infallible and inerrant revelation.

The sermons in this volume demonstrate the exegetical, theological, and homiletical combination which has made former volumes of expository sermons so popular among evangelicals. Of special note is the pastor's theology of the person and work of the Holy Spirit. Deeply sensitive to the work of the Holy Spirit, Dr. Criswell avoids the errors so frequently associated with the doctrine in the present age while lucidly

9

emphasizing the crucial ministries of the Spirit in evangelism and regeneration. Special emphasis is placed on the roll of the Spirit in directing the course of development of the fledgling church.

Notable also are the sermons focusing on the events which transpired on the Day of Pentecost. Messages on "The Price of Pentecost," "The Miracles of Pentecost," and "The Pattern of Pentecost" emphasize the pivotal nature of the event that provided the impetus for worldwide missionary outreach. A unique look at the significance of our Lord's ascension is also the subject of one sermon.

Perhaps the zenith of eloquence and theological insight is achieved in the three moving sermons on the witness and martyrdom of Stephen. Based on Tennyson's poem, the sermon entitled "The Smiting of God's Glory" is a magnificent exposition of the martyrdom of this godly layman. Dr. Criswell has said that the preparation of this sermon blessed him personally more than any other. Those of us who anticipated every word can testify to the impact of that sermon.

The administration and faculty of the Criswell Center joins the membership of the First Baptist Church in Dallas in welcoming the publication of the first volume of sermons on Acts by Dr. Criswell. As you read them, we pray that God will make them as much a benediction to your life as they have been to our lives as we listened to them Sunday by Sunday.

Paige Patterson, President
Criswell Center for Biblical Studies

ACTS
an exposition

1

Great Godly Expectations

The former treatise have I made, O Theophilus, of all that Jesus began both to do and teach. (Acts 1:1)

When the author of Acts refers to a previous book in his words, "a former treatise," we know that he has written another book. It can easily be identified because it also is dedicated to and addressed to Theophilus:

It seemed good to me also, having had perfect understanding of all things from the very first, to write unto thee in order, most excellent Theophilus. (Luke 1:3)

The author refers to Theophilus by using the Greek word *kratistos* which means "most excellent," a man of great and noble stature, of affluence and means.

In the Roman Empire the people were divided into different classes. There were plebes (the common people), there were knights (the people of affluence, dignity, high social standing, and power), and in the highest accolades of government there were senators. *Kratistos*, "most excellent," is the same epithet used for Felix, the Roman governor of Judaea, found later in the Book of Acts, as is used to describe Theophilus.

Evidently Theophilus had become a convert to the Christian faith because his name is a beautiful Christian name which means "the friend of God." Tradition says that he was a noble man who had a slave named Luke who was a doctor, a Greek servant, who won Theophilus to the Lord and to the faith. Out of love for the beloved physician Theophilus gave Luke manumission—he was made free. In turn, out of gratitude for what the noble Theophilus had done for him, Luke wrote

13

his beautiful Gospel, one of the most beautiful pieces of literature in the world.

Luke wrote for Theophilus an additional book, a continuing story of our Lord called the "Acts of the Apostles." Luke is easily identified in the book because there are peculiarities by which he writes that are indicative of his personality.

People can be identified by their own little idiosyncrasies. A writer's works will reveal literary characteristics which are peculiar or special to him. It is so with this man. There are about fifty words or expressions found in his writings not found elsewhere in the Bible. They are scattered throughout the third Gospel of Luke and throughout the Book of Acts. When one looks at those peculiar words that only Luke uses he will find that many of them are medical words. Whoever wrote the Gospel of Luke and the Book of Acts was a physician, which makes it doubly easy for us to identify him.

In Colossians 4:14 Paul refers to Luke as "the beloved physician." In Philemon 1 Paul refers to Luke as his "fellow-labourer." In 2 Timothy 4:11 Paul writes, "Only Luke is with me," after having described his friends who had scattered or had, like Demas, forsaken him. Paul was in the Mammertine dungeon facing inevitable execution under the emperor Nero, and only Luke was with him.

Luke became associated with Paul in Acts 16:10 beginning with the "we" sections. Luke joined Paul in Troas when Paul saw the vision of the man from Macedonia appealing for help. In the three years or more of Paul's imprisonment in Caesarea, Luke saw and visited with the first witnesses in the Christian faith. He wrote about John, the son of Zechariah and Elizabeth, who became known as John the Baptist. He talked with Mary the mother of Jesus and wrote the beautiful stories of Jesus' infancy. His intimate descriptions of the births of John and Jesus were written as only a physician could write.

Almost certainly Luke was a Gentile. In Colossians 4 Paul divides the Jews from the Gentiles, naming those of the Jewish faith, "of the circumcision." Then he names three persons of the Gentile world, one of whom is Epaphras, one is Demas, and the other is Luke, the beloved physician, the only Gentile writer in all the sixty-six books of the Bible.

THE OUTLINE

The Lord gave John the sainted apostle the outline for the Book of Revelation in the first chapter of his Apocalypse. The Lord said:

Write the things which thou hast seen, and the things which are, and the things which shall be hereafter. (Rev. 1:19)

John faithfully followed that outline. First, he wrote the things that he had seen, the vision of the glorified Lord Jesus. Then he wrote the things that are, the seven churches of Asia, which encompass the story of the Christian dispensation to the consummation of the age, to the return of our Lord. Then he wrote of the things after the rapture of the church beginning at chapter 4. He follows that through chapter 22 to the great eternal age by which God will bring to Himself the righteousness that shall fill the whole earth and universe.

So in the Book of Acts we see the Lord's outline for this book. His followers are to be witnesses unto Him in Jerusalem, in all Judaea, in Samaria, and to the uttermost parts of the earth. The Lord presents this great program and outlines its expansion, and Luke follows that outline in writing the book. First is the dispensation of the Holy Spirit poured out upon the disciples in Jerusalem. Then is the evangelization of Judaea in the villages, the highways, the byways. Expanding further the gospel is preached to the halfbreeds, the Samaritans in Samaria. Then presentation of the gospel is made to a proselyte of the temple, a Jew converted out of the Gentile world, the treasurer of Ethiopia under Candace the queen. Luke then follows the preaching of the gospel to a Gentile who is a proselyte of the temple, that is, he forsook his heathen idols and accepted the law of Moses but was still a Gentile. The gospel is preached thus to Cornelius, the centurion of the Roman army in Caesarea, the capital of Judaea. Then the author follows in Acts 11 the preaching of the gospel by the Greek-speaking Jews to the Greek idolators in Antioch. To the amazement of all who knew of the work of the Lord, those idolators came out of their Greek heathenism directly into the Christian faith. Heretofore everyone had come to the faith through Judaism, but the converts in Antioch came directly from their idolatry into the glorious life of the gospel of the Son of God. So amazing was it that they were called "Christians" first in Antioch. It created a repercussion in the entire Christian world. We read in Acts 15 that upon the completion of the first missionary journey, after the Holy Spirit called Paul and Barnabas into the Greco-Roman world, the first Jerusalem conference was held. It was here that the Holy Spirit guided the disciples and apostles in the fact that a man could become a Christian without first becoming a Jew. No matter how lost he was in the deep darkness of heathenism or paganism, he could accept Christ and be saved and be a child of God. We finally see the gospel message brought to the eternal city of Rome. Luke follows the outline that the Lord gave him: the gospel is preached in Jerusalem, in Judaea, in Samaria, then beyond to the uttermost parts of the world.

THE TITLE

Notice the name of the book. In our Bible we have "The Acts of the Apostles." The oldest and finest manuscript that we possess, the Sinaiticus, written in the fourth century A.D., entitles the book "The Acts." I think that is the best name, for it is not just "The Acts of the Apostles," but it is also "The Acts of the Holy Spirit." More specifically it presents "The Acts of the Lord Jesus Christ" which Jesus did directing His work in earth from heaven.

The text begins, "The former treatise have I made, O Theophilus, of all that Jesus began both to do and teach." And that is the gospel, for it tells what Jesus began to do and to teach in the days of His flesh here on earth. Dr. Luke says, "But now we shall follow the acts and doings of our Lord from heaven." What the Lord did in the earth is presented in the third Gospel, the Gospel of Luke. What He does from heaven is the acts of the Lord directing us from glory. We find that the book presents a continuity of what the Lord is doing from heaven of that which He began on earth.

For example, in Acts 2 we read that the Holy Spirit of God was poured out from His gracious hands, a gift from the Lord in glory. The second chapter ends, "And the Lord added to the church daily such as should be saved." What was done was accomplished under the supervision of the Lord from heaven. It is the Lord who adds to His church.

In Acts 3 we read that it is the Lord's name that heals the lame man laid daily at the gate called "Beautiful" in the temple. In Acts 7 we notice that it is the Lord Jesus who stood, who rose to receive the spirit of His first martyr, Stephen. Everywhere else in the Bible the Lord is seated at the right hand of the Majesty, but in this instance, when the first martyr died in earth, the Lord stood to receive the spirit of His saint. It is the Lord in heaven who is guiding His work in earth.

There is no formal ending to the Book of Acts. It follows the story up to the point at which Luke is writing, then it is cut off. There is no ending, no consummation, no reaching out to some marvelous climax. It just stops. The reason why there is no ending is that the story goes on. Our Lord is not done nor will He be until the end of the age.

The story begins in about A.D. 30 and stops in about A.D. 64, a period of about thirty-four years. It ends with the hero in prison, then it just stops. That reminds me of the old serials at the movies that told the story, then left the hero hanging by a shoestring over a four-thousand-foot cliff. That meant there was another chapter, another story. You returned to see what happened to the hero hanging by a shoestring over the cliff. The Book of Acts is like that in that it has no ending, and the reason for it is that God is not done, our Lord is still working, and the great kingdom movement proceeds on and on until the end of the age. The only thing that Jesus finished in His life was the plan of salvation, when He bowed His head on the cross and cried, "It is finished."

HIS GREAT EXPECTATIONS OF US

The apostle Paul writes an amazing word in Colossians 1:14. He says we are to complete what is lacking in the sufferings of our Lord. Does he mean that the sacrifice, the Atonement was not sufficient to save us from our sins? No, what the apostle is saying is that there must be a continuation of the sacrifice and the suffering. The witness and the testimony must continue on. I have a part, Paul says, in the continuing ministry of our Lord who presides over the work from heaven. We also must take our part as an assignment, a mandate in the Lord's ministry, for it is God's work from heaven in the earth today and it grows and grows.

One of the most astonishing things our Lord will ever say to us is that when He is gone and is seated at the right hand of the Majesty on high, greater works shall be done in earth by us than by Him in the days of His flesh. For example, in John 14:12 he writes, "Verily, verily, I say unto you, He that believeth on me, the works that I do shall he do also; and greater works than these shall he do; because I go unto my Father." The greatest work of the Christian faith, the Lord says, has not been done in "what Jesus began to do and to teach," but it will be continuing on in the centuries that follow after.

John 15:8 reads, "Herein is my Father glorified, that ye bear much fruit; so shall ye be my disciples." As Jesus began it in the days of His flesh in the Gospel of Luke, so He is continuing now in His deeds, His works, His actions, His acts in the earth, as He presides over the work from heaven.

Therefore, the Lord is in His church and is in the ministries of His church. It is God's work that we are seeking to do in earth as He guides and encourages and presides over us in heaven. The head of our church is the Lord and the moving Spirit in our church is the Spirit of Jesus. The mandates that we carry out are heavenly mandates. The work that we seek to do is under His gracious and nail-pierced hands. The ministries of our Lord are the ministries that He does in the church through us.

Let me name two or three things that Jesus has been doing through the years and now does through us:

First, is the ministry of our Lord in His church when His hands reach out to bless and encourage in sorrow and death. As it was in the days of His flesh, so He works in the ministries of the church, blessing and encouraging and inspiring. You may have seen or heard about the little English church, Stoke-Pogis. It is surrounded by and sits in the midst of a little cemetery, and almost all English parishes are like that. Thomas Gray in the 1700s wrote a most meaningful poem entitled, "Eulogy Written in a Country Churchyard." You see, the saints who died in the faith wanted to be buried as close to the door of the church as they possibly could, for it is in the ministries of the church that our Lord lays His hand of blessing and hope upon our people just as He did in the days of His flesh.

When my father and mother died we had the services in a little church, and we felt the Lord's presence in our midst just as sweet and comforting and full of hope as it was in the days of His flesh. He comforted Mary and Martha. He promised our own resurrection because of the victory He had won over sin and death and the grave. And it continues on. There is no end to the Book of Acts. There is a twenty-ninth chapter, there is a sixty-ninth chapter, there is a one-hundred-ninth chapter, and it shall continue on chapter after chapter to the end of the age.

Second, Jesus continues His sweet ministry in His church today. He ministers through His church on the mission field, in evangelization, preaching the Good News to those who sit in darkness and in the shadow of death. What a precious and beautiful hope we bring, we whose feet are anointed with the gospel of peace, the message of salvation! A beautiful experience I had recently illustrates this point. It took place in Buenos Aires, Argentina. I was preaching in the downtown Baptist Church, and I was deeply impressed with the pastor of that church. For one thing, every girl would have loved him because he is tall, dark, and handsome. He also is brilliantly educated. He has a doctor's degree in medicine, a doctor's degree in psychiatry, and a doctor's degree in theology. He presides over his church with such grace and gentility. He is absolutely one of the most charming, most gifted, most educated young ministers to be found in our whole Southern Baptist communion.

When I came back to the Southern Baptist Seminary in Buenos Aires I mentioned to the professors in the seminary how impressed I was with that young man. The faculty members said, "You do not know where he came from, do you?" I said, "No." They said, "This afternoon you were a guest in the home of an aged missionary with whom you had tea. You did not know, but years ago that missionary was in a marketplace in Buenos Aires. One day there came to the marketplace a poor, bedraggled woman who had a little baby in her arms. That missionary won the poor disheveled woman to the Lord. The brilliant young minister who impressed you so much was the little baby that the poor woman held in her arms."

I am the first to admit that there are people who are poor and could be called the flotsam and jetsam of human life. But God is not done. He is still raising up Spurgeons, Moodys, and Truetts. He is still saving souls. The Book of Acts continues on, and when we preach the gospel in these places that are so down and out, how do we know but that out of it will come another Chrysostom, another Wesley, a Savanarola, or a Spurgeon? I think it pleases God as He presides over His church that we do it.

The third ministry of our Lord continuing in His church has to do with the child in the home, in the church, and in the school.

Recently I was preaching in New York City to the association of our Southern Baptist churches in that great city. Between the morning and afternoon sessions I walked down the street with one of the pastors in New York City. Our meeting place was one block away from Bowery Street, where humanity dumps refuse of the human race. As I walked down Bowery Street with the young minister I turned my head to talk to him, and suddenly he grabbed my arm and yanked me over. I looked to see why he had done that, and there on the sidewalk in front of me, where I would have stepped on him had the minister not jerked me out of the way, was a poor, miserable, fallen wretch. Part of him was in a doorway and part of him was out on the sidewalk, unspeakably miserable, dirty, and fallen. We have a Bowery Mission, and my heart cannot but thank God for the ministers of Christ who work in that mission doing what they can to help those fallen and miserable men. But there is something better, far better. It is better to keep the man from falling than it is to try to minister to him after he has squandered his life away.

I remember a recommendation that once came from our deacons: "We recommend to the pastor, to the staff, to the deacons, and to the church that we reemphasize our Sunday school and our teaching ministries in the church. It is our Sunday school that we use to visit the lost. It is our Sunday school that is our outreach ministry. It is the Sunday school by which we seek to oversubscribe our giving program. It is the Sunday school that we use to teach the Word of God. We beg our pastor and our people to reemphasize our teaching ministries, to build up our Sunday school, to give it first place and first emphasis in the life of our church."

It is strange how things come to your mind. Almost stepping on the poor, fallen wretch on Bowery Street, I thought about the committee's recommendation to build up our Sunday school. Rather than minister to men when their lives are ruined, why not try to get them for God before they fall.

THE AMBULANCE DOWN IN THE VALLEY

'Twas a dangerous cliff, as they freely confessed,
Though to walk near its crest was so pleasant,
But over its terrible edge there had slipped,
A duke and full many a peasant.

So the people said something would have to be done,
But their projects did not at all tally.
Some said, "Put a fence around the edge of the cliff,"
Some, "An ambulance down in the valley."

But the cry for the ambulance carried the day,
For it spread through the neighboring city.
A fence may be useful or not, it is true,
But each heart became moved with pity,

For those who slipped over that dangerous cliff;
And the dwellers on highway and alley
Gave pounds and gave pence not to put up a fence,
But an ambulance down in the valley.

Then an old sage remarked, "It's a marvel to me
That people give far more attention
To repairing the results than to stopping the cause,
When they'd much better aim at prevention.

Let us stop at its source all this hurt," cried he.
"Come, neighbors and friends, let us rally.
If the cliff we will fence, we might almost dispense
With the ambulance down in the valley."

Better guide well the young than reclaim them when old;
For the voice of true wisdom is calling.
To rescue the fallen is good, but 'tis best
To prevent them when young from falling.

Better build in their hearts the love of the Lord,
Than to deliver from dungeon or galley.
Better put a strong fence 'round the top of the cliff,
Than an ambulance down in the valley.

Ministering in the name of our Lord, let us put our arms around our children and young people, and let us pray that the Spirit of Jesus will work with us in winning them to the faith, in guiding them in the nurture and love of the Lord that they might grow up strong and tall for God and that we do not stumble upon them as fallen wretches in a bowery. That is why I think every one of us who loves Jesus should say, "Pastor, put my name down among those who love the Lord, who support His cause in the earth, who, with whatever talents God may bestow upon us, minister before His throne, in His name, and by His grace."

2

The Greatest of the Promises

And being assembled together with them, commanded them that they should not depart from Jerusalem, but wait for the promise of the Father which, saith he, ye have heard of me. (Acts 1:4)

In all of the Bible there are two continuing and tremendous promises. First, there is a Savior who is coming. The repetition of that refrain is like a recurring theme in a great symphony. The announcement that a Savior is coming is a refrain heard throughout the Bible. After the fall of Adam and Eve, God says that the seed of the woman "shall bruise Satan's head" (Gen. 3:15). Genesis 49:10 reads:

The sceptre shall not depart from Judah, nor a lawgiver from between his feet, until Shiloh come; and unto him shall the gathering of the people be.

Isaiah prophesies:

Therefore the Lord himself shall give you a sign; Behold, a virgin shall conceive, and bear a son, and shall call his name Immanuel. (Isa. 7:14)

For unto us a child is born, unto us a son is given: and the government shall be upon his shoulder: and his name shall be called Wonderful, Counselor, The mighty God, The everlasting Father, The Prince of Peace. (Isa. 9:6)

Someone is coming. The benedictory closing of the Apocalypse states:

He which testifieth these things saith, Surely I come quickly, Amen. Even so, come, Lord Jesus. (Rev. 22:20)

THE SECOND CONTINUING PROMISE

The second continuing promise given by the Father in heaven is that there is to be an outpouring of the Spirit of God. Joel 2:28 says:

22

And it shall come to pass afterward, that I will pour out my spirit upon all flesh; and your sons and your daughters shall prophesy, your old men shall dream dreams, your young men shall see visions.

It is this prophecy to which the Savior refers when He says, "Wait for the promise of the Father."

Why does the Lord call the outpouring of the Spirit "the promise of the Father"? We read in Luke 24:49:

And, behold, I send the promise of my Father upon you: but tarry ye in the city of Jerusalem, until ye be endued with power from on high.

He constantly refers to the outpouring as the "promise of the Father."

In reading the Gospel of John it is apparent why He uses that descriptive word concerning the coming of the Holy Spirit. John 14:16, 26 says:

And I will pray the Father, and he shall give you another Comforter, that he may abide with you for ever;

Even the Spirit of truth. . .

But the Comforter, which is the Holy Ghost, whom the Father will send in my name, he shall teach you all things, and bring all things to your remembrance, whatsoever I have said unto you.

The Greek word for Comforter is *parakletos*. *Para* means "alongside, parallel." *Kaleo* means "call." Therefore the Greek word means "the one called alongside." In many versions of the Bible that Greek word is spelled out and used as such because it is untranslatable into English. It is a tremendous word, and there is no English word counterpart that holds the meaning.

We learn, therefore, that the outpouring of the Spirit is an ascension gift. It is something that must have happened in heaven before the foundation of the world. When the Lord offered Himself to die for our sins, God promised the Son that He would give Him an ascension gift after the Atonement, after the suffering of the cross, after the burial and Resurrection, after His return to heaven. Christ Jesus had the promise of the Father to pour out upon the world the fullness of His presence and of His Spirit. This is the promise of the Father. Someone said that out of all the more than three thousand promises in the Bible, there is only one that is called "*the* promise of the Father." Why is that so signally emphasized in the Word of the Lord? I think we can find an obvious answer.

THE PROMISE FOR STRENGTH AND COMFORT

The promise of the Father, the ascension gift of our Lord, what He did for us when He ascended into heaven in pouring out the fullness of His Spirit, was for our strengthening and comfort. The Lord said to His apostles in John 14:18 when He went away, "I will not leave you comfortless: I will come to you." How does He come to us? This is the context of John 14:16: "I will pray the Father, and he shall give you another Comforter, that he may abide with you for ever; even the Spirit of truth." He comes to us in the presence of His Spirit.

He said in John 16:6-7:

> But because I have said these things unto you, sorrow hath filled your heart. Nevertheless I tell you the truth; It is expedient for you that I go away: for if I go not away, the Comforter will not come unto you; but if I depart, I will send him unto you.

God's presence is with us. Jesus is with us in His Spirit. He is present to strengthen us, to encourage us.

Many Christians through the years can witness to that truth in their experiences. I read one time that a missionary had been seized by cannibals and bound in a thatched hut. Outside was a roaring fire, which was heating a caldron of water in which the cannibals planned to boil and eat the missionary. During the night, while the fire was roaring and the water was getting hotter, the missionary was able to undo his bonds and escape through the thatched hut. He hid in the top of a tall jungle tree. When the cannibals found that he had escaped, they lit torches and searched everywhere through the forest for him. At any moment they could have found him, but he was safe in the top of the tree. In speaking of this experience the missionary said: "I never felt the presence of God so close, so near, so blessedly real as I did that night in the top of that tree, knowing that at any moment they might find me. I wish I could go back to that hour and be back in the top of that tree again if I could just experience the ecstatic closeness of the presence of God as I did then."

In Hong Kong, China, I was with Dr. T. M. Rankin who was the Executive Secretary of our Foreign Mission Board. We were in a little car on the backside of the island. As we drove along he pointed to a place and said: "In that place I was incarcerated in a concentration camp all through the years of World War II. When the Japanese came and seized Hong Kong, I was arrested and interned in that camp. When I was marched into the concentration camp with a Japanese soldier on each side of me I had no idea whether I would live or die. What lay before me could be starvation, disease, and maybe even death. But I never had the sense of the presence of God with me as I did that day when I was marched into the camp with a Japanese soldier on each side of me." Jesus said, "I will be with you until the end of the age. I will not leave you comfortless."

David Livingstone practiced an unusual course of action which some others also practice. When a decision was to be made, David Livingstone would always take his Bible, pray, then let the pages open where they would. The first verse that he read he believed to be God's answer to his prayer.

David Livingstone had strong and unwavering faith. He was the first white man ever to go down the Zambezi River. As he was going down the river, discovering its length and breadth, the friendly natives there said: "You must proceed no further, for there are cannibals down the river. You cannot escape with your life if you go on." David Livingstone took it to the Lord in prayer. After he laid it before God, He placed his Bible on edge, then let it fall open. He looked and the verse that he saw was Matthew 28:20, "And, lo, I am with you alway, even unto the end of the world." David Livingstone said, "Arise, let us go." That is the promise of the Father. That is the Spirit of Jesus with us to comfort us, to strengthen us, to help us, to stand by us, as God's advocate and intercessor.

THE PROMISE FOR POWER

The promise of the Father is for power. Second Corinthians 3 is a magnificent contrast from the pen of the apostle Paul between what he calls the ministration of the Spirit and the ministration of the letter. He calls the ministration of the Spirit, life—the quickening power of God. He calls the ministration of the letter, death. By this he means that the letter of the law, the Word is mere cold print, is without quickening power. Then he speaks of the glory of the ministration of the Spirit. If God is in it, the Word has ability and power to save us. It is like a man filled with the Spirit. Separate the Spirit from him and he is a corpse. The Word of the Lord also is a cold, dead letter until it is quickened by the power of the presence of God in it. It is like Ezekiel's wheel and the wheel in the wheels. They were lifted up by the Spirit of God who lived and moved in the wheels. In that way the Spirit of God takes the Word and makes it powerful to the convicting of our sins, to the saving of our souls, to the regeneration of our lives. This is the promise of the Father

in the ministry of the Word. It is a work of the Spirit of God.
It is the Spirit who convicts us. It is the Spirit who regenerates us. It is the Spirit who sanctifies and cleanses us. It is the Spirit who enables us to do God's work in the earth. It is the Spirit who glorifies us, who shall raise us from the dead. It was the Holy Spirit who raised our Lord from among the dead. It is the same Holy Spirit who shall call us to life from the dust of the ground. For us to attempt the work of God without the presence and the power of the Holy Spirit of God is futile and our efforts would be in vain. A man can pray, but he is saying words unless the Spirit makes intercession for him with groanings which cannot be uttered. A man can preach, but he can preach without power, without the Spirit helping him and enabling him. A choir can sing, but they can also sing without unction and without the presence of God. That is why it is so important for the choir to pray, as well as to practice their notes and lyrics and melodies. It is God in us that makes the difference. Without Him, it is a dead service—it is ritual, it is habit, it is sterile.

After I was called to be pastor I held a revival meeting in a little country church some years ago. It blessed my heart to be with that pastor and his sweet people. That country pastor, who was so uneducated academically, knew God and the truth of the Lord. He was taught of Jesus. He said that he had been preaching without power. No souls were being saved and his own heart was dry. He said that he went to his room, closed the door, fell before God, and with a burdened heart and many tears cried for the Lord to help him and to stand by him. He said the Lord came into his soul in a flame. Then he described how the Lord was with him in his pulpit and blessed him with souls. When he told me that, I knew every syllable of the way. Without the Spirit of the Lord working with you and standing by the preacher, preaching is an exercise, just loudness of speech, just multiplication of sounds and syllables. Jeremiah 23:29 says: "Is not my word like as a fire? saith the LORD; and like a hammer that breaketh the rock in pieces?" The promise of the Father is the promise of the power of the Spirit with us in the work.

THE PROMISE FOR TRUTH

The promise of the Father is for truth. He calls the Holy Spirit of Jesus the Spirit of Truth. All ultimate truth we learn from His teaching. This world is literally a maze of deception, false religions, false cults, false ideologies, false philosophies, false directions, and false doctrines. It is the curse of the world that it is filled with untruth, deception, and lying spirits. When one reads the Bible he will find [when he is sensitive to the truth of God] that one of the things the man of God wrestled with all through the centuries of the old and new covenants was the lying prophet, the deceiving spirit.

In the Old Testament the deceiving spirits sometimes represented heathen gods such as the prophets of Baal, who cried to that false deity on top of Mt. Carmel in the days of apostasy when Elijah sought to bring the people back to the true Jehovah. Paul, in 1 Corinthians 10, says that all of the gods that the Greco-Romans worshiped were demons. How they deceived the multitudes of the people!

The true prophet of God had to wrestle with and confront the false prophet who came forward saying that he was delivering a message in the name of the one true God Jehovah. Do you remember the story of Micaiah and Zedekiah? Micaiah said to Ahab: "The Lord hath said, 'This battle is lost. Your life is lost. You will not come back alive'." Zedekiah, the false prophet, walked over to Micaiah and slapped him on the face and said, "Which way went the Spirit of the LORD from me to speak unto thee?" Micaiah said, "Behold, thou shalt see on that day, when thou shalt go into an inner chamber to hide thyself . . . If [Ahab] return in peace, then hath not the LORD spoken by me" (2 Chron. 18:23,24,27). A man drew an arrow without aiming it and let it fly. It entered between the joints of Ahab's harness and his life's blood flowed out in the chariot. When God speaks, almost always a false prophet will deny it.

Read the story of Jeremiah and Hananiah in Jeremiah 28. Through the streets of Jerusalem the prophet Jeremiah wore a yoke, a sign of the word of the Lord that Nebuchadnezzar would come and carry the people away into Babylon. Hananiah the false prophet came to Jeremiah, broke the yoke from off his neck, and said, "Thus saith the Lord, Nebuchadnezzar will never come nigh this city and these people shall never be carried away into Babylon." Jeremiah said: "You will see the truth of the word when Nebuchadnezzar destroys the city and its temple and carries the people away into captivity. As for you, Hananiah, before the year ends, thou shalt surely die." That was the punishment for misleading the people of God.

Our Lord in Matthew 24:24 said: "For there shall arise false Christs, and false prophets." In 1 Corinthians 14 the apostle Paul writes of those who bring discord, disorder, and disunion into the house of God. The apostle Peter, in 2 Peter 2, warns about false prophets who appear in the church. In 1 John 4:1 we read, "Beloved, believe not every spirit, but try the spirits whether they are of God: because many false prophets are gone out into the world."

How am I to know the truth of God? Our Lord said that who wills to do His will shall know of His doctrine. If I come before the Lord with a humble and teachable spirit, and if I lay before God His inspired and infallible Word and I pray, "Spirit of Jesus, teach me Thy truth," He will not fail. He is the Spirit of truth. There will be the witness in your heart that this is the Word of God and this is the meaning and the message of the Spirit. We have this promise of the Father.

THE PROMISE FOR SALVATION

The promise of the Father, the presence of the Holy Spirit, is for our salvation. Our Lord said that the Holy Spirit will not speak of Himself, He will not glorify Himself. When I see people who greatly magnify the so-called "gifts of the Spirit," and all the things that are a part of such teaching, I often think of the word of our Lord: "He will not speak of Himself. He will not call attention to Himself, but He will glorify Me, for He will testify of Me." If the Spirit of the Lord is in our presence, if the Spirit of Jesus is in the congregation, then our Lord is magnified.

That is why the Bible speaks so seriously concerning the repudiation of the witness of the Spirit of God. In the days of our Lord they said: "He does not have the Spirit of God. He has the spirit of a demon by which He casts out demons." The Lord said:

> Verily I say unto you, All sins shall be forgiven unto the sons of men, and blasphemies wherewith soever they shall blaspheme:
> But he that shall blaspheme against the Holy Ghost hath never forgiveness, but is in danger of eternal damnation:
> Because they said, he hath an unclean spirit. (Mark 3:28-30)

When the Holy Spirit of God witnesses to the deity, the Atonement, and the Saviorhood of our Lord, and a man says that is not so, he commits an unforgivable sin. The author of Hebrews states it this way:

> For if we sin wilfully after that we have received the knowlege of the truth, there remaineth no more sacrifice for sins,
> But a certain fearful looking for of judgment and fiery indignation, which shall devour the adversaries.
> He that despised Moses' law died without mercy under two or three witnesses:
> Of how much sorer punishment, suppose ye, shall he be thought worthy, who hath trodden under foot the Son of God, and hath counted the blood of the

covenant, wherewith he was sanctified, an unholy thing, and hath done despite unto the Spirit of grace? For we know him that hath said, Vengeance belongeth unto me, I will recompense, saith the Lord. And again, The Lord shall judge his people. It is a fearful thing to fall into the hands of the living God. (Heb. 10:26-29)

When the witness of the Spirit says, "This is the Savior of the world," and I reply, "That is a deception and a falsehood," I bring myself to the brink of the abyss. I am liable to the unforgivable sin. When the Spirit calls we must listen. When He pleads we must answer. The Lord has but one Son whom He gave as a sacrifice for our sins. He has but one Spirit to point us to the Savior of the world. If I turn aside from the witness of the Spirit and do despite unto the Spirit of grace, I have no other way. I am eternally lost.

Master, may it be that this day when the Spirit calls, we answer with our lives. When the Spirit testifies, may we say, "Amen." When He leads us to the blessed Jesus, may we follow after into the presence of the Lord Himself and some day enter through the gates of the city into the presence of the marvelous, supreme, universal, ever-living and ever-reigning King.

3

Strategy and World Conquest

When they therefore were come together, they asked of him, saying, Lord, wilt thou at this time restore again the kingdom to Israel?

And he said unto them, It is not for you to know the times or the seasons, which the Father hath put in his own power.

But ye shall receive power, after that the Holy Ghost is come upon you: and ye shall be witnesses unto me both in Jerusalem, and in all Judaea, and in Samaria, and unto the uttermost part of the earth.

And when he had spoken these things, while they beheld, he was taken up; and a cloud received him out of their sight.

And while they looked stedfastly toward heaven as he went up, behold, two men stood by them in white apparel;

Which also said, Ye men of Galilee, why stand ye gazing up into heaven? this same Jesus, which is taken up from you into heaven, shall so come in like manner as ye have seen him go into heaven. (Acts 1:6-11)

Buried in this passage is a tremendous message for us. A Greek word that is found once in a while in the New Testament is the word *strategos*, the word for a general in an army. Our English word "strategem" comes from this word. A "strategem" is a ploy, a scheme, a plan. Our word "strategic" comes from that word as well. An object, a place, a development is "strategic" if it is vital to the execution of the plan. "Strategy" also comes from that word and refers to the art of so deploying your forces as to win your objectives. The Pentagon has a strategy for the defense of America. If we were attacked, our military leaders have a strategy for overwhelming and overcoming the enemy. There is also a distinct strategy of the almighty God in the building of His kingdom in the earth. That strategy in our text is plainly presented in a twofold character.

GOD'S STRATEGY FOR HIS KINGDOM

A part of the strategy of almighty God in building His kingdom in the earth is cataclysmic. It will come suddenly at the consummation of the age. Upon our Lord's resurrection from the dead the disciples said: "Lord, is now the time when you restore the kingdom to Israel?" The prophets spoke of this event in the Old Testament. They presented glorious millennial pictures of the world that is to come when God is ruler and Christ is King. The Lord replied: "That is not for you to know. The time when Jesus Christ shall come is known only to God. As you have seen Him go away in the shekinah glory of God, so will He return in that same glory, accompanied by the hosts of heaven, the saints, and the angels of glory." There is a day coming, a time set when the kingdom will be seen visibly and our King will appear personally. There is a strategy in God's kingdom work that is cataclysmic. Without announcement, without harbinger, the heavens will suddenly be rolled back like a scroll, and God will descend and the kingdom will come.

There is another character in the strategy of almighty God regarding His coming kingdom. The second part is not cataclysmic, it is not suddenly bursting, but rather it is gradual and progressive. The Lord said to the apostles, "Ye shall receive power, after that the Holy Ghost is come upon you: and ye shall be witnesses unto me both in Jerusalem, and in all Judaea, and in Samaria, and unto the uttermost part of the earth." The strategy of God in His coming kingdom is twofold. It is cataclysmic and sudden but it is also gradual and progressive. It is not just that we are waiting for the coming king, but it is also that we are working and evangelizing, teaching, training, witnessing, and discipling.

Recently I preached at the Southern Baptist State Convention in Oklahoma City. I spoke with a man from the First Baptist Church of that city and we began to talk about some of the pastors that church has had through the years. They have had some unusual men pastor that church. One time they had called as pastor a famous evangelist who was an emphatic premillennialist. I think that is good; I am a premillennialist also. But he had a turn to his premillennialism that was unusual. He believed that Jesus was coming very soon, in fact now. He emphasized this so much that the rest of the work of the kingdom was something of an affront to God, as though He were not coming soon. Now we believe that the doctrine of the imminency of the coming of

Christ is what God would have us believe. We are always to be ready and prepared, for we do not know what hour the Lord may come.

But this pastor was driving down the street one day and he saw one of his deacons planting some trees in his front yard. He stopped the car, walked over to the deacon, and addressed him, "Do you know that what you are doing is a repudiation of my preaching?" The deacon in surprise said, "Pastor, I am just planting some trees here in my front yard." The pastor replied, "Do you not know that before the trees could grow up to offer any shade, Jesus will be here?" The pastor was saying that one should not plant trees, one should not plan, for the Lord is coming. That famous evangelist was correct in the gospel that he preached, in that Jesus is certainly coming and we should prepare. His coming is of all things imminent—any day, any hour. But according to the Word of God and my text, we do not know the time when the Lord will come. It is not for us ever to know. The angels do not know. Jesus in the days of His flesh said, "I do not know." The return of Christ is at a set time, a fixed time in God's purposes of election and grace. But in the meantime I must work, I must plan, I must serve, I must struggle, I must agonize, I must try, I must teach, witness, and pray as though His coming were yet another thousand years away.

Let us take the second point: strategy in the kingdom of God as the Lord has mandated it to us. It deals with what we are to do until He comes. The Lord has plainly outlined our assignment. He did it in three tremendous words in the Great Commission in Matthew 28:19-20. He commanded us to go into all the world and *matheteuo, baptizo,* and *didasko. Matheteuo* means "to make disciples." I am amazed every time I read that text that the Lord did not use *euaggelizo,* "evangelize." He did not use the word "evangelize" though we are to evangelize. He used the word *matheteuo.* "Mathematics" comes from that word. *Matheteuo* means "to make students," "to make disciples," "to make followers of the whole world." It has in it *euaggelizo,* "evangelism," and it has in it a world of wealth besides. We are to make disciples of the whole world. We are to form them in churches, baptizing them in the name of the triune God. By one baptism we are added to the body of Christ. We are baptized into the church of the Lord. *Didasko* means "to teach them." "Didactic" comes from that word. . . . "Teaching them to observe all things that I have commanded you. When you do it, I am with you to the end of the age, to the great consummation."

I once had an experience that pressed that strategy upon me as no other I ever had in my life. It has been so constantly with me that I have mentioned it often. In 1950 I was on a three-month preaching mission in Japan. It began at the northern-most island and went down to the southern-most. At one place in the islands an officer in the Japanese government took me to a governmental compound. It was in the days when General Douglas MacArthur, who was a great Christian, ruled the empire of Nippon. MacArthur sought to bring the Christian witness with Bibles and missionaries to the Japanese, and we had an incomparable opportunity to help. Every time I preached we had at least one hundred fifty or more converts. It was the most glorious open door I have ever seen. This officer took me to a governmental compound and assembled the people to whom I would preach. The auditorium was covered with rice mats on which the people sat and listened. When I was through, each one was given a card which was perforated in the middle. The top card read like this: "I accept Jesus Christ as my Savior. I do it now." The bottom card said, "I want to know more about Jesus." After each one in the group had been given the card at the end of my appeal, a man stood up, and pointing to the top card asked me a question, saying, "If I signed this card, then what?" That question burned like fire in my soul. There was no church there, there were no Bibles, there was no pastor, there was no Sunday school, there was no literature, there was nothing. That question covers the gamut of the kingdom of God. It is not enough that a man be saved. It is not enough that a man be evangelized. In the strategy of the work and patience of our Lord there is a discipling, a baptizing, and a teaching. When that strategy given of God is not carried through, faith becomes anemic.

In the last century America saw a tremendously gifted and brilliant pulpiteer by the name of T. DeWitt Talmadge. I have a book in my library entitled, *The Wisdom and Wit of Talmadge.* When he preached his sermon on Sunday in the Brooklyn Tabernacle just across from Manhattan, the next day practically every daily newspaper of the nation from New York to San Francisco printed his sermon. What an astonishing phenomenon. T. DeWitt Talmadge had a gift of seizing upon the occurrences of the day and turning them into tremendous sermons that were pertinent and brilliant. People all over America read them.

I was preaching in the First Baptist Church of Brooklyn and I said to the pastor: "Can you tell me where the Brooklyn Tabernacle was located? It was T. DeWitt Talmadge's church." He said: "I have never been able to find it." Recently I preached in Kansas City to four Baptist conventions. I was eating dinner with Gardner Taylor who is pastor of the Brooklyn Tabernacle, a black church in Brooklyn. I said to Pastor Taylor, "Do you know where the church was over which the great pulpiteer, T. DeWitt Talmadge presided?" He replied: "I have been pastor in Brooklyn for a generation. I grew up in Brooklyn. I have never been able to find its location. I do not know where it was." So completely has the work and the church of that scintillating preacher disappeared that even those who have given themselves to the ministry of the Lord in the same town where he preached have no idea where it was located. It is gone.

FAITHFULLY FOLLOWING THAT STRATEGY

What does that say in letters of livid fire? It reminds us that it is not enough to preach. It is not enough for a pastor to be an able and even brilliant and scintillating pulpiteer. If we follow the strategy that God has given us in this holy Book, there is not only the evangelizing and the preaching but there is also the building up of the church. Paul said to Titus, "For this cause left I thee in Crete, that thou shouldest set in order the things that are wanting, and ordain elders in every city, as I had appointed thee" (Titus 1:5). That is followed by the Apocalypse. This book is for the encouragement of our people in the face of tremendous darkness and opposition. We shall not fail. The victory is finally ours. The whole Bible is for catechumens, for learners, for the teaching, training, and discipling in the Word of the Lord.

We not only have the record of the inspired Word of God, but we have two thousand years of Christian history. What does one find in the two thousand years of Christian history? He finds the same thing. Wherever that strategy has been faithfully followed, there we will find the church growing. We will find the glory of God, the saving of the people, and the strengthening of the work of the Lord. Wherever we find the witnesses of Christ untrue to that strategy, there we will find the work decaying, apostatizing, and finally, in anemia, it disappears from the face of the earth.

Let us look at one or two instances of strategy in the story of Christendom. Out of the island of Iona came missionaries to Scotland who evangelized the Scottish people, winning them to Christ and teaching them the faith. Scotland became one of the great Christian nations of the world. The same thing happened in Ireland. A Baptist preacher named Patrick went there under the power of the Holy Spirit of God and evangelized that entire emerald island. He baptized all six of the tribal chieftains, their warriors, their families, and the court. He won the whole island to Jesus. He built those churches, baptized the people, and taught them the way of the Lord. Ireland became a great Christian nation. What has happened since? In the pulpit of my church the president of one of the Christian colleges of Scotland recently said, "If the apostasy that we have seen in the Christian church in Scotland for the past twenty years continues for the next twenty years, Scotland will be as pagan as it was when Colombo left Iona to evangelize it." When was that? It was in A.D. 500.

Have you been to Scotland? Have you been to England? Have you been there to church? Do you see the whole British Isles and all of continental Europe? It is as pagan as it can be. There are not even 2 percent of the people who attend church. Walking up and down the streets of Stockholm, and riding the bus, I talked to everyone I could, inviting them to the Lord and inviting them to the church. Without exception I had the same repeated answer, "I am not interested." I have never had a variation of that reply. What did we say? We are never but one generation from heathenism, or paganism. What we are seeing develop in England and continental Europe is the loss and the disintegration of a faith. Something else happens when we lose the faith. Look at what is happening economically to England and all of Europe. Knowledgeable men say to me in all sincerity: "It is just a matter of a short time until you will see Europe fall into the hands of the Communists. They can have Italy any time they choose. They can almost have France any time they choose." Fear is even disturbing Mexico. Those who can get out are leaving Mexico, for the country has lost its soul and thereby it has lost its great economic potentiality. The people are afraid.

Our Work Today

Our assignment a million times over again is to evangelize. Are we to *didasko*, to teach the mind of God in Christ Jesus? Yes, a hundred million times. This is the burden of my message. How many people look upon the Christian faith as a speculation! How many people look upon the church as a toy with which to play? How many of them think of the building itself as an architectural ornament? Where is the earnestness and commitment that turned the Greek word *marter* ("witness") into the English word, "martyr"? The martyr laid down his life for the faith. It was blood, it was life, it was eternity, it was God. So many people are half-time Christians. They are quarter-time Christians. Lord, how we need a commitment!

I think we should work to pay life's expenses. Our vocation should be to serve Jesus. We have mortgages to pay, children's mouths to feed, backs to clothe, groceries to buy, but for these things we work just to pay the expenses. Bankers, lawyers, doctors, teachers, clerks, typists all do that just to pay the bills. But our vocation, our calling is to serve Jesus. This is the strategy of the kingdom. Without it the church fails, the nation fails, the home fails, but with it the Lord is exalted and God heals the nation.

4

The Heavenly Ascension

And when he had spoken these things, while they beheld, he was taken up; and a cloud received him out of their sight.

And while they looked stedfastly toward heaven as he went up, behold, two men stood by them in white apparel;

Which also said, Ye men of Galilee, why stand ye gazing up into heaven? this same Jesus, which is taken up from you into heaven, shall so come in like manner as ye have seen him go into heaven. (Acts 1:9-11)

The Bible records eleven different appearances of Jesus after He was raised from the dead. In our text we read of our Lord's eleventh appearance in which, with that little band of eleven apostles, He walked with them from Jerusalem across the Kidron and then up the long slope to the brow of Olivet. When the Lord and the eleven apostles came to the top of the mountain, they paused. They stood there in rapt amazement, in a holy hush, in an intense joy. While the Lord spoke to them, He raised His nail-pierced hands in blessing, and as He did so, the Scriptures say He was taken up. *Epiro* is used to refer to a man who raises his voice. It refers to a man who raises his hands in prayer. The word as used here says that while He extended His hands in blessing, *epiro*, He was lifted up, He was taken up.

A cloud received Him, *hupo lambano*, which means literally "to take from underneath." It was not a cloud such as you would see in the sky, but the chariot of God, the shekinah glory of the Lord, the raiment of deity, clothed Him and He was lifted up from underneath.

37

WHY THE ASCENSION OF CHRIST?

He was taken out of their sight, *ophthalmos*. *Ophthalmos* is the word for "eye." A cloud took Him from underneath, away from their natural eyes. When that happened they stood transfixed, amazed, looking up into heaven. As they stood there in wonder, in rapture, behold, two angels came down from heaven. They were angels not with a sword or even a rod but angels dressed in white raiment who said, "Why stand ye gazing up into heaven?" Sometimes our hearts lead us into actions that are difficult to explain and more difficult to defend. It is like going to a grave to weep. Does it do any good? Does it change anything? No, but it is just something dictated by our hearts. Those apostles, standing there in transfixion and amazement, were asked "Why?" by the angels.

Why was our Lord taken away? He is seen no more with our visible eyes in the congregation of the righteous. His voice is heard no more among the saints. His chair is empty at the table. Why was He taken away?

The two disciples at Emmaus said to our Lord: "Come and abide with us," and they constrained Him to stay. We are like that with our Lord. We would constrain our Lord to stay with us. If He were with us in the flesh we could overcome a thousand frustrations; we could dissolve a million difficulties. If only the Lord were here!

We think His presence would be worth that of ten thousand apostles. If we had His words of wisdom to guide us in every decision and if we had the power of His miracle-working hands, we could bring to Him all our sick. We could even lay our dead at His feet and they would live again. Think of how He could confront the enemies of God—think of the evangelization of the world if only He were leading visibly in the flesh this great army of Christian saints!

In our reading of the Holy Word and in our praying over these pages we find that definite, conclusive, and heavenly answers to that question are revealed as to why the Lord was taken away into heaven and shut away from our physical eyes. He said:

> But because I have said these things unto you, sorrow hath filled your heart. Nevertheless I tell you the truth; It is expedient for you that I go away: for if I go not away, the Comforter will not come unto you; but if I depart, I will send him unto you. (John 16:6-7)

Why is it best for us that our Lord go away?

First, our Lord's ascension was in the plan and purpose of God. We, His sheep here below, are not to suppose that a tragedy has overtaken us and that our Lord has forsaken us. He is there in heaven as alive, as loving, as committed to us as He ever was.

Despisers and scorners say to us: "Your Christianity has spun out. The kingdom of God has come to an end. Your Lord is taken away and you do not know where He is or whether you will ever see Him again. His great power and miracle-working hands are no longer with you. This is the end of your way and the defeat of your message."

That is not so, for our Lord has just changed His field of vision and supervision. He has just left this earth to ascend on high to be seated at the right hand of God. All authority, all power in heaven and on earth has been given to Him. From that vantage and strategic point of glory He surveys the whole field of battle and directs His kingdom's work in the earth. He has not forsaken us. He is there for our sakes to guide and to direct us in all of these vast kingdom commitments, movements, and strategies. Some day He is coming again. It will be in a moment, in the twinkling of an eye, at any hour. The great Leader and King of the marshaled forces of God in the earth will appear.

Second, why did Jesus leave? It was in order that our hearts, prayers, vision, and hope might be lifted upward, heavenward, Godward, and Christward. It is as we read in Colossians and Philippians:

> Set your affection on things above, not on things on the earth. (Col. 3:2)

> For our conversation is in heaven; from whence also we look for the Saviour, the Lord Jesus Christ. (Phil. 3:20)

Our Lord is in heaven. He was raised up into glory that our hearts, our affections, our prayers, our dreams, and our every prospect might be Godward.

To all of us who have found a Savior in Him there is always that pull toward God, that lifting up of our faces, our hearts, and our hands toward Him. There is an upwardness in the Christian faith that is felt and real. We hear God's voice call.

One time I heard of a farmer in southern Louisiana who captured a mallard duck and tied it with a cord to a stake at the edge of the pond. Through the winter the mallard swam around with the domestic ducks and ate from the hand of the farmer. When spring came all of the other wild ducks that had flown south and were wintering in the marshes, ponds, and waters of southern Louisiana began to fly toward the north. When those flocks arose they saw the mallard duck down below on the pond. They called to him from the sky. All of the other domesticated ducks did not hear, did not see, did not raise their eyes to look. They just swam in complacency on the farmer's pond. But when the mallard heard the call from the skies, he lifted up his face, then lifted up his wings and sought to rise. The cord which was tied to the stake pulled him back down. Flock after flock arose, circled, and called. Each time the mallard would rise. Finally, he broke the cord and joined the throng and moved toward the north. People of the world are content here below. Their investments are here, their life is here, their interest is here, their happiness is here, their dreams are here, their purposes are here. Everything they look forward to is here, for they are not children of God. But the child of God hears the call from heaven. He lifts up his heart, his eyes, his ears, and his hands, for his life is hid with Christ and God in heaven. Thus has the Lord done for us who have looked in faith to Him.

For you see, all of Christ's people are gathering in heaven. If you live long enough your mother will be gone and your father will be gone. Every member of your family will be gone. All of your friends will be gone. If they knew the Lord they will be over there in heaven. If the Lord were here and all whom we love are over there, it would be an infinite sadness. The Lord is in heaven; He is waiting there, and gradually our loved ones are crossing over to be with Him in heaven. Some day our time will come for our inheritance is not here, it is there. Our home is not here, it is there. All of our treasures are not here, they are there. We used to sing:

> I am a stranger here;
>   heaven is my home.
> Earth is a desert drear;
>   heaven is my home.
> Sorrows and dangers stand
>   round me on every hand.
> Heaven is my fatherland;
>   heaven is my home.

Our Lord is there awaiting us in our day and in our time. We are to lift up our hearts to heaven where our Lord has gone.

Third, why did the Lord go away? It was in order that we might learn to live by faith and not by sight. The Christian faith is one of spiritual substance and content. If the Lord were here in this world there would be a perpetual embargo and moratorium on faith. People would struggle from one side of this planet to the other to get to Him. We would want to just look at Him, feast our eyes upon Him, bring to Him our sick, and lay before Him our dead. It would be almost unimaginable. But the

Christian faith in its substance is always invisible and unseen. We do not look upon the things that are seen but upon the things that are not seen. The things that are seen are temporal—the flower that fades, the grass that withers. The very heavens and earth shall all pass away. The things that are not seen are eternal.

Paul says in 2 Corinthians:

> While we look not at the things which are seen, but at the things which are not seen: for the things which are seen are temporal; but the things which are not seen are eternal. (4:18)

The realities of God are always invisible and spiritual; they are eternal and never temporal.

That is why in the Christian religion we are looking up. Our expectancy is in heaven. Our sanctuary is in heaven. Our altar is in heaven. Our sacrifice is in heaven. Our great High Priest is in heaven. We have in Him a spiritual faith and a spiritual religion which is not seen with the naked eye but is hidden away from our natural eyes that we might see with the eyes of faith.

Hebrews 11 speaks of Moses:

> By faith he forsook Egypt, not fearing the wrath of the king: for he endured, as seeing him who is invisible. (v. 27)

It is a poor faith that has to place its fingers in the nail prints in His hands, that has to thrust the hand in the riven scar of His side.

Fourth, why did our Lord ascend into glory? Because He is there, our faithful High Priest, our mighty mediator, our omnipotent intercessor and Savior for us who are down here in this world. He is our representative in heaven, there to secure for us an eternal salvation and an everlasting inheritance.

Who is it who entered heaven? Who is it who ascended from the top of Mt. Olivet? Some say that the disciples saw nothing but a melting phantom and a disappearing apparition. The disciples were standing there gazing up at a mist and a dream. Is that so? Who is this who ascended up into heaven? It is the Lord Jesus Christ who is the same yesterday, today, and forever. It is the God-man of flesh and bone. It is the risen and resurrected Lord who entered heaven.

Paul quotes an early Christian hymn in 1 Timothy 3:16 that says that God who was manifested in the flesh and justified in the spirit was also "seen of angels." Those angels had watched Him in eternity and they were present when He was born. They continued their interest, surveillance, care, and love throughout His ministry. They saw Him buried in the tomb when He was crucified. They rolled away the stone and were present when He was raised from the dead. They welcomed Him back to glory.

If you want to read of His reception into heaven, read Revelation 5. If you would know how it was that He entered into heaven read Ephesians 4 when He ascended up on high carrying captivity captive. It is the Lord Jesus who entered into heaven, and who is there at the right hand of the Majesty on high, our brother who lived our lives, walked our earth, died our death, suffered our sorrows, and wept our tears. He was touched with the feeling, the sympathy of our infirmities. That is why the author of Hebrews is so bold to avow in Hebrews 7:

> Wherefore he is able also to save them to the uttermost that come unto God by him, seeing he ever liveth to make intercession for them. (v. 25)

Romans 5 says:

> For if, when we were enemies, we were reconciled to God by the death of his Son, much more, being reconciled, we shall be saved by his life. (v. 10)

What life is that? Is it His life down here in the earth? No, it is His life in heaven. We are now forever saved by His life in heaven. He ever lives to make intercession for us. Our salvation is assured. We shall certainly inherit what God has prepared for us who have looked in faith to Him.

If I could send a representative to heaven to secure for me my inheritance in glory, if I could choose the ablest among men to be my representative in glory, he might fail. But our Lord will not fail. My assurance is forever. My life down here is hid in His. My life in heaven is hid in Him. Whether I live here or I live there, it is the Christ life that I live. If He tarries, and if a garden tomb and a winding sheet await me, the same Holy Spirit who raised Him from the dead shall raise me from the dead, for "the Lord himself shall descend from heaven with a shout, with the voice of the archangel, with the trump of God: and the dead in Christ shall rise first" (2 Thess. 4:16). We are identified with Him. He is alive and we cannot die.

THE AGE OF THE HOLY SPIRIT

Fifth, why did our Lord ascend into heaven? He said:

> Nevertheless I tell you the truth; It is expedient for you that I go away: for if I go not away, the Comforter [parakletos] will not come unto you; but if I depart, I will send him unto you. (John 16:7)

Parakletos means "the helper," "the one alongside," "the one who is here."

Where is the Lord? He is here. He is here with each one of us. If two thousand of us bow our heads to say grace at the table at our noonday meal, He will be listening. Wherever we are, there He is.

Do you want to know the way? He will tell you. Ask Him. Do you need strength for some assignment that is beyond you? Ask Him. Do you need grace when the doctor tells you that your illness is terminal? Ask Him. He will be there to sustain. Do you need assurance that when your body is laid in the grave your soul will be taken to heaven? That is why He went away. He is preparing for the day of our coming. He is walking, working, comforting, helping, and ministering by our sides that we might be assured of our heavenly inheritance.

In a great art museum I saw a picture entitled "Christ Among the Lowly." The artist had drawn a very poor home and a very poor family. In the picture a father, a mother, and ragged children are seated at a table. They are bowing their heads saying grace over a few crumbs. The artist drew above them the Savior with His hands extended in blessing. Would you rather be in a palatial home without Jesus or would you rather be in that poor man's cottage with the Lord's hand extended in blessing? Those riches are ours in Christ Jesus. They are ours forever.

5

When Jesus Comes Again

And while they looked stedfastly toward heaven as he went up, behold, two men stood by them in white apparel;

Which also said, Ye men of Galilee, why stand ye gazing up into heaven? this same Jesus, which is taken up from you into heaven, shall so come in like manner as ye have seen him go into heaven. (Acts 1:10-11)

There has been no time in recorded history when men have not dreamed of a golden age. The poets and the philosophers of ancient East as well as the poets and philosophers of the western world in Greece and in Rome often spoke of the day that was yet to come. It would be a day when there would be no more wars and peace would cover the earth, a day when iniquity would be abolished and righteousness would fully reign. It would be a day when the earth would bring forth her increase and storms would rage no more. The Old Testament prophets repeated by inspiration an incomparable refrain that there was coming a golden age.

Micah wrote of it in his famous fourth chapter:

. . . and they shall beat their swords into plowshares, and their spears into pruninghooks: nation shall not lift up a sword against nation, neither shall they learn war any more. (v. 3b)

Isaiah wrote of it in the eleventh chapter of his prophecy:

The wolf also shall dwell with the lamb, and the leopard shall lie down with the kid; and the calf and the young lion and the fatling together; and a little child shall lead them.

And the cow and the bear shall feed; their young ones shall lie down together: and the lion shall eat straw like the ox.

They shall not hurt nor destroy in all my holy mountain: for the earth shall be full of the knowledge of the LORD, as the waters cover the sea. (vv. 6-7,9)

The New Testament carried that refrain to its ultimate and final consummation. In the New Covenant the word used to describe that golden age is one which we have taken over into our English language out of the Latin Vulgate, "millennium." "Mille"—a thousand, "annus"—a year, means a thousand years. The New Testament says that all history is moving toward the final consummation called "the millennium." That is to be followed by new heavens and a new earth. The very heaven shall be purged and purified and this planet will find its rest in the harmony of the spheres. These are the dreams of the golden age of the poets and the philosphers and they are the inspired foretellings of the prophets and the apostles. Who is going to introduce and usher in that golden era?

The Preaching and Teaching I Used to Hear

When I was growing up, and even as a student in college and in the seminary I heard one doctrine, one explanation, and one supposed inspired revelation of how that new era is to be introduced. Without exception, I was taught by the preacher and by the professor that the golden era would be introduced by the preaching of the gospel. The watchword was: the world is growing better and better. The affirmation of the gospel was seen in the progress that humanity was making in the arts, sciences, and the cultures of the nations. By the operation of the Holy Spirit, by the preaching of the message of Christ, and by the diffusion of the gospel of peace, we were going to usher in that new millennial age. Christ will reign in the hearts of men and the Lord will lead in the councils of the nations. The tiger will forget to bare its fangs. The leopard will change his spots.

Now this is a glorious vision. We, by our preaching and by our counseling and by our progress in all of the areas of human life, will introduce this glorious golden age of a thousand years at the end of which Christ shall come. The only thing the matter with the doctrine I found out in my study of the Bible was this: it contradicted the Word of God. I see no intimation of any such doctrine as I read the Bible.

The Real Truth in the Scriptures and in Experience

For example, take the plain and simple parable of our Lord of the sower and the seed. The sower went out to sow and only one-fourth of what he sowed bore fruit to God. Part of it fell by the wayside and the birds ate it up. Some of it fell on stony ground and the sun scorched it. Some of it fell among thorns and the worldly cares choked it to death. Only some seeds fell upon good ground. No preacher will ever be able to convert a whole people, for they will not all turn.

Another error I found in this doctrine was that it forever precludes the coming of our Lord for any practical purpose in human life. If we are going to get better and better, and finally usher in the kingdom at the end of which thousand years the Lord will come, then for all practical purposes the coming of the Lord has no meaning to us at all. The Lord's admonition when He said, "Watch, therefore, for ye know neither the day nor the hour wherein the son of man cometh" (Matt. 25:13) is an extraneous and impertinent statement by our Savior, for He is not going to come until the end of a thousand years when we have ushered in the millennial reign.

Another thing I found in my reading of history and in my looking at the world in human experience is that it is denied by everything I read and everything I know. The world is not getting better, period. There are millions more people today who do not know the Lord than when Christianity began. As for progress, you see progress from a Model-T tin lizzy to a beautiful limousine made by the same motor company. You see progress in radio, you see progress in television, you see progress in the incandescent lamp, and you see progress in scientific achievement. But you also see progress in atomic warfare. You see progress in the use of the media for the propagation of lies and the destruction of the liberties of a people. Progress in human life is a sorry illusion. It does not exist. Men, when they were in the stone age, killed with an ax and with a club. Then in their progress they killed with a bow and an arrow. Then in their progress they killed with gun powder and bullet. Today we kill with hydrogen bombs and atomic-headed missiles. There is no evidence in human life or experience that the world is getting better.

Let us return to the Word of the Lord. What does God say to us about the human race? What does God say about the millennial age? What does the Lord say about the coming of our Christ? Let us, therefore, build our hopes, preach our doctrines, and teach our word as the Lord has written it on the sacred page.

WHAT THE WORLD WILL BE LIKE WHEN CHRIST RETURNS

When the Lord comes again, how is this age going to be introduced? How are we to enter this millennial reign of our Lord? "Ye men of Galilee, why stand ye gazing up into heaven? this same Jesus, which is taken up from you into heaven, shall so come in like manner as ye have seen him go into heaven" (Acts 1:11). Notice the phrase, "in like manner." What was the world like when He came the first time? He is coming in like manner. As I read the Bible I notice the mention of Caesar Augustus. Who was Caesar Augustus? He was the first undisputed dictator of the civilized world. He liquidated his rivals, Antony and Lepidus. He assassinated three hundred senators and three thousand knights. He confiscated the lands of the aristocrats and gave them to his soldiers. He forever destroyed the republic of Rome and made it into a dictatorship. He took to himself a word that was reserved only for God—namely, Augustus. That sounds like a world dictator, does it not? That fits the picture of the great and final antichrist. That is the kind of a world into which Jesus came the first time.

As we read through the pages of the Bible about our Lord's first coming we are introduced to Herod the Great. Herod is doubtless the bloodiest petty monarch who ever lived. Someone may ask why Josephus, who wrote much about the life of Herod didn't mention the story of the slaughter of the babes at Bethlehem. The answer is obvious. The reason Josephus never mentioned it is that it was a peccadillo in the life of Herod. He killed so many thousands as his daily menu of hatred and jealousy (including his own family) that to speak of killing the babes in Bethlehem would have been a detail not worthy of mention. It was that kind of a world into which Jesus came.

We read in the Bible of scribes, elders, and chief priests. There never was any time in the history of Judaism when their religion was as low as it was when Jesus was born into the world. Simony, intrigue, and murder were on every hand in the life of the religious Jewish nation. Then we read that His second coming is "in like manner."

What kind of a world was it when the Lord went away? The last time the unbelieving world ever saw the Lord Jesus was when they watched Him die in shame on the cross. Their voices were raised in shouts, "Crucify him!" No unbeliever has ever seen Him since, nor will any unbeliever ever see Him before He comes in power and glory.

When the Lord was tried before Caiaphas, the high priest said, "I beg of you, by the living God, that you tell us whether you are the Christ, the Son of God." The Lord answered, "You have said it." In the most emphatic affirmation that the Greek language can avow, the Lord answered, "I am." Then He added, "Hereafter shall ye see the Son of man sitting on the right hand of power, and coming in the clouds of heaven" (Matt. 26:64). The next time the unbelieving world will see the Lord Jesus will be when He comes again introducing the kingdom to men.

What kind of a world will it be when the Lord returns? It will be "in like manner." The Lord has plainly revealed to us that when He returns it will be "as it was in the days of Noe," "as it was in the days of Lot." The Lord expressly taught us that same truth in the parables of the mysteries of the kingdom. When the Lord returns the earth will be as wheat and tares that are separated and the tares are burned with unquenchable fire. It will be as fish caught in a net and the bad are cast away. It will be as a shepherd gathering his flock and separating the sheep from the goats. It will be as the sixth seal in the sixth chapter of the apocalypse: "And the heaven departed as a scroll. . . . And [they] said to the mountains and rocks, Fall on us, and hide us from the face of him that sitteth on the throne, and from the wrath of the Lamb: For the great day of his wrath is come; and who shall be able to stand?" (vv. 14,16-17). That reveals something to us. The great millennial reign of our Lord is introduced not by the preaching of the gospel but by the judgments of almighty God. First is the terrible tribulation from Revelation 6 through Revelation 19. Then these judgments are followed by the ultimate blood bath in the battle of Armageddon in which battle the Lord comes and the kingdom is introduced by His omnipotent and almighty hand.

The Blessed Hope of the People of the Lord

What is the destiny and the hope of us who have looked in faith to the Lord? What of these who have fallen asleep in Jesus, who have died, are buried, and the Lord still has not come? This is the blessedness of the hope that God has placed in the hearts of us who live in a world that faces inexorable and inevitable judgment, and we who live in a body that is decaying and dying: Christ remembers us all. He is coming for us all, both the dead and the living.

When Jesus returns He will come, secretly, unannounced. He is coming for His saints. Before the judgment falls, before the terrible tribulation, before the awesomeness of Armageddon, the Lord will come to take away His people. The Bible says that it will be like Enoch walking along with God and then suddenly he was gone. It will be as it was in the days of Noah. God took him and those who believed with him and put them in the ark and shut the door. No flood could fall, no judgment could come until first Noah was safely hidden away. It will be as it was in the days of Lot. The angels seized him and said, "We can do nothing until thou come thither." Judgment cannot fall until God's people are safely tucked away. They laid hands upon Lot and took him out of Sodom. The fire could not fall, the brimstone could not burn as long as righteous Lot was in the city. It will be as it was in the days of the Passover. Before the death angel could pass over, God's people had to be hidden under the blood. It will be as it was in the days of Rahab. Before the trumpet sounded and the city fell she had to be hidden behind the scarlet line. So it will be with God's people in the earth. Before the judgment falls, and before these terrible, indescribable visitations of judgment can come, God's people must be taken away. They must be hidden out of sight. They must be caught up to God in heaven.

Look around you. As long as the dead are in their graves, He has not come. As long as God's saints are living in the earth, He has not come. For when the Lord comes, the dead in Christ shall rise first. Then we who are alive and remain shall be caught up with them to meet the Lord in the air. So shall we ever be with the Lord. When Jesus comes "in like manner," the world will be lost. Blaspheming men will be judged, but God's saints will be taken up to their everlasting home in heaven. No Christian is ever fully Christian when he is discouraged and dismayed. We may die, but God shall raise us up again. We may be weak and feeble before the tyranny of a whole world, but God is the refuge and defense of His own. We may face incomparable problems, but the light of the hope of Christ shines in our hearts to that beautiful, perfect, and glorious day when Jesus comes again.

6

This Same Jesus

And when he had spoken these things, while they beheld, he was taken up; and a cloud received him out of their sight.

And while they looked stedfastly toward heaven as he went up, behold, two men stood by them in white apparel;

Which also said, Ye men of Galilee, why stand ye gazing up into heaven? this same Jesus, which is taken up from you into heaven, shall so come in like manner as ye have seen him go into heaven. (Acts 1:9-11)

I would like to divide this text into three parts: the place, the promise, and the Person. First,

THE PLACE

When Jesus comes the second time, He will return first to the Mount of Olives. On the west of Olivet is Mount Moriah with its temple. Between the two mountains lies the valley in which "the winepress," *Gethsemane,* is located. Up the slope to the height of the mountain on the east of the city is the mountain called the Mount of Olives which will receive the feet of our Lord when He comes down from the sky. The prophecies in the Bible are not only general covering vast eras, but many of them are decidedly specific, sometimes in smallest detail. The return of our Lord is specifically revealed.

In Zechariah we read:

And his feet shall stand in that day upon the mount of Olives, which is before Jerusalem on the east

. . . and the LORD my God shall come, and all the saints with thee.

. . . but it shall come to pass, that at evening time it shall be light.

And the LORD shall be king over all the earth: in that day shall there be one LORD, and his name one. (14:4a,5b,7b,9)

As He went away from the Mount of Olives, so shall He some day return to that same place. When His feet touch the mountain it shall be riven, split in two. Oh, the wonder of the infinitude of the power and presence of Christ the Lord when He comes back to this earth!

When Jesus came to earth the first time, the place where He was to come was specifically identified. Micah the prophet said:

But thou, Bethlehem Ephratah, though thou be little among the thousands of Judah, yet out of thee shall he come forth unto me that is to be ruler in Israel; whose goings forth have been from of old, from everlasting. (Micah 5:2)

The eternal God, the Prince of Glory, shall be incarnate, and the prophet declared that in the little town of Bethlehem the Savior of the world would be born.

God's prophecy is specific also as to the exact location of the second coming of Christ. The glorious, triumphant return of our Lord will be on the Mount of Olives, on the east side of the holy city of Jerusalem.

THE PROMISE

"This same Jesus, which is taken up from you into heaven, shall so come in like manner as ye have seen him go into heaven." The first-century Christians carried a secret with them. They suffered indescribable, merciless persecution. They were burned at the stake, fed to the lions, exiled, and exposed. Their property was confiscated. They were hated, hounded, and hunted. But they faced their martyrdom with a song on their lips and with praise in their hearts. What was the secret of those first-century Christians who laid down their lives gladly for their faith? They had a promise. As they would bid each other a farewell, they would say "*Maranatha*," which means, "Our Lord comes." Beyond the blood, suffering, and persecution of this life they saw the glorious return of their living Lord. It was their hope and strength. Paul wrote, "If in this life only we have hope in Christ, we are of all men most miserable" (1 Cor. 15:19). Beyond the grave, the death, and the night we have the light of the glorious coming of Christ our Savior.

When one looks at the philosophies and religions of the world he finds that many of them have numerous favorable features. They have fine teaching and splendid morality. There are noteworthy qualities in Confucianism, in Shintoism, in Hinduism, in Buddhism—but they are like a bridge that starts on one side and rises, but in the middle of the abyss it breaks off. There is nothing beyond.

Christianity, the faith of our Lord, is fulfilling and complete. Not only is the Christian faith grounded in this earth and rewarding and blessed in this life, but as the faith rises and soars it goes over and beyond the dark abyss and finds its other foundation in life on the shores of the kingdom of God in heaven. The secret of the faith is woven into the warp and woof of the Christian religion itself. All through the Scriptures we can find the promise of the coming victorious reign of our Lord. We read of that promise:

> For the Son of man shall come in the glory of his Father with his angels; and then he shall reward every man according to his works. (Matt. 16:27)

> For as the lightning cometh out of the east, and shineth even unto the west; so shall also the coming of the Son of man be. (Matt. 24:27)

> But because I have said these things unto you, sorrow hath filled your heart. Let not your heart be troubled: ye believe in God, believe also in me.
> And if I go and prepare a place for you, I will come again. (John 16:6, 14:1,3a)

> This same Jesus . . . shall so come in like manner. (Acts 1:11)

> For our conversation is in heaven; from whence also we look for the Savior, the Lord Jesus Christ. (Phil. 3:20)

> For the Lord himself shall descend from heaven with a shout, with the voice of the archangel, and with the trump of God. (1 Thess. 4:16)

> I have fought a good fight, I have finished my course, I have kept the faith:
> Henceforth there is laid up for me a crown of righteousness, which the Lord, the righteous judge, shall give me at that day: and not to me only, but unto all them also that love his appearing. (2 Tim. 4:7,8)

> Looking for that blessed hope, and the glorious appearing of the great God and our Savior Jesus Christ. (Titus 2:13)

> . . . unto them that look for him shall he appear the second time without sin unto salvation. (Heb. 9:28b)

> Be ye also patient; stablish your hearts: for the coming of the Lord draweth nigh. (James 5:8)

> . . . the Lord cometh with ten thousands of his saints. (Jude 14)

> Behold, he cometh with clouds; and every eye shall see him, and they also which pierced him: and all kindreds of the earth shall wail because of him. Even so, Amen. (Rev. 1:7)

> He which testifieth these things saith, Surely I come quickly. Amen. Even so, come, Lord Jesus. (Rev. 22:20)

The secret of the Christian faith lies in its eternal, unbounded, and never-dying optimism. There is a great day coming! The Lord, this same Jesus, will so come in the same manner He went to heaven.

THE PERSON

Who is this who is coming? So many have spiritualized and rationalized our Lord's promise until the Lord Himself is lost in it. I am not referring to men of the school of higher criticism who look upon the Bible as a collection of legends and myths. I am speaking now about men of great spiritual stature who spiritualize the incomparable promise of the return of this same Jesus. They do it in many ways.

Some of them say the Lord came in the destruction of Jerusalem in A.D. 70. There are others who say that the Lord came in the conversion of Constantine in A.D. 320, when the Christian faith became the official religion of the Roman Empire. There are those who say that the Lord Jesus comes in the diffusion of the Christian gospel message in the world. There are those who say that Jesus has come in the advancement of Christian civilization and culture. There are those who say that the Lord comes in death.

We need not so spiritualize the coming of our Lord as to say that He is enmeshed and lost in history or war or destruction or death. When His glorious appearing shall be ushered in, it will be the same Lord Jesus who went away. The same holy face, the same blessed voice, the same nail-pierced hands. He said, "If I go away, *I* will come again." Who is that "I"? It is Jesus for whom we pray. It is Jesus for whom we wait. It is Jesus whom we expect.

Our Lord has not lost His identity. He is still the same blessed Lord Jesus. Though immortalized in flesh and bone, though transfigured, though glorified, He is still the same blessed Jesus. His identification never varies. When He was raised from the dead, Mary recognized Him by the way He pronounced her name. The two on the way to Emmaus recognized Him by the way He spoke the blessing at the table. When John entered the empty tomb he believed because he recognized the way Jesus folded up a napkin. When Jesus held up His hands, there were nail prints in His hands. When the Lord showed His side, there was a great riven scar in His side. Thomas cried, "My Lord and my God."

Through the centuries since, there have been those who have seen the same Lord Jesus. When Stephen, the first martyr, was thrown to the ground by the stones cast at him, he looked up and saw the Lord Jesus standing at the right hand of the majesty on high. Saul of Tarsus, hurling slaughter and intimidation against the church, met Him in the glory of a light above the Syrian midday sun, and blinded by that light, fell at His feet and asked, "Who art thou, Lord?" He replied, "I am Jesus of Nazareth." On the lonely isle of Patmos, exiled there to die of exposure and starvation, John saw a vision. He saw the Lord walking in the midst of the seven golden lampstands. In the glory of that vision John fell at the feet of the Lord as one dead. The Lord reached forth His hand and touched him saying, "Be not afraid."

A story that moves me every time I hear it is about my famous predecessor in the First Baptist Church. He was on a hunting trip with the chief of police of the city of Dallas, when his gun accidentally went off killing the chief of police. The great pastor was plunged into an indescribable and abysmal sorrow. He felt that because he had killed a man he could never preach again, but the Lord appeared to him in the night. He appeared and spoke a second time. The Lord spoke a third time and called the pastor again to the incomparable ministry the Holy Spirit endowed him with for forty-seven years in that pulpit. This is the same Lord Jesus.

WE WANT TO SEE JESUS

Who is it we want to see? It is Jesus Himself we long to see. We have seven letters from Jesus in the Revelation, but it is not enough to have letters from our Lord. It is not enough that we have the story of His life so beautifully portrayed in the four Gospels. It is not enough that we read His words of wisdom. It is not enough to have His Spirit in our hearts. We would see Jesus! We want above all things to see Him. Some day we will be seated at the marriage supper of the Lamb, but what would it be without the bridegroom? If the bride is there and the groom is absent, there is no marriage. There is no gladness, no joy. It is when He comes for His own that we are seated at the marriage supper of the Lamb. We shall look full into His glorious face and rejoice as we break bread together.

It is Jesus we want to see. Some day we shall see Him face to face!

7

Prayer and Pentecost

These all continued with one accord in prayer and supplication, with the women, and Mary the mother of Jesus, and with his brethren. (Acts 1:14)

When the Lord was crucified His brethren did not believe on Him. Raised from the dead, the Lord appeared to James and through him won all of His family to the faith. In this pre-Pentecostal prayer meeting those present were the apostles, Jesus' mother, the women who followed Him from Galilee, and His brethren. Together they numbered something like one hundred twenty.

They were with one accord pouring out their souls before God in prayer and supplication. There is an amazing amount of doctrinal study in our text that one does not realize as he casually reads through it. Why should the followers of Jesus be praying when Pentecost was as set in the programming of God as any other great day in the life of our Lord? There was a set day when the Lord was to be born. There was a set day when He was to be crucified. There was a set day when the Lord was to be raised from the dead, three days after His crucifiixion. There was a set day when He ascended into heaven. There is a set day known to God when the Lord is coming back to this earth again. Just as set is the day of the outpouring of the Holy Spirit.

The Lord had said to His disciples:

And I will pray the Father, and he shall give you another Comforter, that he may abide with you for ever. (John 14:16)

. . . It is expedient for you that I go away: for if I go not away, the Comforter will not come unto you; but if I depart, I will send him unto you. (John 16:7)

THE PROMISE OF THE FATHER

The outpouring of the Holy Spirit is an answer to the prayer of Jesus Christ. That is why it is called "the promise of the Father." Our Lord says, "Wait [in Jerusalem] for the promise of the Father, which . . . ye have heard of me" (Acts 1:4). All of the outpouring of the Spirit of God is something that Christ has done for us.

Pentecost is an ascension gift, something our Lord won for us when He died for our sins, was raised for our justification, and ascended up to glory. Pentecost is the answer to the prayer of Jesus that the Holy Spirit be given to the world.

The Holy Spirit marks a new dispensation, a new era, a new age. This is the age of the church, the age of the preaching of the gospel, an age which the prophets never saw. When someone finds the church in the Old Testament, he is finding something that is not there; therefore, he does not find it. The church is a mystery that God kept in His heart, hidden away, until He revealed it to the apostles. The Holy Spirit came to gather together out of the Jews, out of the Gentiles, and from all the families of the earth, a new body, a new creation, which is called the church. It is something that God brought to pass, this marvelous day of Pentecost composing the body of Christ.

WE ARE TO PRAY FOR THE HOLY SPIRIT

Why this praying and supplication? There are those who say that such praying and supplication are extraneous and beside the point. They say that we are not to pray in this manner, that our asking for the Holy Spirit has no place in the Christian's life.

God has a vast sovereign purpose that He began working out when He poured out the Spirit of God upon the earth in Pentecost. God also has a plan for us, something that we are to do. Look at Luke 11:1:

> And it came to pass, that, as he was praying in a certain place, when he ceased, one of his disciples said unto him, Lord, teach us to pray.

In verse 5 He talked to the disciples about importunity in praying. We are to knock at the throne of grace until God answers from above. The Lord tells the disciples about a man who had a friend who came to him for food but the man had no food to give him. He went to the neighbor and said, "Trouble me not: the door is now shut, and my children are with me in bed; I cannot rise and give thee." And then the Lord said, "I say unto you, Though he will not rise and give him, because he is his friend, yet because of his importunity he will rise and give him as many as he needeth" (Luke 11:7-8). The man needed rest, so in order to get rid of the man he would give him as many loaves as he needed. That is what the Lord says about importunity. Look at the application of the parable:

> And I say unto you, Ask, and it shall be given you; seek, and ye shall find; knock, and it shall be opened unto you.
> For every one that asketh receiveth; and he that seeketh findeth; and to him that knocketh it shall be opened.
> If a son shall ask bread of any of you that is a father, will he give him a stone? or if he ask a fish, will he for a fish give him a serpent?
> Or if he shall ask an egg, will he offer him a scorpion?
> If ye then, being evil, know how to give good gifts unto your children: how much more shall your heavenly Father give the Holy Spirit to them that ask him? (Luke 11:9-13)

Our heavenly Father desires in His elective purpose that we ask for the fullness of the Spirit as much as He purposes in His sovereign will that the Holy Spirit be poured out upon the earth.

As Elisha walked with Elijah, he said, "[Master] I pray thee, let a double portion of thy spirit be upon me" (2 Kings 2:9). As these men of God opened their hearts, so He wants us to be open to the filling of His Spirit. Though Pentecost was a set date, the followers of Christ gave themselves to prayer and supplication and continued asking in importunity for ten days.

In John 20 the Lord is with His disciples, as we read:

> Then the same day at evening, being the first day of the week, when the doors were shut where the disciples were assembled for fear of the Jews, came Jesus and stood in the midst and saith unto them, Peace be unto you.
> And when he had so said, he shewed unto them his hands, and his side. Then were the disciples glad, when they saw the Lord.
> Then said Jesus to them again, Peace be unto you: as my Father hath sent me, even so send I you.
> And when he had said this, he breathed on them, and saith unto them, Receive ye the Holy Ghost. (vv. 19-22)

There is a turn in a word in this passage in John that is hidden in the English translation. The Greek word is *labete*, translated "receive ye the Holy Ghost." In the English translation it sounds like a command. *Labete* is an imperative from *lambano*, "to take." The Lord actually said to His disciples, "Take ye the Holy Ghost."

In John 18 the word is from Pilate, "Take ye him, and judge him according to your law." In John 18 the word *labete* appears again: "Take him and crucify him." In John 20 He breathed on His disciples and said,

"Take the Holy Ghost." The disciples prayed and after ten days they were ready to *labete*, to take the Holy Spirit, and Pentecost came down.

We also are to take the Holy Ghost. In our praying and supplicating we are preparing to take from the hands of God His most wondrous and precious gift, the fullness of the Spirit. Without the praying and supplicating, I do not know whether we would be ready for the filling of the Spirit, so we also have a part. God's sovereignty pours out the Spirit upon us in this earth, and then we see what God does with a people who pray, intercede, and yield themselves to the fullness of the Spirit of Jesus!

In my reading I came across an incident in history which did not identify the contestants but just told the events that happened. In the Middle East a tyrant proposed to vanquish and lead into subjection a free people. The people whom he was attempting to subdue were godly and praying people. The tyrant gathered his army together to invade the land of this free people. When they saw the tyrant coming they gathered their forces together to confront the tyrannical invader. Before the battle began, those who were defending themselves all bowed down in prayer. The tyrant said to his generals: "Look, they are already cowering. They are already surrendering." One of his counselors who knew the people said: "Sir, they are not cowering and surrendering. Before the battle begins they are praying to their God." When the battle was over, the tyrant and his armies were destroyed.

It pleases God when we pray. Even though in God's sovereign, elective grace He has His hands on this world until the ultimate end of the age, He wants us to be on our knees in prayer and supplication.

8

The Pre-Pentecostal Church

These all continued with one accord in prayer and supplication, with the women, and Mary the mother of Jesus, and with his brethren. (Acts 1:14)

In our preaching through the Book of Acts we have come to the gathering in a ten-day prayer meeting of one hundred twenty souls who were waiting for the promise of the Father. In Acts 2 we read:

And when the day of Pentecost was fully come, they were all with one accord in one place. . .
And they were all filled with the Holy Ghost. (vv. 1,4a)

Simon Peter delivered his great message on that day and three thousand souls were added to the church. What a day, waiting for the new dispensation! The believers were ready and waiting, praying expectantly.

As we look forward we must remember that the Lord has many and great things planned for His church. No matter where we are in the history of time, God always has a greater day coming. God always moves forward. His creation is followed by redemption. His redemption is followed by sanctification. His sanctification is followed by glorification. Always one moves onward, upward, and outward, as the Lord leads Him step by step. So we look at this little congregation of one hundred twenty followers of Christ against whom God has matched the darkness and heathenism of the world.

GOD IS WITH US AND FOR US

Standing poised on the brink of the new dispensation of grace, they were characterized by some things that ought to characterize us. First, they were conscious of the truth that God is with us. The Holy Spirit is in us. The purpose of God's grace is to use us. God is never against us. The Holy Spirit never interdicts us in the purposes of God. Certainly there are numerous times when we seem frustrated and defeated, and because of our human weakness we fall into despair. But no matter what the providence, God is with us and God is for us.

We read in Romans:

> And we know that all things work together for good to them that love God, to them who are the called according to his purpose. (8:28)

God is with us. When a pastor stands to preach or when he witnesses to a man privately, regardless of how hardened the heart of the sinner, God's Spirit is moving and working.

One of the saddest experiences I have ever read about is the following report of a man about his church. Listen to him: "I go to God's house and find no God. I do not hear His voice in song or sermon. His grip is not in the hand of fellowship. I hear no yearnings for the lost in the message of the preacher, nor do I see it in the faces of the people. There is no God in the temple where my people worship." What a tragedy! O that the church might open its heart and soul heavenward and that God might come down and fill us with His moving Spirit so that when a stranger comes in the door he will immediately feel the presence of God among us.

If the spiritual mercury is low, then God's engineer is ice bound and there is no traffic in the kingdom of God. Nothing moves. A refrigerator may, for awhile, preserve things that are already dead, but it never generates life. Even an egg has to be warmed under a mother hen's wing or in an incubator if the baby chick is to burst into life. When the wires are heavy and down, the electricity is cut off from the city and it dies. No baby is ever born that is not first bathed in the warm blood of a mother's womb. The matrix in which children are born into the kingdom of God is in the warmth and prayers and in the love and tears of His people. When Zion travails, sons and daughters are born into the kingdom. The only difference between the iceburg that sank the *Titanic* and the bosom of the ocean that bore up the ship is a matter of temperature. So it is in the church. O that God could be with us as He was in the midst of that little Pentecostal group, that we might be filled with the Spirit! When we bring the Spirit with us into the house of worship, then something is felt and seen and done in the congregation of God's saints. Lord, make our churches resplendent with the filling of Thy Holy Spirit.

THE CHURCH BASED THEIR HOPE
ON THE WORD AND PROMISE OF THE LORD

Second, they were persuaded that the Word of God is immutable. The little band of followers of the Lord stood on the word and promise of God. The Lord had said:

> . . . that they should not depart from Jerusalem, but wait for the promise of the Father, which, saith he, ye have heard of me. (Acts 1:4b)

The Word of the Lord does not lie and does not deceive us, and it was on this immovable rock the little band took their stand. That is where the church of Jesus Christ must stand also.

In Hebrews we are told:

> For the word of God is quick, and powerful, and sharper than any two-edged sword, piercing even to the dividing asunder of soul and spirit, and of the joints and marrow, and is a discerner of the thoughts and intents of the heart. . .
> . . . but all things are naked and opened unto the eyes of him with whom we have to do. (4:12-13b)

Jeremiah says:

> Is not my word like as a fire? saith the LORD; and like a hammer that breaketh the rock in pieces? (Jer. 23:29)

If Jesus delays His coming a thousand years, may every year bring to us a deeper love for the Word of the Lord. That is why I love to hear a choir sing Handel's *Messiah*. One of the reasons that I have a profound affinity for that oratorio is that every syllable in the text of the score is from the Word of God. Wherever we worship our Lord let His Word be magnified.

CHRIST AND HIS GOSPEL ARE ABLE TO SAVE

Third, they believed that Christ and His gospel can save. Three thousand souls were added to that little congregation that day, with one hundred twenty praying at the meeting. Oh, the ableness of our God to save!

When the Charles A. Sammons Cancer Center at Baylor University Medical Center was dedicated, I was seated next to the speaker who is a famous movie and television star. He has a brother who is also a movie star and actor even more famous than he. His brother is an alcoholic. But this famous speaker had been marvelously converted, and he witnessed to the grace of the Lord Jesus in his life. Seated there at the dinner preceding the dedication ceremony, the actor was talking to me about the conversion experience of a beautiful actress and singer, who, when she sang about Mary, the mother of Jesus, wept openly and unashamedly. He remarked that her testimony was such a shining example of what the Lord can do in a yielded life. As I looked at the man talking to me, I thought, "And my brother, God has done a wonderful thing in saving you." God has performed a miracle in saving all of us. He can and does save. His ministry in the earth is to save all who will ask Him into their hearts.

GOD ANSWERS PRAYER

Fourth, they believed that God answers prayer. I saw God do something at the First Baptist Church several years ago, but I never dreamed He would do it again. Many years ago the deacons voted to borrow a million dollars and build the chapel building across the street which cost about $1,750,000. To borrow that much money was truly a big endeavor. While that building was getting started, the property on the other side of Patterson Street came up for sale. When I presented the news to the deacons, they said: "Pastor, we have borrowed to the limit of reason. We just cannot buy that property." I said: "I understand. You are correct." Standing on the curb of Patterson Street with our Minister of Music, we were looking at the building. I said: "This is a sad day. Someone will buy that expensive property and build a forty-story building on it and then we will lose it forever. We so desperately need that property." He said, "Pastor, why do not you ask God for it?" That was astonishing! Such an idea had never occurred to me. I thought I was to ask the deacons for it. So I took it to the Lord and told God all about it.

Within a few days I received a telephone call from a parishioner who said, "Pastor, I hear you are on your knees praying about the property on Patterson Street." I said, "Yes." She said, "How much does it cost?" I replied, "I do not know, but I will find out right away." Upon learning that the price for the property was $550,000, I called her back. She said: "Go buy it. I will give you the money." She gave me $550,000 and we bought that property.

Some time later she called me again and asked, "Pastor, what do you want to do with the property now that you have bought it?" I said: "The city was crowding us to death during the week. I want to build a parking and recreational building." She said, "How much will it cost?" I said, "I do not know but I will tell you soon." When I informed her that the price to build the building would be a little over a million dollars she said, "I will give the money to you." So the building went up, and only the donor knew anything about who gave the money.

Who could imagine that God would do that again. But He did. For a long time we in the First Baptist Church needed more room as did the nursery. Both the Academy and the Mission Department desperately needed recreational areas for their work, so I prayed: "Lord, there is no way. We have no place to turn. What shall we do?"

Then one day I was told, "Pastor, the city of Dallas wants to give you Patterson Street." Did you ever hear of anyone in the city wanting to give you a street? If you think that's not unusual, just go to the city and tell them, "I want a street," and see what happens. I could hardly believe what I heard.

God's graciousness to us is like the story of the soldier in the army of Alexander the Great who had done a heroic thing and Alexander wanted to reward him. Alexander said to the soldier, "What would you like?" The soldier made a stupendous request and Alexander's men said to the great general, "The request of this soldier is beyond what he ought to ask." Alexander the Great replied, "But it is not beyond what Alexander the Great can give." God is like that. He is a great and mighty God. He loves His people and bows His ear to hear them when they cry and when they pray. He is delighted to answer in kind.

O Lord, we bless Your name with every fiber of our being. Let everything that has breath praise the Lord. What a great and wonderful God!

9

The Price of Pentecost

> These all continued with one accord in prayer and supplication, with the women, and Mary the mother of Jesus, and with his brethren.
>
> And when the day of Pentecost was fully come, they were all with one accord in one place.
>
> And suddenly there came a sound from heaven as of a rushing mighty wind, and it filled all the house where they were sitting.
>
> And there appeared unto them cloven tongues like as of fire, and it sat upon each of them.
>
> And they were all filled with the Holy Ghost, and began to speak with other tongues, as the Spirit gave them utterance. (Acts 1:14; 2:1-4)

There is a twofold purpose of God for His people. First, God's will is that we be filled with the Holy Spirit. This is not a new development in the kingdom, far back in the old covenant Joel the prophet said:

> And it shall come to pass afterward, that I will pour out my spirit upon all flesh; and your sons and your daughters shall prophesy, your old men shall dream dreams, your young men shall see visions.
>
> And also upon the servants and upon the handmaids in those days will I pour out my spirit. (Joel 2:28-29)

The first chapter of Acts says, "But ye shall receive power, after that the Holy Ghost is come upon you: and ye shall be witnesses unto me both in Jerusalem, and in all Judaea, and in Samaria, and unto the uttermost part of the earth" (Acts 1:8). It is in the purpose of God that we be filled and endued with the Holy Spirit of heaven. In fact, God commands that we ". . . be filled with the Spirit" (Eph. 5:18).

It is a disgrace to our Lord when we are dull and lethargic. We should have a more deepening interest in the house of God and in the worship and work of our Lord than on any field of athletics, in any movie theater, or anywhere else in this earth. A dull, dreary service is an affront to God. Indifferent and phlegmatic Christians are a disgrace to the name of our Lord. We are commanded to be filled with the Spirit of God.

Second, it is the purpose of the Lord that we be filled again and again. We should not think of having just one tremendous experience, but we should look for a continuous experience of the filling of God's Holy Spirit.

There was a Jerusalem Pentecost. There was a Samaritan Pentecost. There was a Caesarean Pentecost. There was an Ephesian Pentecost. There was a Corinthian Pentecost. There was a Roman Pentecost. All through the ages we are to experience this marvelous outpouring of the presence and power of the Lord.

That is why there is no formal conclusion to the Book of Acts. We come to chapter 28, but the book reaches no consummation or has no formal ending. The reason is obvious. The Holy Spirit is not finished. He writes a twenty-ninth chapter of the Book of Acts, a three hundredth chapter, a three thousandth chapter—and He is still writing. The purpose of God is that we be filled with the Spirit of the Lord and that we experience that divine infilling, that holy endowment again and again.

That leads to a discussion of the price and preparation for a Pentecost. How do we have that power? Jesus tells us to *labete*, which means "take" or "seize" the power. Poured out upon the world, He is ours to possess. How do you have the Pentecostal presence and power of God in your life? The outline for us is given in the Word of the Lord.

PRAYER AND WAITING UPON GOD

First, there is no other way to receive His Holy Spirit but by prayer. We do not have two alternatives or ten choices. There is one and one way only in which God mediates to us the power of His presence and Spirit and that way is through prayer. The same Lord God who made the universe that follows certain laws decided and purposed that we should have the presence and power in our lives through intercession and through prayer.

A mission in Africa had fallen into despair. No one was converted. And one day the mission was plunged into despair when the tribal chief appeared before the mission and said: "I hereby renounce the Christian faith. I am going back to my heathen gods. When I worshiped my tribal gods I was happy. After I became a Christian, I became miserable. I am denouncing the faith and going back to my heathen ways." In desperation the mission quit its work and bowed before the Lord in prayer and intercession. They stayed before God. The result is what you could have expected. A revival broke out. A great, sweeping Pentecostal presence of the saving grace of God swept through the tribe. Even the tribal chief began preaching the gospel of the Son of God. I cannot pronounce the word that the chief was using for his language is one that I cannot fathom. But when we translate the word he used, the word meant "joy is killing me." The same must be true with us. We can hone all the machinery of our church. We can grease all the wheels that turn in the organized life of the church, but the church will finally come to a dead halt, a standstill, unless it is bathed in prayer and the whole foundation is laid upon intercession and appeal to God.

Let me read from a godly minister named Richard Newton, a preacher of great power in the nineteenth century.

> The principal cause of my leanness and unfruitfulness is owing to an unaccountable backwardness to pray. I can write or read or converse or hear with a ready heart; but prayer is more spiritual and inward than any of these, and the more spiritual any duty is the more my carnal heart is apt to start from it. Prayer and patience and faith are never disappointed. When I can find my heart in frame and liberty for prayer, everything else is comparatively easy.

One need not decry the organized life of our church any more than he would decry the minister's preparation in study. But God does not work only in the brilliance of the pastor, nor does the Spirit necessarily move in the finely-tuned organized life of the church. There has to be something over and beyond if power is to come from God.

You can build a house without prayer. You can build a corporation without prayer. You can run a business without prayer. You can live in the carnal world and enjoy it without prayer. But you cannot do God's business without the Lord. There has to be the presence of the convicting power of the Holy Spirit with us or else what we do is in the strength of human flesh. Only God can convict a man of sin and regenerate his soul. All the organizations brought to bear on any family in the earth are just so much human carnality unless the effort is done in the moving, saving Spirit of God.

Let us hear what the men who belonged to William Carey's brotherhood in the mission in Serampore, just eighteen miles from Calcutta, had to say about prayer:

Let us often look at David Brainerd in the woods of America, pouring out his very soul before God for the perishing heathen.

Prayer—secret, fervent, believing prayer—lies at the root of all personal godliness. A heart given up to God in closet religion—this, more than all knowledge, or all other gifts, will fit us to become the instruments of God in the great work of human redemption.

Those men saw the secret of the successful Christian life. If they had any ableness to convert the heathen Hindu in India, that power had to come from God.

We used to think of the heathen there and of God's sainted people here. The frontier of the mission line runs today through every town and state, every government and nation, every language and tribe under the sun. There is no such thing as "the heathen there and the Christian saved here." The heathen are everywhere and are becoming increasingly so. The pagan are in every nation and city around this world. The frontiers of our mission program are in Dallas as well as in Calcutta or Hong Kong or any other place in the earth. If we have any power to witness in this dark and heathen land, the power lies in the presence of the Holy Spirit of God working with us.

An Acknowledged, Recognized, Stated Dependence Upon the Holy Spirit

Second, we should have an open and stated recognized avowal of our dependence upon God. However gifted, learned, trained, or able we might be in ourselves, our efforts are still in the strength of the flesh without God. We are dependent upon God; therefore, let us boldly and honestly say that to God and one another. We cannot do God's assignment in ourselves. We cannot convert the soul of even the humblest little child. God has to help us. The Lord must work with us. We confess to Thee, O God, our inability, our human weakness and unableness. Dear God, we look to Thee for the victory and answer and power and presence and infilling and help.

In the Bible there is a moving picture in 2 Chronicles 20. Good King Jehoshaphat is on the throne of Judah. He is surrounded by enemies that threaten to destroy his land and people. He prays before God and says:

. . . we have no might against this great company that cometh against us; neither know we what to do: but our eyes are upon thee.

And all Judah stood before the LORD, with their little ones, their wives, and their children. (vv. 12-13)

Can you see that picture? A king, who in his inability to face the foes that surrounded him on every side, stood before God with his hands upraised in humble supplication and by his side stood the men of Judah and their wives and children with eyes facing heavenward. You know the rest of that story. God bared His great, mighty arm to save and to deliver. He never forsakes us or neglects us or refuses us. He just waits for a yielded heart and a surrendered life in which and through which to do His work in the earth.

Any great work for God that has ever been done has been done in the power and grace of the Holy Spirit. Bring a Christian is not enough; he must also have an enablement from heaven for the work to which God has called him. Each of us has his assignment. As Paul would say, "Each one of us has a gift." God may have given you the gift to pray with power, the gift may be to be wise in the government of the church, or your gift may be in presenting the gospel. All of us have our gifts and we use them only in the ableness and power of God. Beside our conversion and regeneration, there is also an infilling. There is a visitation from above. There is an experiential part of a man's religion. Not only did Christ die for our sins, not only does the Lord write our names in the Book of Life when we look in trust to Him, but there is also an experiential part to the Christian faith. God moves my soul when He speaks. He enables me to do His work, whatever my assignment may be. Any work that is done for God is always done in the power of the Holy Spirit.

Elisha was a child of God before Elijah met him, but Elisha was not prepared for the prophetic ministry until he had a double portion of the Spirit of prophecy fall upon him. That is why the exclamation of Elisha is so marvelously meaningful in the story. As Elijah and Elisha walked along, Elijah said to the young man, "Ask what I shall do for thee, before I be taken from thee." The young man said, "I pray thee, let a double portion of thy spirit be upon me" (2 Kings 2:9). I think Elijah was taken back by the unusual request. He must have been expecting something else. But he told Elisha that if he saw him when he was raptured, his prayer would be answered. Suddenly a chariot of fire and horses of fire appeared. Elijah was raptured up to glory in a whirlwind. And Elisha cried, "My father, my father, the chariot of Israel and the horsemen thereof." His request was fulfilled. He picked up the mantle that had fallen from the hands of Elijah and went to the edge of the waters of the Jordan and smote them and said, "Where is the LORD God of Elijah?" The waters parted on either side. The sons of the prophets of Jericho looked upon him and said, "The spirit of Elijah doth rest upon Elisha" (2 Kings 2:12,13). How did they know that? When a man has the Spirit of God in him, his face shines. The Spirit is in the very timber of his voice, in the very gesture of his hands, in the way he walks, in the way that he is.

Jesus was a child of God when He was born. He had a holy infancy, a spotless youth, a manhood without reproach. But before He was prepared for His messianic ministry, He first had to be anointed from God. Jesus was anointed at His baptism when the Spirit of the Lord came down in the form of a dove and lighted upon Him, and God said, "This is my beloved Son."

The disciples were Christians before Pentecost, but before they were ready for their witnessing to that pagan world, they first had to be endued with power from on high.

Saul of Tarsus was converted on the road to Damascus. In the light of the glory of the presence of Jesus he fell down, blind. He said, "Lord, what wilt thou have me to do?" (Acts 9:6). Led by the hand in his blindness, he came to Damascus. After he had prayed and fasted for three days and three nights, Ananias was sent to him by the Lord and said to him, "Brother Saul, the Lord, even Jesus, that appeared unto thee in the way as thou camest, hath sent me, that thou mightest receive thy sight, and be filled with the Holy Ghost" (Acts 9:17). That is the ministry of the apostle Paul.

Paul was learned and educated and brilliant and equipped. He could speak Aramaic, Hebrew, Latin, Greek, and Sicilian. He had sat at the feet of Gamaliel, one of the seven rabbanim of the Talmud. He was learned in the theology of the Jews. He was perfectly at home with an Athenian group, quoting their own poets to them. He could converse with a Roman centurion face to face. In whatever culture or society he moved, whether in Rome or Corinth, he was perfectly at home. Paul was an able and gifted man in himself, trained and educated. How did he preach? Let me quote from 1 Corinthians 2:

> And I, brethren, when I came to you, came not with excellency of speech or of wisdom, declaring unto you the testimony of God.
>
> For I determined not to know any thing among you, save Jesus Christ, and him crucified.
>
> And I was with you in weakness, and in fear, and in much trembling.
>
> And my speech and my preaching was not with enticing words of man's wisdom, but in demonstration of the Spirit and of power:

That your faith should not stand in the wisdom of men, but in the power of God. (vv. 1-5)

Our Praying and Dependence Upon the Holy Spirit

I admire any man who stands to witness for Christ and speaks gloriously. But there is no power in the oratory or learning of a man as such. The power lies in another area in the man's heart and the man's life. Some of the men who have had that power have been men who were without formal training such as John Jasper or Dwight L. Moody. There is a secret in the church. There is a secret in the life of the Christian, and there is a secret in the Christian's power in the earth which does not lie in the man but in Christ; not in human ingenuity, but in the presence of God.

Richard Cecil, born in 1748, was an English preacher of tremendous ability who said:

There is a manifest want of spiritual influence on the ministry of the present day. I feel it in my own case and I can see it in that of others. I am afraid there is too much of a low, managing, contriving, maneuvering temper of mind among us. We are laying ourselves out more than is expedient to meet one man's taste and another man's dislike. The ministry should find in us a simple habit of spirit and a holy but humble indifference to all consequences.

Let us pray that there might be less and less of ourselves in our work and more and more of God until there is nothing of ourselves and everything of the Lord.

10

The Miracles of Pentecost

And when the day of Pentecost was fully come, they were all with one accord in one place.

And suddenly there came a sound from heaven as of a rushing mighty wind, and it filled all the house where they were sitting.

And there appeared unto them cloven tongues like as of fire, and it sat upon each of them.

And they were all filled with the Holy Ghost, and began to speak with other tongues, as the Spirit gave them utterance.

And there were dwelling at Jerusalem Jews, devout men, out of every nation under heaven.

Now when this was noised abroad, the multitude came together, and were confounded, because that every man heard them speak in his own language.

And they were all amazed and marvelled, saying one to another, Behold, are not all these which speak Galilaeans?

And how hear we every man in our own tongue, wherein we were born? (Acts 2:1-8)

Pentecost is significant in typology and in the ritual of the Mosaic legislation. There is significance in the timing of the new dispensation's coming to pass at Pentecost. The Greek numeral for "fifty" is *pentekonta*. The substantive form of the word is *pentekoste*, the Greek word for "fiftieth"—the fiftieth day. The word refers to the fiftieth day after the Passover. The Passover was followed by the Feast of Weeks, the Feast of Unleavened Bread. In those seven weeks that followed, forty-nine days, the fiftieth day was called the Feast of Pentecost.

In typology in the Old Testament, among many other things, after the Passover on the day of the beginning of the Feast of Unleavened Bread, a sheaf of the barley harvest was offered to God, and that sheaf

71

was of the firstfruits. When the Lord was crucified on Passover, He was raised on the first day of the week. He was the firstfruits to God and that sheaf represented His marvelous and heavenly resurrection, which was the beginning of the harvest, the beginning of the firstfruits to the Lord. Seven weeks later the Mosaic legislation offered unto God a loaf of wheat bread which represented the gathering together of the final harvest.

At Pentecost the ingathering, the harvest of the wheat was offered to God. So at Pentecost the peoples and nations of the world were gathered into the family of Christ, into the body of our Lord. It is therefore deeply significant that this new era, this new dispensation, this new age of grace is introduced to us at Pentecost, the gathering together of the harvest of the Lord.

THE EXTERNAL PHENOMENA OF THE HEAVENLY GIFT

When the day of Pentecost was come, some miraculous and marvelous things happened to the 120 followers of Christ. However the archaeologists and the geologists push back the age of the world, and however the anthropologists and biologists push back the age of life in this earth, they are forced to acknowledge that there were phenomena in the world at one time that men no longer know and no longer experience. There were things long ago that shaped this universe and life and living that no longer are to be found in modern human observation and experience.

So it is that in the first chapter of Genesis there was a new creation. The Holy Spirit of God brooded over the dark chaos of this primeval world and out of it brought the beauty of the new creation and the Garden of Eden in which the Lord set our first parents. Likewise, there are miraculous phenomena that accompanied this new introduction that are not experienced by our people today.

First, "Suddenly there came a sound from heaven as of a rushing mighty wind, and it filled all the house where they were sitting." There was no wind or tornado. There came a *sound* from heaven as of a rushing mighty wind which is in itself of tremendous typological, exegetical, and revelational meaning and significance.

In the Bible the word for "spirit" is "breath" or "wind." It is the Hebrew word *ruach*. In Greek the word is *pneuma*. A pneumatic tire refers to a tire that is filled with wind.

The Lord said in John 3:

Marvel not that I said unto thee, Ye must be born again.
The wind bloweth where it listeth, and thou hearest the sound thereof, but
canst not tell whence it cometh, and whither it goeth: so is every one that is born
of the Spirit. (vv. 7-8)

In John 20, when the Lord appeared to His disciples after He was raised from the dead, He breathed on them the breath of God and said, "Receive ye the Holy Ghost." This is the phenomenon that happened at Pentecost: the breath of God, the presence of the Lord, the very Spirit of the Lord was poured out upon the apostles.

Second, "There appeared unto them cloven tongues like as a fire, and it sat upon each of them." The phenomenon was that while they were there praying, a mighty shekinah glory came down from heaven and as it came down, the glory became cloven; that is, it separated. As the great light came down, it glowed over the head of each one of them. This also is a tremendous symbol.

The Lord could have let down from heaven a burning, flaming sword and placed the hilt of it in the hand of each one of those disciples. But He did not send the sword. What He sent was a tongue like as a fire which burned over the head of each one of them. The propagation of the faith of the gospel of Christ is never to be by the sword. Presenting Christ is never to be by coercion or force, but by the witnessing, preaching testimony of God's people.

In Revelation 12 we read: "And they overcame him by the blood of the Lamb, and by the word of their testimony" (v. 11a). Revelation 1:16 says, ". . . and out of his mouth went a sharp two-edged sword. . . ." "The pen is mightier than the sword," is a saying that is everlastingly true. The word is mightier than the force, the coercive agent. To prove that fact, simply look around you. The explosive power in a word is something that cannot be killed, such as the explosive power of the idea of communism. In traveling through Russia and East Germany, and having stood on the border and looked into the interior of China, I think of the explosiveness of the words of Karl Marx and Fredrich Engels. There is power in an idea. There is explosion in a word. God's great assignment for us who are His witnesses in this earth is to use the idea, the witness, the testimony, and the spoken word to evangelize the world. Our weakness is that we do not speak. We do not testify. We do not deliver the message. We are indifferent about the faith, so there does not flame and burn and rise upward from our souls any desire to tell others about His saving grace. The great phenomenon in this verse was that there appeared to those in the upper room tongues like as fire that burned over the head of each one.

Third, "And they were all filled with the Holy Ghost, and began to speak with other tongues, as the Spirit gave them utterance." Those who were present at that Pentecostal feast said:

> And how hear we every man in our own tongue, wherein we were born?
> Parthians, and Medes, and Elamites, and the dwellers in Mesopotamia, and in Judaea, and Cappadocia, in Pontus, and Asia,
> Phyrgia, and Pamphylia, in Egypt, and in the parts of Libya about Cyrene, and strangers of Rome, Jews and proselytes,
> Cretes and Arabians, we do hear them speak in our tongues the wonderful works of God. (Acts 2:8-11)

God intends that every tribe and language under the sun hear this glorious message in their own speech and language. There should be missionaries in every language of the world preaching the glorious good news of Jesus. One of the miraculous things of the message of the gospel is that no matter what language one uses, when he translates the message of Christ, the people who read the truth of the Savior say, "That is the most marvelous message I have ever heard."

A Hottentot was talking to an English missionary and said, "I am sorry for you people over there in America." The missionary said, "Why are you sorry for us?" He said, "Because you cannot read the Bible in Hottentot and you do not know how John 3:16 sounds in Hottentot." It is a marvelous thing for each to be listening to the Word of the Lord in his own language.

In Revelation 7 we read:

> . . . What are these which are arrayed in white robes? and whence came they?
> And I said unto him, Sir, thou knowest. And he said to me, These are they which came out of great tribulation, and have washed their robes, and made them white in the blood of the Lamb. (vv. 13-14)

Out of every nation, tongue, and tribe there were those who praised God, and that was Pentecost, the gathering together of all of God's saints in the earth. Some day when this age of Pentecostal grace is done, we shall all be together, raptured up before the Lord from every family, nation, tribe, tongue, and language in the earth.

Fourth, look at a marvelous change that came into the life of Simon Peter. Only seven weeks earlier he cowered before a little damsel who said, "Aren't you one of His disciples?" He cursed, swore, and denied that he ever knew the Lord. Now look at him. We see Simon Peter standing before those people and he is saying to them, "Him, being delivered by the determinate counsel and foreknowledge of God, ye have taken, and by wicked hands have crucified and slain" (Acts 2:23). This same man is bold now before all Jerusalem and accuses them of crucifying and with wicked hands slaying the Prince of Glory. He repeats the accusation. "Therefore let all the house of Israel know assuredly, that God hath made that same Jesus, whom ye have crucified, both Lord and Christ" (Acts 2:36). Such a transformed heart was a miracle in the life of Simon Peter.

Fifth, "Now when they heard this, they were pricked in their heart, and said unto Peter and to the rest of the apostles, Men and brethren, what shall we do?" (Acts 2:37). The Lord spoke in this same place to these same people in Jerusalem, but when He spoke to them, they were infuriated, irritated beyond compare, and they put a price on His head saying that if anyone could find Jesus and lay hands upon Him, they were to bring Him in for judgment. And Judas betrayed the Lord for thirty pieces of silver. Our Lord was crucified by these same people. What has happened now? Jesus said:

> . . . It is expedient for you that I go away: for if I go not away, the Comforter will not come unto you; but if I depart, I will send him unto you.
> And when he is come, he will reprove the world of sin, and of righteousness, and of judgment:
> Of sin, because they believe not on me. (John 16:7-9)

The Lord said in John 14: ". . . greater works than these shall ye do; because I go unto my Father" (v. 12). Look at that miracle. These people to whom the Lord spoke became infuriated and crucified Him. Simon Peter now spoke to the same people of their sin in crucifying the Son of God and they were convicted in their hearts and cried: "What shall we do? Where shall we turn?"

When the Spirit of God came upon John Wesley, he wrote: "I preach the same sermon, using the same text. Before, people did not come. Now they come." The difference is the Spirit of God, the breath of the Lord.

Dwight L. Moody made the same confession. After his wonderful spiritual experience, he said: "I preach the same sermon. I use the same text. But now they come and they come and they come." The difference is the Holy Spirit of the Lord, the breath of God. The miracle of the foundation of the new spiritual day of grace was as great a miracle as when the Spirit of God brooded over the face of the deep and brought beauty and order out of the chaotic universe. We are living now in that day of grace.

O breath of God, fall fresh on me.

11

The Pattern of Pentecost

And when the day of Pentecost was fully come, they were all with one accord in one place.

And suddenly there came a sound from heaven, as of a rushing mighty wind, and it filled all the house where they were sitting.

And there appeared unto them cloven tongues, like as of fire, and it sat upon each of them.

And they were all filled with the Holy Ghost, and began to speak with other tongues, as the Spirit gave them utterance. (Acts 2:1-4)

In our preaching through the Book of Acts we are following the pattern of events that occured at Pentecost. After the Holy Spirit filled these devoted followers of Christ, we see the marvel, the wonder, and the awe that fell upon the vast concourse of Jews who had gathered there for Pentecost from the ends of the earth. They said one to another: "How can these men speak like this? Are not all of them Galileans?" The educated people of Jerusalem said they were not men of the schools, of the seminaries, of the universities, or of education. They were rude, rough, and crude fishermen from Galilee. "How is it that we hear from these men in our own *glossa* (language), the marvelous works of God?" This is the beginning of a new dispensation, the beginning of the dispensation of the Holy Spirit, of the grace of God poured out upon His church. Every new era of God is always introduced by wonders, signs, and miracles.

SOME OF GOD'S MARVELS AND MANIFESTATIONS
ARE NEVER REPEATED

77

When God created matter, He accomplished that which was of a miraculous nature. Then it was never done again. The miracles stopped; just the substance continued. Since the days in the beginning when God created the heavens and the earth, not one atom of matter has been created. God created matter one time only.

The same thing happened when God introduced the era of the Mosaic legislation, the Mosaic law, and the Mosaic covenant. God's presentation of the Mosaic covenant was attended by marvelous signs and wonders, such as manna, in Egypt, at the Red Sea, and in the wilderness wanderings. But the manna ceased. For years the children of Israel gathered the wonder of the gift of God in the wilderness, then when they entered the Promised Land, the sign ceased. No more do we see those wonders done in Egypt—no more the crossing of the Red Sea with the waters banked on either side, or the gathering of the manna in the morning. There is only one other dispensation that remains, that is, at the consummation of the age in the second coming of Christ. Then, also, there will be marvelous wonders, miracles, and signs such as the world has never seen.

THE CONFIRMING SIGNS OF THE NEW ERA OF GRACE

This age of the Holy Spirit was introduced at Pentecost and was attended, as God always confirms His works, by wonders, signs, and miracles. First was the sound as of a rushing, mighty wind. Second was the flame of the shekinah glory of God moving upward. Third was the Holy Spirit, filling those apostles who spoke with languages, *glossa*, declaring to those visitors from the ends of the earth the marvelous proclamation of the new age of grace in Christ Jesus and the calling out of the church of the Lord.

As Acts continues, the third sign was seen when the gospel was preached to the Gentiles in the household of the Roman centurion, Cornelius, at Caesarea. Simon Peter, describing it, said in Acts 11:17, "Forasmuch then as God gave them *the like gift* as he did unto us, who believed on the Lord Jesus Christ; what was I, that I could withstand God?" That is, they spake with *glossa* and magnified the Lord in languages.

The same marvelous sign was seen also in Ephesus where men also spoke with *glossa* in that great capital city of the Roman province of Asia. They magnified the Lord with *glossa*.

Again, in the church at Corinth, they magnified the Lord with languages. When the unusual sign and phenomenon occurred in Corinth, Paul wrote, "and *glossa* shall cease." The sign has never been seen or heard again.

First Corinthians 13:8 says, ". . . tongues, . . . shall cease." Tongues have never been given again. After Paul wrote 1 Corinthians, he wrote the letter to the Romans which is a doctrinal treatise of the Christian faith. The *glossa* are not mentioned. After Paul wrote 1 Corinthians he wrote 2 Corinthians. The tongues are not mentioned. After Paul wrote 1 Corinthians he also wrote Galatians. The sign of tongues is not mentioned. After Paul wrote 1 Corinthains he wrote Ephesians, which is written to all the churches of all time. He does not refer to tongues. After Paul wrote 1 Corinthians he wrote Philippians. Again he does not refer to tongues. The same can be said of Colossians, 1 and 2 Thessalonians, 1 and 2 Timothy, Titus, and Philemon. Why? Because the sign of tongues has ceased.

From Hebrews we can go through the rest of the books of the New Testament to the Book of the Revelation, and there is no hint, not even an approach to any sign or wonder of the *glossa*, for the sign of tongues has ceased. The same can be seen during the two thousand years of Christian history. The great leaders of the Christian faith today are known to us intimately, and not one of them has ever engaged in any such practice as attempting to speak in an unknown tongue.

John Chrysostom was called "John the Golden Mouth." He was the incomparable preacher of the imperial court of Constantinople which began to flourish in A.D. 350. John Chrysostom knew nothing about speaking in tongues.

Ambrose, the bishop of Milan, Augustine, the great theologian of the church, Savanarola, John Huss, John Wycliffe, John Wesley, Charles G. Finney, Dwight L. Moody, Charles Haddon Spurgeon, Martin Luther, and John Calvin were all great Christian leaders. They never attempted to speak in an unknown tongue.

All over the world recordings have been made of so-called unknown tongues. They have been taken to the greatest linguistic institutions in the world, but at no time has a language ever been identified.

What is it that remains of Pentecost? What remains is for us to share in all of its glory and wonder. When I open the Bible and read in Acts and the rest of the Bible I see the marvel and glory of the presence of

God. What continues when Pentecost is repeated is the driving, moving presence of the Holy Spirit.

Dwight L. Moody said: "I believe that Pentecost was but a specimen day. I think the church has made a woeful mistake in believing that Pentecost was a miracle not to be repeated. I believe that now, if we looked upon Pentecost as a specimen day, and began to pray, we would have the Pentecostal fire here again today." I believe every word of that. Pentecost was given to us as a pattern, and it can be repeated again and again. Pentecost was the introduction, the opening of the door, the lifting up of the curtain. There are four marvelous phenomena that attended Pentecost that are to be repeated again and again today and to the ends of the earth.

Four Phenomena That Attended Pentecost That Are to Be Repeated Again and Again

First, we read in Acts, "And they were all filled with the Holy Ghost." We turn the page and read, "And he was filled with the Holy Ghost." We read further, "And they were filled with the Holy Spirit." We read in Acts 20, "And they were filled with the Holy Spirit." We read in Ephesians 5:18 where Paul writes, ". . . be filled with the Holy Spirit." This is the Pentecostal gift that is repeated again and again and can be repeated anywhere in this earth. Somewhere in the world there is an outpouring of the Spirit of God. There is always this fullness of the Pentecostal outpouring of the Holy Spirit of God.

From much reading and experience I prepared the following statement:

Always, Somewhere, the Fulness of the Spirit Is Outpoured

1. When the church at Jerusalem was lost in Judaizing legalism the churches at Ephesus and at Antioch were abounding in spiritual glory.

2. When waning piety in Antioch turned the church into an empty shell, the Spirit of God was waxing strong in Milan.

3. While the churches of Alexandria and Carthage and North Africa were sinking into formalism, the churches of Gaul were battling the voices of imperial oppression and winning converts from the dark depths of barbarianism.

4. While the church at Rome was falling into empty pretense, all Ireland was turning to the holiness and beauty of the Savior.

5. While Mohammed was destroying the churches of Syria, Egypt, and

Asia Minor, the scholars of Iona were studying the Bible and their preachers were evangelizing all of Scotland.

6. While the papal court of Avignon was disgracing the name of religion in luxury and in vice, pious men were writing books, preaching sermons, and practicing godly virtues in the cities of Germany.

7. When Italian fields were covered over with worthless, rotten stubble, Bohemia was ripening white unto the harvest.

8. When the night of religious superstition and despotism was getting darker in continental Europe, the morning star of the Reformation was rising in England.

9. While the Unitarian defection was emptying the churches of New England, the pioneer preacher was pressing beyond the Alleghenies, across the frontiers of the wilderness and of the prairies, establishing the churches and the Christian institutions that bless us and our children today.

10. While the voices of a thousand sterile, decadent church leaders decry mass evangelism, Billy Graham is preaching to the greatest throngs in human history.

11. While the fetid breath of liberalism is destroying the witness of the mainline denominations in America, there is revival of unusual proportion in Indonesia, in South Korea, and on the continent of Africa.

That is Pentecost, and it is intended for all of God's people through the ages. The dead church is a disgrace to the name of Christ. There ought to be power, life, quickening presence, and revival among our people. God intends His church to be alive and growing.

Second, look at the boldness of Simon Peter. This is the man who, a few days earlier, cowered before a little maid when she said, "You are one of His disciples." He swore and denied that he ever knew Christ. This is that same Simon Peter who is standing at Pentecost and, bold and courageous as a roaring lion, is accusing the very men who cried for the blood of Jesus and who nailed Him to a cross. This is a miracle of boldness in the faith.

In my first little country pastorate I said to one of my men: "You know, I just cannot talk to anyone about the Lord. I am just so timid and afraid." He said to me, "Young pastor, do you know what the matter is?" I said: "No. I don't." Polished, cultured, educated people will always observe the amenities of life. They will always be nice and often will not be honest and forthright. An uneducated, uncultured, unlettered rural man sometimes will tell you frankly and openly what he thinks. He said,

"The trouble with you is you ain't got no religion." I was his pastor! I stood in the pulpit of that little church on Sunday and opened the Bible and preached to him. The nerve of that fellow telling me I "ain't got no religion.!" But he made an impression on me I have never forgotten.

Certainly, if I do not have any religion, I have nothing to share with anyone. I have nothing to say. No wonder I fear and tremble and am hesitant and timid. I have no Good News to tell. If a man were starving and I had bread, would I be timid? If I met a man who was thirsting to death and I had water to give him, would I be too shy to offer it? The sweetest thing I could ever share, the noblest gift I could ever bestow, the grandest news this side of heaven itself is the Good News—Jesus. That is the gift of the Spirit of God. We are to be bold in the faith.

Third, the marvelous power of conviction and conversion that followed the witness of the preacher is of God. We cannot convict anyone. We cannot convert anyone. When Simon Peter delivered that message from the Lord filled with the Spirit, the people were convicted in their hearts and cried out saying, "Men and brethren, what shall we do?" Peter said, "Repent, and be baptized." At that moment God added to His church three thousand souls.

John Wesley came to America to convert the American Indian, but when he went back to London miserable and discouraged, he wrote, "I went to America to convert the Indian, but who shall convert me?" A Moravian witnessed to John Wesley and he was marvelously filled with the Spirit. Then John Wesley wrote in his journal: "I called and they did not come. Now I call and they come."

In 1821 the Holy Spirit of God filled the lawyer Charles G. Finney and set him on fire. People by the thousands came and were converted. The city of Rochester, New York, at that time had a population of fifty thousand. And one hundred thousand souls were saved in that revival of Charles Finney.

In 1871 the same experience became Dwight L. Moody's. Moody said: "I preach the same sermons. I use the same text. I make the same invitations, but now they come." What is the difference? It lies in the filling of the Holy Sprit of God. Pentecost is repeated.

Fourth, an indescribable lift comes into a man's heart and life when he gives his soul to Jesus. "And they, continuing daily with one accord in the temple, and breaking bread from house to house, did eat their meat with gladness and singleness of heart, praising God, and having favour with all the people. And the Lord added to the church daily such as should be saved."

A man was wonderfully converted. He went back to his job the next morning, and his fellow workers made fun of him. They said: "So you have been converted. Don't you know that the Bible has more than ten thousand mistakes?" He said: "I don't know about that. All I know is that since I gave my heart to Jesus, I have been so happy I cannot sleep." That is a wonderful way to be.

If religion for us is dull and dry it is because we have lost the Spirit. When we are filled with the Spirit, we want to go to church. We want to pray to the Lord. We want to sing the songs of Zion. What a difference Pentecost made! What a difference the repeated Pentecost continues to make!

12

With One Accord

And when the day of Pentecost was fully come, they were all with one accord in one place. (Acts 2:1)

There is a word that Dr. Luke loves to use which is peculiar to him, and a word that he will use again and again. Only one time does another author use that word and that is Paul, who incidentally uses the word in Romans 5:6. Other than that, only Luke uses the word *homothumadon*, translated "of one accord," "with one mind." *Homothumadon* is an adverb composed of two basic words. *Homo* means "the same." Homogeneous means the same constituency all the way through. If a man is a homosexual he is attracted to the same sex. If milk is homogenized it is the same all the way through, it does not separate. The other Greek word is *thumos* which refers to heat, to anger, or to a volatile spirit. When the Greeks put the words together in the word *homothumadon*, the word refers to one in spirit, one in heart, one in accord.

Look at the repeated use of the phrase "with one accord":

These all continued with one accord in prayer and supplication, with the women, and Mary the mother of Jesus, and with his brethren. (Acts 1:14)

And when the day of Pentecost was fully come, they were all with one accord in one place. (Acts 2:1)

And they, continuing daily with one accord in the temple, and breaking bread from house to house, did eat their meat with gladness and singleness of heart,
Praising God, and having favour with all the people. (Acts 2:46-47)

And when they heard that, they lifted up their voice to God with one accord, and said, Lord, thou art God. (Acts 4:24)

And by the hands of the apostles were many signs and wonders wrought among the people; (and they were all with one accord in Solomon's porch. . .

And believers were the more added to the Lord, multitudes both of men and women.) (Acts 5:12,14)

The followers gathered here in the presence of the Lord were united in one heart and in one spirit.

A United People in Spirit

First, the followers of the Lord were united in their inward commitment to God and to one another. They were not divided. It is so easy for us to fall away from a oneness in spirit and to yield to the temptation to be critical and to find fault with one another.

When the Lord left His little group of 120 followers, they had only a Savior and a promise. They had no guns, no tanks, no armies, no social standing, no political power, no status. They resolved to pray together and to stay together, and while they did so the Pentecostal power fell on them. This is the first thing Luke tells us of the faithful group of the Lord's followers. With one accord they were together in supplication before God.

I can imagine 120 people looking at Simon Peter and saying: "There is Simon Peter. You know, I feel he is still following afar off. How in the world can anyone ever forget that he denied he even knew the Lord? I have no confidence in him." I can imagine 120 people looking at Thomas and saying: "Look at Thomas. He is still doubting. He drags his feet. He is no encouragement to us in Jesus' work. He is still full of doubt. He does not fully believe." And how about John and James: "I believe they are still as ambitious as they ever were. All they want to do is to be exalted. They want to be presented. They are just as selfish as they were when we first began to follow the Lord Jesus. I do not have any confidence in them." It is easy to do that even today in the house of the Lord. All of us have our faults and failures. It is easy to remember them and say, "I have no confidence in that person."

United in Presence

Second, the band of followers were one in their convocation and presence. The apostles were there. The women were there. One of the glorious things about the Christian religion is that it is also for women. It is a mother's religion, a wife's religion, a girl's religion. There is room in

God's house for dedicated women to shine and serve in the work of the Lord.

One-hundred-twenty followers launched the Christian faith, and most of them were laymen. We think that the preacher is the one to pray, win souls, and visit. The preacher does his part, but the church is a mighty and powerful witness when it is filled with dedicated laymen.

One of the greatest preachers of all time was a layman. All of his life he was known as "Mr. Moody." He was never an ordained preacher; he was never licensed. When he started going to church after he was saved (in those days the pews were rented), he took a whole section of the church and paid for the pew rental. He filled the pews every service with men and women, boys and girls who needed the Lord. Finally, he started teaching the people in a Sunday school class. Then God so blessed Mr. Moody that he began preaching to the people. God continued to bless him further so that he began to preach all over America. And he also preached all over England. But he was always "Mr. Moody." Oh, what a wonderful church when you have consecrated ministers and elders, and by their side a glorious band of laymen and laywomen!

The young people were there. Peter says this was the fulfillment of Joel's prophecy when Joel said, "And it shall come to pass afterward, that I will pour out my spirit upon all flesh; and your sons and your daughters shall prophesy, your old men shall dream dreams, your young men shall see visions" (2:28). The young people there were dreaming dreams and getting ready for the greatest assignment God ever gave to young people: serving Jesus in manhood and in womanhood.

God's People Fall Into Divisiveness

There is a tragic weakness in the Christian faith which is the tendency to bog down in the morass and quagmire of divisiveness, criticism, and bitterness. Look at Israel as an example. In Exodus 20 God gave to His chosen seed the Ten Commandments. In Exodus 19 He said, "Israel is to be unto me a kingdom of priests and a holy nation." What is a kingdom of priests? Priests are people who represent us to God and represent God to us. That is, the Lord chose Israel to be the missionaries, teachers, and preachers to the whole world.

What did Israel do? Instead of being the missionaries of the world, they wrapped their garments around themselves and called everyone else a Gentile dog. In the New Testament the family of God has divided into Pharisees, Sadducees, and zealots, and they all bitterly are warring against each other.

Christians are worse. The divisiveness that enters into the body of Christ is unholy, ungodly, and unbelievable. In the first Christian centuries the entire civilized world was being evangelized. Literally it was set upon new hinges. But then the entire Christian world at the end of the first three centuries fell into an actual war over *homoousios*, "the same essence," and *homoiousios*, "of a similar essence." The question dealt with whether Christ was the same as or similar to the Father. The estranged and enraged bishops divided and tore apart the entire Christian faith and actually went to war over the altercation.

Edward Gibbon wrote the greatest history in human speech, *The Decline and Fall of the Roman Empire*. In the volume he sarcastically said, "The Christian church divided the entire civilized world over a Greek iota"—the difference between *homoousios* and *homoiousios*.

Baptists are the worst of all. When they call us "the fighting Baptists," they surely know us well. Our churches will divide over anything. The division that comes into our fellowship is almost unthinkable. When I was in seminary all the professors used a church they were familiar with as an example of how Christians can go to war over an inconsequential matter. This battle was over the piano—whether to place it in front of the pulpit or near where the choir was seated. All the seminary professors went to the church to try to settle the fight over the piano. They failed. Others went to settle that battle. They failed. So the church split wide open.

Those who moved out organized another Baptist church, and I was called to be a pastor in the original church. To my amazement, the old war-horse who led that battle in the other church was in the church to which I had been called. He was living in a little cottage with his maiden sister, Lizzy, and I went to visit him. He had become senile, but all I had to do to resurrect him to life was to say, "Brother Q. J., tell me about that piano." He had a gold-headed cane and would sit and beat on the floor as he told me how he fought over that piano. One evening, as he was telling me the same story, I put my hand on his arm and said: "Wait a minute Brother Q. J., where did you want that piano? Did you want it in front of the pulpit or on the side?" The old man began to think and think. Then he began to tap on the floor with that gold-headed cane. Finally he lifted up his voice and said, "Lizzy, where did I want that piano?" Isn't that typical? Most of the things over which we war and fight are inconsequential. Lord, if there is anything that ever separates us, let it to be hell itself. Keep us together in the faith and the body of Christ with one accord.

What pulls people together is a tremendous commitment, a dedication, a vast assignment. Jesus told His followers to wait and pray because He was committing into their hands the evangelization of the whole world. Think of matching these souls, just 120 in number, against the world! Such an assignment bowed them to their knees and in *homothumadon*; in a common determination they faced the evangelization of the civilized world.

One-hundred-fifty years ago our Baptist churches were tiny groups scattered up and down the eastern seaboard. In those days Adoniram and Ann Hasseltine Judson, and their friend Luther Rice, found themselves as Baptists in India. It was decided that Luther Rice would return home and tell these Baptist churches that they had a missionary couple, Adoniram and Ann Judson, on the mission field. Up and down the eastern seaboard he visited the little churches and told them about the evangelization of the world and the great mission enterprise. He organized them into associations and conventions and founded Columbia College in Washington, D. C. for the education and preparation of the great mission endeavor. Our Baptist churches pulled together. Our preachers began to pray together. They forgot their fifth Sunday debates, and they forgot their bitternesses and arguments, and they found themselves together, *homothumadon*, in one accord. That is what the Christian faith needs.

When we fall into divisiveness it is because we have turned aside from the great assignment and we are beginning to look at little things. The whole world lies upon our hearts. The vast mission enterprise has been committed to our souls. We must be together, *homothumadon*. We must pray together. We must dedicate our lives together for the saving of the lost and for the winning of these souls to the Lord.

13

The Baptism of the Holy Spirit

And when the day of Pentecost was fully come, they were all with one accord in one place.

And suddenly there came a sound from heaven as of a rushing mighty wind, and it filled all the house where they were sitting.

And there appeared unto them cloven tongues like as of fire, and it sat upon each of them.

And they were all filled with the Holy Ghost, and began to speak with other tongues, as the Spirit gave them utterance. (Acts 2:1-4)

As I read through the text I am amazed, for there is a phrase for which I am looking but do not find. The phrase is the "baptism of the Holy Spirit." There is no such phrase as that in the Bible. In the Greek the phrase used is the "baptism in the Holy Spirit." In the King James version of the Bible the translation is "baptized with the Holy Spirit." Since the phrase, "baptism of the Holy Spirit," is not in the Bible, I then look for the word "baptism," and I do not find that word in this passage. Maybe inerrancy has fallen into error. Maybe inspiration has dropped away from its inbreathing of God. Maybe infallibility is no longer infallible. Maybe God has made a mistake and He left out the word for which I am looking.

What is God saying? I discover as I study the Book that the "baptism with the Holy Spirit" is said just one time. In Matthew 3 John the Baptist said, "I indeed baptize you with water unto repentance: but he that cometh after me is mightier than I, whose shoes I am not worthy to bear: he shall baptize you with the Holy Ghost, and with fire" (v. 11). This passage is the only place where the phrase is mentioned in the Bible.

In Acts 1 Jesus referred to that one saying of John the Baptist. In Acts 11 Simon Peter referred to that same saying of John. Other than that, the word "baptism" is not mentioned.

If the word "baptism" is not used, then what word is used? All we have to do is to open the sacred Book and read: "And they were all filled with the Holy Ghost." Again and again we read: "And they were all filled with the Holy Spirit." There is never any deviation from the use of the word "filled." Always they are "filled" with the Holy Spirit, and not "baptized."

Then there must be some tremendous doctrinal revelation that God is teaching us. There is. God's presentation is fundamental and dynamic. Because we do not understand God's teachings is the reason we fall into such heresy and error. When one understands, God's Word is true and plain.

The "Baptism" and the "Filling"

Now let us look at those two words, "baptism" and "filling." John the Baptist used the word "baptize." He is the only one who ever said it. Then all of the recounting thereafter is the "filling" of the Holy Spirit. What is the difference between the prophecy of John the Baptist concerning Christ, "He shall baptize you with the Holy Spirit," and the story as it unfolds before us of the filling of the Holy Spirit? God plainly reveals the difference to us. With relationship to Christ, He is the baptizer in a once-for-all sense, and that only. That is, the outpouring of the Holy Spirit is an ascension gift of our Lord when He returned to heaven. After He was crucified, buried, and raised from the dead, He returned to His father and there He kept the promise He made to the disciples that He would pour out upon them the Spirit of presence and of power. And that happened only once. In that sense Christ is the baptizer with the Holy Spirit.

Why did He give the Holy Spirit just once? Because that ascension gift of the pouring out of the Spirit is the beginning of a new era, a new dispensation. It is the beginning of the day of the calling out, the gathering together of the body of Christ made up of Jew and Gentile. Paul, in Ephesians 3, describes the event as a *musterion*, a secret that God hid in His heart until He revealed it to His holy apostles. In one sense and in one time only is Christ considered the baptizer, and that was on the day of Pentecost.

The Holy Spirit baptized us into the body of Christ, for 1 Corinthians

12:13 says, "For by one Spirit are we all baptized into one body." When you became a Christian, the Holy Spirit baptized you and joined you to the body of Christ. That is the baptism of the Holy Spirit. First, it is a once-for-all ascension gift of Christ as He poured out the Holy Spirit upon the earth. Thereafter the Holy Spirit is the baptizer and He baptizes us, when we are saved, into the body of Christ.

The filling of the Holy Spirit of God is an experience that is ours now and forever and is repeated again and again and again. "And they were filled with the Holy Spirit in Jerusalem." "And they were filled with the Holy Spirit in Samaria." "And they were filled with the Holy Spirit in Ephesus." And they were filled with the Holy Spirit in Dallas. We are filled with the Holy Spirit of God today.

What is the difference between the "baptism" and the "filling"?

First, never in the Bible is there anything even approaching a command that we be "baptized with the Holy Spirit." But we are commanded to be "filled with the Spirit." It is a command of God (Eph. 5:18). A dry Christian without life, without quickening, without joy, without gladness is a travesty upon the faith. It is a disgrace to the name of the Lord. Thus, we are to be filled with the Spirit of God; we are to be bright, radiant, happy, singing, praising the Lord. Our church services, our prayer meetings, our Sunday school lessons, our witnessing, the whole life of the Christian is to be quickened and uplifted.

Second, the baptism is a once-for-all operation of God, but the filling can happen again and again, and this can be seen in the language that the Scriptures use.

Translating Greek verbs exactly as they are into English is almost impossible because the Greek language has a different verbal system than English. In English one cannot speak without tense because every verb must be placed in time. In the Greek language the verbal system expresses kinds of action. An action is considered a point happening one time or maybe going on and on.

Look at these verbs. In 1 Corinthians 12:13 we find: "For by one Spirit are we all *ebaptisthemen*, 'baptized'." That is one time. Only once are we all *ebaptisthemen* into the body of Christ.

Look at the verb in Ephesians 5:18, "But be filled with the Spirit." It is be ye *plerousthe* with the Spirit. The word connotes continuous action. Again and again we are to be filled with the Spirit of God.

Third, in the baptism we are talking about a positional operation of God. The way God gives His Holy Spirit is similar to what happens when we are converted, for God writes our names in the Book of Life. That is something God does and it is positional. A man can stand so tall but no taller. But God writes my name in the Book of Life in the third heaven beyond the highest stars. I am baptized into the body of Christ. He creates for me my relationship with the Lord, and places me in the body of Christ. We are all fellow members of the body of our Lord, joined to Him by the Holy Spirit of God. For that positional work of the Holy Spirit, the Bible uses the word "baptized."

The filling is experiential. It is something that happens to a man in his heart, and happens again and again. It may be that when you were saved you shouted, cried, or laughed, or it may be you were filled with the holiness of God. There are so many ways that we respond when we are converted and filled with the Holy Spirit of God. Then sometime later, maybe in a prayer service, in a dedication, in a kitchen corner, out in a field, or driving along crying to God, you can have another marvelous experience. You are filled with the Holy Spirit of God. Times without number I have felt the infilling as I met with God's people. And that filling recurs again and again. Nor do we ever reach any high plateau where God has nothing else for us. No matter how we have been filled, and no matter what wonderful experience we have had with Jesus, there is always something more and something beyond. We are filled again and again and yet again. God continues to bless us with some great, glorious thing.

THE MARVELOUS EFFECTS OF THE FILLING

Now let us examine the effects of the filling of the Spirit upon people, and a good example would be to look at the effect of the filling upon the apostles. Our text says, "And they were all filled with the Holy Ghost." The effect on the apostles was that they were new men. They were not the same. In the four Gospels the twelve apostles appeared quarrelsome, ambitious, and selfish. They were always vying with each other as to which one was going to be greatest in the kingdom of heaven. The argument was precipitated by who would be seated at the right hand and at the left hand of our Lord. While they were quarreling and trying to further their own selfish interests, the Lord took off His clothes, which is the humblest thing a man can do. A man without his clothes is a man without dignity, prestige, or power. A naked man is just flesh. The Lord took off His clothes and girded Himself with a towel and began to wash the apostles' feet. He dried their feet with the towel with which He was girded and said to them, "He that would be greatest in the kingdom of heaven must be the humblest servant of all." At the most sacred moment in the life of our Lord, His apostles were quarreling.

They were full of doubt. One of the finest apostles, Thomas, said: "I do not believe that He lives. You cannot convince me that dead men rise. Nor shall I be convinced until I put my finger in the scars on His hands and thrust my hand in the scar in His side."

A little girl in the household of the high priest accosted the big fisherman, Simon Peter, and pointed a finger at him and said: "You are one of His disciples. You talk like Him." He cowered before a little maid in the house swearing and cursing and said: "I never saw Him. I do not know Him." These were the men that we read about in the four Gospels.

After they were filled with the Holy Spirit they were bold, fearless, and courageous like lions. They rejoiced that they were even counted worthy to suffer for the name of Jesus. They filled the whole world with the faith that He is raised from the dead and He lives forever more. For those who find refuge in Him, He is for them also an everlasting Savior. These are the same men, but they are transformed men, they are new men. They have been filled with the Spirit of God.

The effects of the filling of the Holy Spirit are evident. Look at the effect that the filling of the Holy Spirit of God has upon sinners outside the church. These are the men who crucified Jesus and to whom Simon Peter is addressing this sermon. Their hands have been dipped in the blood of the Son of God. These are the men to whom Peter says, "Ye with wicked hands have taken and crucified the Son of Glory." He repeats the accusation boldly, courageously, facing those men and charging them with slaying the Prince of Peace. What is the response of those men who perpetrated the most heinous crime in human history, the crucifixion of the Son of God? Do we read that they rose in fury, seized the apostles, and threw them to their death off the highest pinnacle or stoned them outside the city? No. What we read is that they were cut to the heart, filled with conviction, and said: "Men and brethren, what shall we do? The blood of the Son of God is on our hands." They cried for mercy. As a result, not a mere half dozen, but 3000 souls that day were saved and added to the church.

In Acts 4 we read how 5000 *andron* believed. *Andron* is the word for "man" as opposed to "woman." Five thousand men were added to the faith. The Bible says that a great company of the priests became obedient to the faith. That is, they took a position of openly confessing their sins and being baptized by water as disciples of the despised Nazarene. Such a transformation of men's lives is a miracle, a wonder. It is the power of the gospel to reach hearts that are obstinate, steeped in sin, or given to vituperative denial and opposition.

A humble preacher was once seated in a hotel lobby along with a loud and blasphemous infidel. The infidel said to the preacher: "You and your prayers! Let us see you pray for me and convert me." The preacher in that hotel lobby knelt down by the side of the blatant infidel and prayed for his soul that he might be saved. When the infidel stood up he laughed and said; "Ha, I'm just the same. Nothing has been changed in me." The preacher humbly replied: "But wait. God is not done yet." Sometime later that humble preacher was looking at a newspaper from another town in which there was an article about a layman who was holding a heaven-sent, Spirit-filled revival meeting in that town. The preacher saw the name of the layman who was leading the revival, and it was the infidel for whom he had prayed in the hotel lobby.

If you want to look at the power of God unto salvation to change men's lives, look around you. It is everywhere. It is a miracle, the effect the filling of the Holy Spirit has upon sinners outside the fold of grace.

Look at the people whom God added to the first-century church. They continued steadfastly in the apostle's doctrine and fellowship, in the breaking of bread, and in praying. They ate their meat with gladness and singleness of heart, praising God, and finding favor with all the people. That is what a church is like when it is filled with the Spirit of God. There is no bickering, no quarreling, no vying, no selfish ambition. Master, fill us with the Spirit of God.

14

What We Must Do to Be Saved

> Therefore let all the house of Israel know assuredly, that God hath made that same Jesus, whom ye have crucified, both Lord and Christ.
>
> Now when they heard this, they were pricked in their heart, and said unto Peter and to the rest of the apostles, Men and brethren, what shall we do?
>
> Then Peter said unto them, Repent, and be baptized every one of you in the name of Jesus Christ for the remission of sins, and ye shall receive the gift of the Holy Ghost.
>
> For the promise is unto you, and to your children, and to all that are afar off, even as many as the Lord our God shall call.
>
> And with many other words did he testify and exhort, saying, Save yourselves from this untoward generation.
>
> Then they that gladly received his word were baptized: and the same day there were added unto them about three thousand souls. (Acts 2:36-41)

Many knowledgeable scholars have said that the word "repent" in our text is a poor translation. It is difficult to find a suitable English word for the Greek word, *metanoeo*. To us, the word "repentance" carries an overtone of sorrow or remorse. There is a Greek word *metamelomai* which means "to be sorry" or "remorseful," but *metanoeo* has nothing of emotion or feeling or remorse in its meaning. The literal meaning of *metanoeo* is "to change your mind, your way, the way you think and do, the direction in which you go." The word means "to turn." You have been going in one direction; turn around.

Let us look at the most famous verse quoted by those who believe in baptismal regeneration, that is, that the water washes our sins away. One may not be willing to relinquish his persuasion that the actual water washes away sin, but he can examine the Word of God. These who

95

believe in baptismal regeneration will use the word "for" instead of "in order to" be baptized. They translate the word *eis*, "for," to "in order to." One must not forget that in English as in Greek, "for" can mean "because of," as it means "in order to." In English we will say, "He is decorated for bravery." The meaning is not "in order to," but "because of" his bravery. Or we will say, "He has been cited for good grades." The meaning is not "in order to," but "because of" his good grades. Or we will say, "He is electrocuted for murder." The meaning is not "in order to" but "because" he was a murderer. So it is in Greek—"be baptized every one of you in the name of Jesus Christ for (because of) the remission of sins."

Look for a moment at how the Greek uses the word *eis*, "for." "He that receiveth a prophet in the name of a prophet, *(eis)* shall receive a prophet's reward" (Matt. 10:41a). He receives the reward because he is a prophet. It is not because he is a rich man or that he could repay, or not because of fame and fortune. "He that receiveth a righteous man in the name of a righteous man *(eis)*" (Matt. 10:41b). Because he is a righteous man he will receive a righteous man's reward. The last verse in Matthew 10 says, "And whosoever shall give to drink unto one of these little ones a cup of cold water only *(eis,* because he is a believer in Christ) in the name of a disciple, verily I say unto you, he shall in no wise lose his reward" (Matt. 10:42).

We look at Matthew 12:41: "The men of Nineveh shall rise in judgment with this generation, and shall condemn it: because they repented *(eis)* at the preaching of Jonas; and, behold, a greater than Jonas is here." They repented "because of" the preaching of Jonas. So the word is used here: repent and be baptized every one of you in the name of Christ, *eis*, because of the remission of your sins.

First John 1:7 says, ". . . and the blood of Jesus Christ his Son cleanseth us from all sin." Water cannot wash the stain of sin out of our hearts, even if we scrub with lye soap. This is a spiritual holiness between us and God. Someone else cannot do it for us. A preacher can baptize us, but he cannot wash your sins away. The blood of Christ washes our sins away. In the memorial of the Lord's Supper when the Lord took the cup, He said, "For this is my blood of the new testament, which is shed for many for the remission of sins" (Matt. 26:28). We are washed clean and white by the blood of the Lamb.

In Simon Peter's preaching in Acts 10 he concluded his message, "To him give all the prophets witness, that through his name whosoever believeth in him shall receive remission of sins" (v. 43). When Peter said that the Holy Spirit came upon them, He then stated:

> Can any man forbid water, that these should not be baptized, which have received the Holy Ghost as well as we?
> And he commanded them to be baptized in the name of the Lord. (Acts 10:47-48a)

First, they were saved by trusting in the Lord's blood and atoning grace for the remission of sins. Then on that confession and commitment they were baptized into the fellowship of the church of the Lord.

Acts 2:40 says, "And with many other words did he testify and exhort, saying, Save yourselves from this untoward generation." What did Simon Peter mean when he said, "And with many other words did he testify and exhort, saying, Save yourselves"? By reading this sermon in Acts 2, and by reading the sermons of Simon Peter that follow after, these are the things he said.

We Are All Lost Sinners Before God

First, all of us before God are lost sinners. There is a common ground upon which every man stands, and it is that he is a lost person. I have often been asked, "Pastor, in days past, when you preached to the Stone Age Indians in the Amazon Jungle, when you preached to the Hottentot in darkest Africa, when you preached in Australia and in the Orient, what did you say?" The answer is simple and plain. I began talking to them about the sin in our hearts. There is not one man who has not sinned nor are there any degraded so low but that they have a deep moral consciousness in their souls. I began with our sins, the black drop in our hearts. Sin is universal. By nature we are sinners. A man does not have to be taught to sin. A child does not have to be taught to sin. By nature he has affinity for evil. By volition and choice we are sinners, and education or culture or environment cannot change our sinful inclinations.

If a poor sinner becomes wealthy, he will be an affluent sinner. If an unlearned and uneducated sinner goes to school, he will be an educated and academic sinner. If a rude, crude sinner is taught the amenities of life and he moves among high society, he will be a cultured sinner. There is no difference. All of us sin and come short of the glory of God. Sin is the one common denominator upon which all men stand.

We All Face Death and the Judgment

Second, we face inevitable death and judgment. Hebrews 9:27 says,

"And as it is appointed unto men once to die, but after this the judgment." We shall certainly die, and no less so shall we certainly stand some day before the judgment bar of almighty God.

In Revelation 20:15 we read, "And whosoever was not found written in the book of life was cast into the lake of fire." This is the second death. A man can die two times. First, he dies in his physical frame. Second, he dies in his soul, when he is separated from God. The sorrow of all sorrows and the sadness of all sadnesses is when a man dies without God.

GOD'S LOVE AND GRACE ARE EXTENDED TO US ALL

Third, God in His love and grace has extended salvation and invitation to all men everywhere. He has never failed in any century nor in any generation. The arms of the Lord are always outstretched to dying sinners. God is always for us; He is never against us. In Ezekiel 33:11 the Lord says, "As I live, saith the Lord GOD, I have no pleasure in the death of the wicked; but that the wicked turn from his way and live: turn ye, turn ye from your evil ways; for why will ye die?" Why would a man choose to be lost and damned and spend eternity away from God when the way to be saved is so near and so dear?

In Isaiah 1:18 we read, "Come now, and let us reason together, saith the LORD." God is not far out or unreasonable. God is the most reasonable person one could ever know. He does not delight when a man is destroyed. He does not delight when a man chooses ways that ruin him. God delights when a man turns and faces the Lord and talks to Him about the finest and best in his life here and in the life that is yet to come. "Come now, and let us reason together, saith the Lord: though your sins be as scarlet, they shall be white as snow; though they be red like crimson, they shall be as wool" (Isa. 1:18). God always opens the door of salvation and invitation for us. He has never failed to be the Savior to all through the centuries and generations who call on Him.

When our first parents were driven out of the Garden of Eden, God placed cherubim on the east side of the gate, the emblems of His mercy and grace. They were there to teach fallen man how to come back to the Lord.

In the days of the terrible judgment of the deluge, God instructed Noah to build an ark. For 120 years righteous Noah pointed to the door of that ark. Not only was the ark big enough and wide enough for elephants to lumber in, but it was big enough and wide enough for a man to enter. One-hundred-twenty years Noah pointed to the door of the ark beseeching men and women to be saved, and they mocked, laughed, and ridiculed. The Bible says that God closed the door. There is a line unseen that crosses every path, the dividing line between God's mercy and His wrath. But before the judgment falls, God always provides a way of escape.

A way of escape was also provided in the days of the Passover. Not only could an Israelite save his home by placing sprinkled blood in the form of a cross on the lintel and each side of the doorposts, but an Egyptian could have done that and he would have been saved. Had anyone followed the Lord's commandment to place the blood on his house, he would have been saved. When the death angel passed over, he was looking for the blood. Those who found refuge under the blood were saved. God's open invitation to the lost of the whole world is that we all be saved.

In the days when the sinners of Israel were bitten and dying from the bite of a small snake, God said to Moses: "Make a brazen serpent and raise it in the midst of the camp. If any man is bitten and is dying, and he looks up, he will live." Had there been a Midianite passing by who had been bitten by one of those fiery serpents, and had looked up, he would have lived. Any man can look and live.

> Look and live, my brother live.
> Look to Jesus Christ and live.
> 'Tis recorded in His word, Hallelujah.
> It is only that you look and live.

Cities of refuge were found all through the kingdom of Israel. If a man found himself facing condemnation and execution, he could flee to the city of refuge and be saved. I often think of preachers who change the directions to the cities of refuge. People are lost, not knowing where to go or what to do. But God has made provision for us. He has given directions that point to the cities of refuge; He tells us how we might be saved. Of all the things God has done, nothing is so wondrous, so simple, and so life-changing as what He has done for us in Jesus our Lord.

We sing a little chorus:

> Oh, oh, oh, oh, what he's done for me.
> He lifted me up from the miry clay.
> Oh, oh, oh, oh, what He's done for me.

God has opened to us the gates of heaven and grace! We read in John 3:

> And as Moses lifted up the serpent in the wilderness, even so must the Son of man be lifted up:
> That whosoever believeth in him should not perish, but have eternal life. (vv. 14-15)

What God has done for us! This is the way to be saved.

WHAT WE MUST DO

First, a man must listen, and he must hear. He cannot be saved if he does not listen and if he does not hear. A man has not only physical ears and eyes, but his soul also has eyes and ears. He must listen with his heart. He must shut out the din of this noisy and busy and empty and sterile world, and he must listen to the voice of the eternal God. "Faith cometh by hearing, and hearing by the Word of God" (Rom. 10:17). Isaiah 55:3 says, "Incline your ear, . . . hear, and your soul shall live." We must listen. We must hear. We must open our hearts Godward, heavenward, and Christward.

Second, a man must turn. "Then Peter said unto them, *metanoeo*." If a man is walking down a road that leads away from God, away from the Lord's people, and away from the Lord's will, he must turn around. He must face God. He need not be afraid to face God, because Jesus died for his sins that he might be saved. The Lord offers the omnipotence of heaven as a sinner's eternal inheritance. God is for us, not against us. We are to turn and face God.

When a man turns and faces God, the Lord God will always point to Jesus the Son, whether it be God the Father or God the Holy Spirit. "This is my beloved Son, in whom I am well pleased; hear ye him" (Matt. 17:5b). God the Father will always speak of Jesus the Son.

God the Holy Spirit also will always point to Jesus. In John 16 we read these words concerning the Holy Spirit:

> For he shall not speak of himself; but whatsoever he shall hear, that shall he speak: and he will shew you things to come. (v. 13b)

When a man faces God, He will point him to the blessed Jesus. That leads to his entrance into the kingdom, for the moment he opens his heart to the Lord Jesus, the moment he calls upon His name, the moment he trusts Him and believes in Him, that moment he is saved.

> All hail to the Father,
> All hail to the Son,
> All hail to the Spirit,

The great three in one.
Saved by the blood of the
crucified One.

The Word of God points to the Lord Jesus. When a man truly preaches the Word of God, and when the listener goes out the door, he will have met in a new and beautiful and precious way the Lord Jesus. If you have a prayer meeting, and the Lord has been in it, you will have a feeling of having been in the presence of the Lord Himself. If the services are moved by the Spirit of God, they will be an exalting of the Lord Jesus. That is why I love to hear a choir sing powerful songs that magnify the Lord. There are no weaknesses in the Word. When we look at the Bible we look full into the face of the Lord and are transfigured.

Third, "They that gladly received his word were baptized; and the same day there were added unto them about three thousand souls." When a person opens his heart Christward, joy, gladness and strength overflow. The saved man immediately wants to confess his faith. He cannot keep from saying: "I have found the Lord. I have given my heart to Jesus. I am a born-again child of God." That confession is to salvation itself. Paul wrote it like this:

That if thou shalt confess with thy mouth the Lord Jesus, and shalt believe in thine heart that God hath raised him from the dead, thou shalt be saved.

For with the heart man believeth unto righteousness; and with the mouth confession is made unto salvation. (Rom. 10:9-10)

Or as the Lord would say it:

Whosoever therefore shall confess me before men, him will I confess also before my Father which is in heaven. (Matt. 10:32)

Being baptized is a form of confession. A man has put on the uniform of the Lord. He belongs to the people of Christ. This is an open avowal, an open commitment. Coming down the aisle is an open publication to the world that a man has given his heart and life to the blessed Jesus. When the Lord sees us make a public confession of faith, He is glad for us. He sees us through.

15

The Christian Community

Therefore let all the house of Israel know assuredly, that God hath made that same Jesus, whom ye have crucified, both Lord and Christ.

Now when they heard this, they were pricked in their heart, and said unto Peter and to the rest of the apostles, Men and brethren, what shall we do?

Then Peter said unto them, Repent, and be baptized every one of you in the name of Jesus Christ for the remission of sins, and ye shall receive the gift of the Holy Ghost.

For the promise is unto you, and to your children, and to all that are afar off, even as many as the Lord our God shall call.

And with many other words did he testify and exhort, saying, Save yourselves from this untoward generation.

Then they that gladly received his word were baptized: and the same day there were added unto them about three thousand souls.

And they continued stedfastly in the apostles' doctrine and fellowship, and in breaking of bread, and in prayers.

And fear came upon every soul: and many wonders and signs were done by the apostles.

And all that believed were together, and had all things common;

And sold their possessions and goods, and parted them to all men, as every man had need.

And they, continuing daily with one accord in the temple, and breaking bread from house to house, did eat their meat with gladness and singleness of heart,

Praising God, and having favour with all the people. And the Lord added to the church daily such as should be saved. (Acts 2:36-47)

The first impression we get from the inspired description in our text of the first Christian community is one of infinite gladness, of rejoicing and praise. It is written thus in the text, "Then they that gladly received his words were baptized . . . And they, continuing daily with one

102

accord in the temple . . . did eat their meat with gladness and singleness of heart, Praising God. . . . And the Lord added to the church daily such as should be saved." To be glad in the Lord is a part of what it is to be saved, to belong to the Christian community.

> I am happy in Him.
> My soul with delight
> He fills day and night
> For I am happy in Him.

One of the most tremendously meaningful sermons I have read was delivered by B. H. Carroll, the giant man who was founder and first president of our Southwestern Baptist Theological Seminary located in Fort Worth. The sermon is entitled, "My Infidelity and What Became of It." In the days of the Civil War B. H. Carroll was an outspoken and crude infidel. He had a violent reaction against those who believed in God and in Christ. When the days of the war were over he came home, crippled by an injury. While he was living at home, a tremendous outpouring of the Spirit of God fell on the community where he lived.

One night after a revival service, he came hobbling home on his crutches. He walked through the kitchen of the house and up to his room to lie down. A little nephew in the kitchen watched him and went to B. H. Carroll's mother and said:"Uncle B. H. is acting so strange. He is crying and singing at the same time!" His mother, a godly, praying woman, went upstairs and into the room where her son was lying on the bed with his hands over his face. She took her hands and pulled his hands away from his face, looked long and searchingly into his eyes, and exclaimed: "Son, you have found the Lord! You have been saved!" She saw the glory of God in her boy, and the little nephew heard God's glory in the gladness of B. H. Carroll's song.

There is often a strange response from a man when he is saved. He is so happy he cries, just out of the overflowing of the saved heart. To be a Christian is to be glad in soul, to sing, to praise God. This praise creates a fellowship like the first Christian community.

What could be more unhappy or tragic than for one to have just enough religion to make him unhappy. A war is always going on in his heart. Struggle and strife go on between his loyalty to Christ and a worldly amusement or a selfish covetousness. He has just enough religion to make him miserable and unhappy, but how happy he could be if he would just let God have all of his heart and all of his life.

The First Christian Community
Gave Everything to God

One of the secrets of this first Christian community in Acts 2 was that they gave everything they possessed, and all that they did, to the Lord. The Scripture says:.

> And all that believed were together, and had all things common;
> And sold their possessions and goods, and parted them to all men, as every man had need. (vv. 44-45)

They gave everything to the Lord, and were happy in Him.

A devout, godly, and affluent couple, who were faithful in the church, faithful in their devotion, and faithful in their gifts illustrate this. They prayed, they gave to missions, they supported the work of the Lord. They had one daughter who, one day, came home from school and announced to her father and mother that she had felt God's call to be a missionary and was now preparing her heart to go to a foreign field and represent our Lord as a missionary. The parents at first took the news hard. They said: "We have given our money, our prayers, our time, our love, and our devotion, but child, you are the only child we have. To see you leave and go to a foreign field is almost too much." They resolved that they would take the matter to God and tell Him in prayer all about it. When they finished their praying, they had found an infinite peace and rest in Him. "Lord, not only the money we have, not only the prayers of our hearts, not only the devotion of our lives, but Lord, we also give to Thee this only child." What a marvelous attitude!

Everything we have we ought to give back to Him. I breathe God's air. I live in God's world. My hands and feet were created by God and He gave them to me. God's heart and soul lives within my physical frame, which is God's holy temple. It all belongs to God. When we come to the place in our lives where we can just say that all is His, how happy we are!

The Fellowship of God's People

"And they continued stedfastly in the apostles' doctrine and fellowship, and in breaking of bread, and in prayers." There are four things that the Holy Scriptures avow characterize that first church. I choose one of them. The verse says, "doctrine and fellowship, and in breaking of bread [our Lord's Supper], and in prayers." I want to refer to fellowship.

The Greek word *koinonia* is a beautiful word for "fellowship." A communion service is the "communion," the fellowship, the common bond between our Lord and us. The purpose of God from the eternal ages has been that there be a church, a body of Christ, an assembly of the saints which, in the New Testament, is called a *koinonia*, a fellowship. God did something precious for us in placing us together in the body of our Lord where we belong to Him and to each other. We are not saved in the plan of God and left alone or forsaken. The purpose of the Lord is always that we are joined to the *koinonia*, the "body," the "fellowship," the "assembly," the "family of God."

One of the most beautiful and meaningful of all the verses in the Psalms is Psalm 68:6, "God setteth the solitary in families." Thus does He rear His little children in the circle of a home. A forsaken child brings tears to our eyes. God never meant it that way. He placed the solitary in families. He does the same thing when we are born into the family of God. We are added to the church, added to the body of Christ. We become fellow members of the assembly of God's saints.

One of the most touching of the new gospel songs is entitled, "The Family of God." Just to think that I am a part of God's family moves me. I am a part of the family of God, the *koinonia*, the fellowship, the communion of the saints.

To illustrate a point about fellowship I would like to use mutual funds and their owners, such as the Metropolitan Life Insurance Company. They are actually mutual companies; no one owns them. One day I asked an insurance executive of one of those companies, "Who owns the billions of dollars in your company?" He said, "Well, of course, all the people who have policies in it do, but actually all of this money would ultimately belong to the last surviving policyholder." Then I began to think that if I were the last surviving policyholder, all the others would be gone. I could have billions of dollars, and could buy everything I wanted, but I would be alone. It is the last thing in the world I would want, for fellowship with friends makes life sweet and precious. Without friends it is dust and ashes. The preciousness of God's gift to us is one another, the *koinonia*, the fellowship of the saints. That is why the Lord said, "I go to prepare a place for you." That is why He leaves us in Christian communities to encourage each other in the faith until the day He gathers us home.

The Christian community is like an island in a vast and endless secular world. The sea of worldliness surrounds us on every side. We live in that kind of a world; but we Christians are an island in it. In the world of materialism we can possess in Christ our hearts, homes, and families and we can live godly, spiritual, and heavenly lives.

In Moffatt's translation of the New Testament he refers to the church as a "colony of heaven," when speaking of the church at Philippi. I think that was inspired. Through the preaching of the word we continue to see people gathered into this fellowship, and this fills us with joy.

A young man recently said to me: "I was discharged from the Army. I descended into the gutter and was wretched, miserable, and in the depths of sin. One Sunday evening I happened to be in Dallas, walking through one of those downtown streets, wretched and miserable. A godly couple saw me, stopped me, and said: 'We are going to church to the First Baptist Church. Would you go with us?' I told them: 'I have nothing else to do. I will.' We came to the church that night and I listened to you preach. That night I was wondrously saved. God came into my heart. I took my GI bill and went to school and to the seminary and I am now pastor of a fine little church in northern Louisiana."

My brethren, if we never did anything in our lives but invite someone to church, it will have been worth it. Invite someone to come and walk with you, and to belong as a member, to the family of God.

16

The Heavenly Fellowship

And they continued stedfastly in the apostles' doctrine and fellowship, and in breaking of bread, and in prayers. (Acts 2:42)

Our text for the message today is a beautiful fourfold characterization of the first mother church and the paragon church in Jerusalem. Four fellowships are mentioned: a fellowship with the apostles and all of the great teachers of the truth of God in the doctrine, a fellowship with one another in the *koinonia*, a fellowship with our Lord in the breaking of bread, and the fellowship we have with God our Father in prayer.

It is not without symbolic significance that the holy and beautiful new Jerusalem is foursquare. We read in Revelation:

And he that talked with me had a golden reed to measure the city, and the gates thereof, and the wall thereof.

And the city lieth foursquare, and the length is as large as the breadth: and he measured the city with the reed, twelve thousand furlongs. The length and the breadth and the height of it are equal. (21:15-16)

This is a picture of the beautiful and heavenly fellowhip of the saints of the Lord in their communion, in their coming together as a body of Christ. They are full and complete, a perfect cube. The height, the length, the breadth, and the depth are all alike. We see this characterized in the first church in Jerusalem.

THE APOSTLES' DOCTRINE

"And they continued stedfastly in the apostles' doctrine." The Greek word, *didasko*, means "to teach." The substantive of the verbal form,

107

didaxa, means "what is taught," "the doctrine." This is the word that is used in the text. Through the years the body of the revelation of the truth of Christ has been mediated to us through the prophets, the apostles, the martyrs, and the witnesses of God. In that line and in that train we also belong. We have a fellowship with them as we also preach, teach, and witness to the truth of the Lord.

One of the tremendous chapters in the Bible is the chapter of the heroes of faith in Hebrews 11 which begins with Abel and continues with Noah, then Abraham, Isaac, Jacob, David, and the prophets. Having called that glorious roll of those who witnessed to the grace of God, the author of Hebrews begins chapter 12 with this word:

> Wherefore seeing we also are compassed about with so great a cloud of witnesses, let us lay aside every weight, and the sin which doth so easily beset us, and let us run with patience the race that is set before us,
> Looking unto Jesus the author and finisher of our faith. (vv. 1-2a)

We belong to a great company which surrounds us as we in our generation and time also witness to the grace of God in Christ Jesus.

THE KOINONIA

A fellowship with one another in the *koinonia* is a communion, a fellowship that God has given us who have been added to the body of Christ and who belong to the church of our Lord. It is fellowship with one another—a communion of love, sympathy, encouragement, forgiveness, patience, and understanding. Our Lord said in John 13:

> A new commandment I give unto you, that ye love one another; as I have loved you, that ye also love one another.
> By this shall all men know that ye are my disciples, if ye have love one to another (vv. 34-35)

That ought to be the cement that binds together all the hearts, souls, lives, and families that belong to the body of Christ. It is a fellowship, a communion of love, sympathy, care, and understanding.

The famous love chapter in 1 Corinthians in the authorized King James version reads like this:

> Though I speak with the tongues of men and of angels, and have not charity
> . . .
> Charity never faileth. (13:1a,8a)

All through 1 Corinthians 13 the word "charity" is used. "Though I give my body to be burned and though I bestow all my goods to feed the poor, and have not charity." Why is the word "charity" used?

I think the reason goes back to a deep and profound meaning. In the Greek language there were several words for love. One is *philos*. Another is *agape*. They are often used in the New Testament and they characterize the people of the Lord. But there was a word in the Greek language far more common than either *philos* or *agape*, and that is the word *eros*. But we will not find the word *eros* once in the Bible. That was the word that characterized all the unbelievable promiscuities of the gods who lived on Mt. Olympus. One would define *eros* actually in the Christian nomenclature "lust." So it was when Jerome translated the Vulgate, which is the great basic document that lies back of the translation of the King James version. The Latin word, *amor*, was used in the same way that *eros* was used in Greek. When Jerome sat down to translate that word *agape*, he had before him the Latin word *amor*. But looking at it, he felt that there was far more of the depth and meaning of God in the word *agape* than just *amor*, so he chose another Latin word, *caritas*, which means "dear," "precious," "in high and heavenly esteem." Translate *agape* into the Latin Vulgate *caritas* and the result in our English language is the word "charity," which refers to the endearment, the high esteem and loving regard, the infinite preciousness in which we hold and value each other. That is the *koinonia*, the fellowship of God's people in the church. This is what the apostle John meant when he wrote that we love one another.

An ancient legend comes to us about the aged apostle John, who is now more than one hundred years of age and is yet pastor of the church in Ephesus. One Lord's Day, with an elder holding him up on one side and an elder holding him up on the other side, the aged apostle comes to the pulpit for a message to his people. As they listen for a word from their old pastor, he says, "Little children, love one another." Then he repeats himself twice more. One of the men who is sustaining him says: "John, we have heard you say that. Is there not some word more?" The aged pastor replies: "It is enough. Little children, love one another." If in the congregation of the Lord you find that *caritas*, that high esteem, that heavenly preciousness, that love of God in our hearts for each other, you will find the *koinonia*, the fellowship of the saints.

A group of men were talking together and one of them asked a minister in the group, "Preacher, do you have to join a church in order to go to heaven?" The preacher replied, "No." The man patted him on the back because of his broadmindedness, and congratulated him for a good answer. Then the preacher turned to the man and asked, "Sir, may I ask you a question and will you answer me quickly?" The man said, "Yes." The preacher said, "Why would you want to go to heaven that way?" Why would a man want to go to heaven when he does not like to associate himself with the people of God in this world? We must remember that in heaven we will be with each other, and with our Lord. We will sing the songs of praise, magnify God with our worshiping, adoring souls, and love one another forever and forever. Why would one want to go to heaven and leave out of his life the *koinonia*, the fellowship.

THE BREAKING OF BREAD

"And they continued stedfastly in breaking of bread." This is a communion, a *koinonia*, with our Savior. The bread which we break, is it not the communion of the body of Christ? The cup which we drink, is it not the communion of the blood of Christ?

In the Lord's Supper we identify ourselves with Him. He figuratively becomes a part of us. We are a part of Him. When we eat the bread and when we drink the cup, we are dramatizing the sufferings of our Lord that identify us with Him. This is also our fellow suffering with the Lord. Paul said in Philippians 3:10, "That I may know him . . . and the fellowship of his sufferings." In Colossians 1:24 he wrote one of the most unusual verses in the Bible, "[That I might] fill up that which is [lacking] of the afflictions of Christ in my flesh for his body's sake, which is the church." Knowing that the sufferings of Christ were all adequate for us, what could be lacking in the atonement of our Savior? What is lacking in what Christ has suffered for us? Yet Paul writes, "That I might fill up that which is lacking." The explanation of that is something deep and spiritually profound.

Not only did Christ suffer for us and in that atonement once and for all provide sufficient grace, but He paid for all our sins of yesterday, today, and forever. Nothing need be added to what Christ has done to save us. But the apostle says that there are also sufferings that we are to dedicate to Christ in order to mediate that love and grace to the world. There are prices we must pay. There are works that we must do. As our Lord provided for us the glory, the beauty, and the wonder of a new life, a new day, and a rebirth, so we must also with Him suffer that others might know His name, that they might be saved by His grace and be won to His loving care. I also have a part in the sufferings of my Lord, a *koinonia*, a fellowship in His sufferings. I must also offer to God what I can that His grace might be mediated to the world.

I had been in Nashville, Tennessee, at a Southern Baptist convocation. While standing in the airport waiting for the plane to return to Dallas, a man, who was obviously affluent, approached me. He was tall with gray hair, beautifully dressed, and he called me by name. He asked if he could say a word to me. He introduced himself and he said that five years earlier I had been in Nashville preaching at an evangelistic conference. He said "You did something that night that I had never seen or heard before. When you got through with your message that night you made an appeal to the laymen who were there in words something like this: 'In behalf of a man that you know, would you consecrate your life that he might be saved? If you would, get up out of your seat, walk down the aisle to the front, and kneel while we pray together a prayer of consecration.' I was seated in the top balcony in the last row. I stood up out of my seat and came down the stairway and down the aisle and knelt there before you. I consecrated my life in behalf of a businessman in my city who was not a Christian. For four years I witnessed to that man and asked him in the most prayerful way I knew how to come to Jesus. For four years the man was adamant. That year I went to him for the last time and said, 'You know, I am afraid I have been a nuisance to you. Every time I have seen you I have talked to you about the Lord and have invited you to Christ. I have come to you about the Lord for the last time. I want to apologize to you. I did not mean to bother you and I did not mean to be a nuisance to you. I have come to ask your forgiveness. I will not speak anymore in His name.' That man looked at me searchingly and said: 'Oh, no. Pray for me, keep on asking me, do not stop. Talk to me about the Lord.' That year the businessman gave his heart to the Lord. He and his family were baptized. He is a fine member in his church."

That made my heart sing. That is what God meant when He said, "We are to fill up what is lacking in the sufferings of Christ." He died for our sins and was raised for our justification according to the Scriptures, but we must also testify and witness to the world of the grace of God extended to us in our Lord Jesus. It is the fellowship of our Lord in the sufferings of Christ.

The Prayers

The fourth characterization of the mother church in Jerusalem is fellowshiping with God our Father in prayer. From Greek the translation into English is "in the prayers." There is private prayer, family prayer, but there is also stated and public prayer. When the congregation comes together, we pray as an assembly of God's people, continuing stedfastly in the prayers. It pleases God that we bow, that we pray, that we ask, that we talk to Him as our Father. We go further on our knees than in any other way, retreating to advance, falling to rise, stooping to conquer. Oh, the fellowship we have with God in intercession!

When they found Livingstone dead, he was by his bed on his knees. In the heart of Africa, those faithful natives who accompanied him all night long never entered into the little hut in which Livingstone was living, because the master was on his knees. In the morning when they looked in he was still there on his knees and they went to him and touched him. While he was praying at night his spirit had fled away. What a wonderful way to die!

I read of a president of a Christian school who overheard what his doctor said. Turning to the physician, he asked, "Did you say I was dying?" The doctor replied, "Yes." The president then said, "Would you put me on my knees by the side of the bed?" They lifted him up and placed him on his knees by the side of the bed and he began to pray, and when he could no longer form the words and his voice failed, he whispered the words. His spirit then fled away and he died there on his knees. A great revival broke out in that school. Every student in the school was saved, and the revival spread to the countryside around. Oh, that we had leaders, presidents, and pastors like that who know God in prayer and who so stedfastly continue in intercession that the last breath they breathe is a prayer to God for the people. This is the perfect and heavenly fellowship of God's saints.

17

Christian Communism

> Then they that gladly received his word were baptized: and the same day there were added unto them about three thousand souls.
>
> And all that believed were together, and had all things common;
>
> And sold their possessions and goods, and parted them to all men, as every man had need. (Acts 2:41, 44-45)

The passage in our text gave birth to the communist dictum, "From every man as he is able, to every man as he has need."

That same thing is avowed in Acts 4:32, ". . . neither said any of them that ought of the things which he possessed was his own; but they had all things common."

There are two kinds of communism: political communism and religious communism. In the development of communism in the story of modern life the two types are altogether different. They move in different worlds.

Political communism is coercive communism. It is communism by the gun and by the bayonet. Political communism can be seen in the Bolshevik Revolution in Russia and in the communist takeover of Mao Tse-tung in China. This is a communism in which the army in the hands of a tyrannical dictatorship assumes all the property, takes all the wages of all the people, takes the church houses and all that is done in the house of the Lord, takes all the farms and other possessions of the people and assumes the ownership of everything in the state. This is political communism which today is Marxist and inevitably atheist.

Karl Marx said, "Communism begins where atheism begins." Without atheism there would be no communism, for its values are fundamentally material and secular. Atheism and communism comprise a secular society that denies spiritual value and spiritual reality.

Under political communism the hand of the state reaches into every area of human life and possesses it. The lives of your children—their education, the assignment of their jobs, what they can do, where they can live, what traveling is permitted—the whole area of human life is encompassed in political communism. Political communism is coercive and is a regime held in power by the hand of brute force.

Religious communism moves in a different world. It is voluntary. Any group meeting together can say they will share all things they possess. They live in a commune, such as the Shakers of Pennsylvania and Kentucky who lived upon vast, beautiful farms and had everything in common—a communist society. Many years ago I visited the House of David in the state of Michigan which was a communal society. It was religious communism.

POLITICAL OR RELIGIOUS COMMUNISM WILL NOT WORK

Whether it is political or whether it is religious, in either case communism does not work. It inevitably fails. Let us speak first of political communism.

That is the brutal force that thrives in Russia and in China. There is no communist nation that can feed itself. Were it not for the free Western world, they would starve to death. People in a communist nation mine by forced labor, gold, silver, platinum, and other things such as they are able to produce. They sell these products to the free world in exchange for wheat, corn, and bread.

The communist world has ability and fertility as does the Western world. For example, I have flown over the great Ukraine of Russia. It is beautiful, rolling land such as you see in Wisconsin, Iowa, and Illinois. Communism cannot produce food for their hungry mouths because communism has built in it failure, scarcity, need, poverty, and want. Their leadership does not lift up the people to the level that some of them enjoy; instead, they pull everyone down to the lowest common denominator and there they grovel in poverty, need, and want alike.

On a streetcar in Prague, the capital of Czechoslovakia, I was seated next to a woman who began to extol to me the virtues of communism, and one of the things she said was: "There are no poor in a communist nation. There are no poor in Czechoslovakia. There are no poor in Prague." I asked her, "Do you know why?" She said, "It is because of communism." I said: "The reason there are no poor in a communist nation, in Czechoslovakia, and in Prague, is because all of you are poor. You are all alike. You have the bare necessities of life. Were it not for the Western world, you would starve."

You might wonder why the communists of Russia and China do not change their system, and in a free enterprise produce food. The answer is it would be a denial of their Marxist ideology, and they dare not admit that their system is futile and failing. Wherever there is political communism in the world, it is a failure and will continue to be. There is no such thing as prosperity in a socialist country. The people there increasingly fall into debt and despair.

It no less fails religiously. There is no such thing as a successful religious communist enterprise, not ultimately. Did you know that when the Pilgrims came to America they established a communist society? In those years of their commune, from 1621 until 1623, they suffered hunger and nearly starved to death. The Pilgrims were deeply religious, but they were so hungry that they stole food from their starving fellow workers. From 1621 to 1623 they had a communist society in Plymouth, Massachusetts.

About ten years ago a copy of a document written by the governor of Plymouth Plantation was found which explains this. I read from it:

> Some complained they were too weak to work. Young men complained because they had to work hard to feed other men and their wives and children.
>
> Women rebelled when ordered to cook for men not their husbands, or when asked to wash their clothes. They said they were little better than slaves, and their husbands said they would not permit their womenfolk to do that kind of labor.

In 1623 they turned away from that communist communal property and the common storehouse, and they gave each family a parcel of land for its own use. Then a miracle took place. I quote again from William Bradford:

> Women went into the fields willingly, taking their children along with them. All women, men, and children planted as much corn as they felt they could possibly work.
>
> People who had formerly complained that they were too weak to dig or hoe, declaring that it was tyranny to make them undertake such work, gladly began to plant and cultivate for themselves.
>
> When the harvest was brought in, instead of famine, there was plenty. So they all gave thanks to God.

They had a day of Thanksgiving and praise to God which is where our American Thanksgiving celebration originated.

Religious communism does not work any more than political communism, nor did it here in the Bible. Our text says that on the first day those who believed had everything in common. They sold their possessions and goods, parted to all as they had need. No one said that any of the things he possessed were his own but they had all things in common. Let us see what happened.

Acts 5 begins with trouble. Communism always breeds trouble. Chapter 5 of Acts says:

> But a certain man named Ananias, with Sapphira his wife, sold a possession,
> And kept back part of the price, his wife also being privy to it, and brought a certain part, and laid it at the apostles' feet.
> But Peter said, Ananias, why hath Satan filled thine heart to lie to the Holy Ghost, and to keep back part of the price of the land?
> Whiles it remained, was it not thine own? . . .
> And Ananias hearing these words fell down, and gave up the ghost. (Acts 5:1-4a, 5a)

In a little while his wife came in.

> And Peter answered unto her, Tell me whether ye sold the land for so much? And she said, Yea, for so much.
> Then Peter said unto her, How is it that ye have agreed together to tempt the Spirit of the Lord? behold, the feet of them which have buried thy husband are at the door, and shall carry thee out.
> Then fell she down straightway at his feet, and yielded up the ghost. (Acts 5:8-10a)

Trouble, trouble, trouble.

Chapter 6 begins with a similar circumstance. "And in those days, when the number of the disciples was multiplied, there arose a murmuring of the Grecians against the Hebrews, because their widows were neglected in the daily ministration" (v. 1). The Greek-speaking Jews said: "When it comes to the parceling out of the common storehouse, they do not treat our widows right. They show favoritism to these Aramaic, Palestinian widows." There was trouble and more trouble. Communism does not work; it never has and it never will. Thereafter in the Bible communal life was never mentioned again.

That leads us to a real problem in the house of the Lord. If equal sharing does not work, then how is the church to sustain itself? The Lord has given to us a vast assignment, the evangelization of the whole world. How could the Lord mandate to us such a tremendous work and then give us no guidelines to sustain it and how to do it? Would the Lord do that? It would be unthinkable, unimaginable. God knew and provided a way for us that we might sustain the work of the church and that we might underwrite and undergird its prosperity and its fulfillment of the Great Commission. I will speak from the Scriptures first and from experience second how God mandated to us the way in which we are to sustain the work of the Lord.

A WORD FROM THE SCRIPTURE

In the Bible there are fundamental, foundational principles that we learn from the Holy Scriptures for living, for working, for being, for building, for ministering, for preaching, for evangelizing, and for all of the many things God has laid upon our people to do.

The Bible says nothing against slavery. The only thing the Bible says is, "Slaves, be obedient to your masters." But the great Christian principles of the Bible destroyed the institution of slavery forever. How? By teaching the brotherhood of the saints. Paul says in Philemon: "I send Onesimus back to you, no longer a slave, but a brother beloved. Receive him as such." The Spirit of brotherhood destroyed the institution of slavery.

Look at crucifixion. Under the Romans crucifixion was a universal institution. It was a common sight in the Roman Empire to go down a highway and see numerous crosses with the felons dying, suffering, and agonizing on them. Is there anything in the Bible against the institution of the execution? No. But it was destroyed by the spirit of kindness and sympathy, such as found in Ephesians 4:32, "And be ye kind one to another, tenderhearted, forgiving one another, even as God for Christ's sake hath forgiven you." The spirit of kindness and sympathy destroyed that awesome figure of execution.

The problem of drinking is the curse of modern society. Why am I not at liberty to drink? Paul said in 1 Corinthians 8:13, "Wherefore, if meat make my brother to offend, I will eat no flesh while the world standeth, lest I make my brother to offend." One out of nine social drinkers becomes a problem drinker. Six out of nine problem drinkers become confirmed alcoholics. When I by my example in social drinking could cause a young man to destroy his life, I will not drink as long as the world shall stand. That is the Christian principle. That is what God teaches us out of His Holy Book.

These same great principles come into use when we speak of sustaining the work of the Lord. We are not told to sell all that we have and live in a commune, out of a common storehouse, in a religious communism. Such a practice is not blessed of God. We sustain the work of the Lord by applying the great principle found in 1 Corinthians 16:2: "Upon the first day of the week let every one of you lay by him in store, as God hath prospered him, that there be no gatherings when I come." The great principle for the sustaining of the work of God is simply: we are to give as God has prospered us. Our proportionate giving is always dedicated to the work of the Lord.

What proportion? I am to dedicate to the Lord a proportion of everything God gives to me. Now some people may feel this is going to yoke us with the bondage of the law. Let us discuss that for a moment.

I do not deny that tithing, giving a tenth, is in the law. Leviticus 27:32b says, "The tenth shall be holy unto the LORD." Malachi 3:10 says, "Bring ye all the tithes into the storehouse . . . and prove me now herewith, saith the LORD of hosts, if I will not open you the windows of heaven, and pour you out a blessing, that there shall not be room enough to receive it." The Lord said to the scribes who were hypocrites, "Ye pay tithe of mint and anise and cummin, and have omitted the weightier matters of the law, judgment, mercy, and faith: these ought ye to have done, and not to leave the other undone" (Matt. 23:23b).

I admit that tithing was incorporated into the law, but let me point out something to you. Long before there was any Moses or law, long before there was any Mosaic legislation, in the day of grace God's saints set aside one-tenth as sacred for Him.

Was Abraham under the law? Abraham lived four hundred years before the law. The Bible says in Romans 4:

> What shall we say then that Abraham our father, as pertaining to the flesh, hath found?
> For if Abraham were justified by works, he hath whereof to glory; but not before God.
> For what saith the scripture? Abraham believed God, and it was counted unto him for righteousness.
> Now to him that worketh is the reward not reckoned of grace, but of debt.
> But to him that worketh not, but believeth on him that justifieth the ungodly, his faith is counted for righteousness. (vv. 4:1-5)

Abraham was under grace. He was saved by faith just as we are. We are the spiritual children of Abraham by faith.

Let us look at another passage from the life of Abraham and Melchizedek:

> And Melchizedek king of Salem brought forth bread and wine . . .
> And he blessed him, and said, Blessed be Abram of the most high God . . .

And blessed be the most high God, which hath delivered thine enemies into thy hand. And he gave him tithes of all. (Gen. 14:18-20)

Abraham gave one-tenth of everything he possessed to Melchizedek, the priest of the most-high God.

In Genesis 28 we read of the marvelous experience of Jacob at Bethel. When Jacob saw the ladder reaching up to heaven, he said: "This is a dreadful place. God is here and I did not realize it. If God will bless me so that I come back in peace to my father's house, the Lord Jehovah will be my God. Of all that God shall give me, I will surely give a tenth back to Him." Jacob lived more than three hundred years before the law.

We are the spiritual children of Abraham, Isaac, and Jacob by faith. These great patriarchs who lived hundreds of years before there was such a thing as the law dedicated a tithe to God. The law was but to teach us how far we fall short. The great principle of the New Testament is found in Hebrews 7:8 describing Abraham as he gave a tithe to Melchizedek. The author says, "And here men that die receive tithes; but there he receiveth them, of whom it is witnessed that he liveth." Jesus our Lord is a priest forever after the order of Melchizedek. The Aaronic priesthood, though a dying priesthood, received tithes. How much more spiritual Melchizedek, the type of our Lord, received tithes of whom it is witnessed that he lives forever. This is the great Christian commitment.

18

The Day of Revival

Then they that gladly received his word were baptized: and the same day there were added unto them about three thousand souls.

And they continued stedfastly in the apostles' doctrine and fellowship, and in breaking of bread, and in prayers.

And fear came upon every soul: and many wonders and signs were done by the apostles.

And all that believed were together, and had all things common;

And sold their possessions and goods, and parted them to all men, as every man had need.

And they, continuing daily with one accord in the temple, and breaking bread from house to house, did eat their meat with gladness and singleness of heart,

Praising God, and having favour with all the people. And the Lord added to the church daily such as should be saved. (Acts 2:41-47)

What a remarkable era, what a day of revival! Lord, how we need a revival, an outpouring of the Pentecostal Spirit of God!

Look at the mathematics of verse 47. If the Lord added to the church daily those who were being saved, a minimum would be one a day. A minimum in the course of one year would be three hundred sixty-five. There are very few churches in the world today who baptize as many as three hundred people a year. In fact there are only a handful that baptize as many as one hundred people a year. Lord, how we need revival!

Look at the mathematics of the world. A newspaper reporter called me when I was speaking at a convention in another state and said: "What is this I hear? You are saying that by the year 2000 the Christian faith will be practically extinct." I said, "Do you have a pencil and paper?" He said, "Yes." I said: "Take this graph. One hundred eighty-five years ago, twenty-five percent of all the population in this world were evangelical Christians. In 1970 the number was eight percent. By 1980 it will be four percent. By the year 2000 it will be two percent. You graph it and see what will be the ultimate end and outcome of the sterile faith of the Christian people who live in this present and modern age." Lord, how we need revival!

The spiritual dearth and drought that surrounds us on every side is like the endless Sahara of shifting, barren sand. I can call any group together and upbraid, castigate, and criticize them for their powerlessness, but they can look at me in helplessness and say: "I do not know how to do God's work."

Let me ask you a question: How long has it been since you walked down the aisle of your church bringing someone to the Lord? Has it been a month? Has it been a year? Is it a lifetime? Did you ever do it? Many of you will pause in utter helplessness and powerlessness. There is no unction from God.

Thirty years ago I was in Spurgeon's Tabernacle, seated with that little band that remains in the greatest Baptist church that ever existed. Back of me were two old men who were talking. One of them said to the other, "Did you ever hear Spurgeon preach?" He replied: "Yes, many times. He was my pastor." The man asked him: "How was it? How did he preach? What was Spurgeon like?" The man replied: "Sir, I do not like to criticize the preachers of today, but it seems to me that they just talk, just lecture. But when Spurgeon stood up to preach, sir, there was power in his preaching."

How many times do I stand in my pulpit saying words, repeating clichés, doing what has been habitual for us to do all our lives? At a certain hour we are here. At another time we do this or the other. At this time we listen to a sermon. Then at this time we look for the benediction. Then at a certain time we go home and forget it.

> Lord, send the old time power,
> The Pentecostal power!
> Thy floodgates of blessing
> On us throw open wide!
>
> Lord, send the old time power,
> The Pentecostal power,
> That sinners be converted
> And Thy name glorified!

We assemble ourselves in the presence of the Lord to worship. As we listen to Him we should ask what He would have me do.

What we are to do is not a secret or a mystery. We are to be filled with the power and ablility to witness for God in soul-saving strength. He has outlined our assignment on the sacred page. We are to listen to the Lord and obey His heavenly commands.

In the middle of the last century in Greenville, South Carolina, four scholarly men of the Southern Baptist communion founded the Southern Baptist Theological Seminary, which later moved to Louisville, Kentucky. They were Dr. John A. Broadus, Dr. James Pettigrew Boyce, Dr. Basil Manley, and Dr. William Williams. Then came the tragedy of the war between the states. It seemed as though the seminary would die. Those four men met together and placed their hands one upon the other. They said, that though the seminary might die, they would die first. This resolve can be illustrated by the following story.

In the days of the Civil War a little company of Confederate soldiers was standing on a hill after the battle had swept past them. They were surrounded by the slain men. An officer rode back from the front and saw them standing there on the hill. He rode up to them and asked, "Sirs, where is your general?" One of the soldiers pointed to a prostrate form and said, "There he lies." The officer asked, "Where is your captain?" Another soldier pointed and said, "There he lies." The officer then asked, "Then what are you doing here?" A third soldier replied: "Our general said that this hill was a vantage point that must be kept and defended unto the death. We are doing just that."

The faithfulness of men in times of war to the orders given to them should be practiced by the soldiers in the army of the Lord. How indifferently and casually we often listen to and carry out the great heavenly mandates of the Son of God who is the hope of the world.

What did the Lord say? He said we are to be filled with power from on high and are to go forth in that power carrying out His commands.

WE ARE TO PRAY TOGETHER

In Luke 24 and in Acts 1, before the Lord ascended to the right hand of the throne of God, He said: "Tarry ye in the city of Jerusalem, until ye be endued with power from on high." They were to "wait for the promise of the Father, which, saith ye, ye have heard of me." While the disciples waited and tarried before God, "these all continued with one accord in prayer and supplication." They tarried and waited before God.

The prayerlessness of many people is an astonishment to me. The prayerlessness of my own heart and life is a rebuke to me and a disgrace to my ministry. There is no unction without it. There is no ability without it. There is no converting without it.

God kept the promise made to His Son and poured out the ascension gift of the Holy Spirit. It was the greatest phenomenon that ever came to pass in all of the history of God's dealing with men. God never intended for Pentecost to be the big end of the horn and then to diminish to vanity, futility, emptiness, and barrenness. God meant for Pentecost to be the little end of the horn and that faith was to grow in power and might. Jesus said, "Greater works than these shall ye do because I go unto the Father." John 3 says that God "giveth not the Spirit by measure unto him." God does not measure it out as though He were stingy, miserly, or unable, but He gives the Spirit without measure. There is no limit to the power of the Spirit of God to work with us if first we wait upon Him.

"And when the day of Pentecost was fully come, they were all with one accord in one place." The apostles were there, including Matthias who was elected to take Judas's place. All of the laymen were there too because there were only twelve apostles, but there were one hundred twenty in that first congregation. That meant that the greatest part of the group were laymen. The women were there because they are explicitly named. The young people were there because in his Pentecostal message Peter began, "This is that which was spoken by the prophet Joel. And it shall come to pass in the last days, saith God, I will pour out of my Spirit upon all flesh: and your sons and your daughters shall prophesy, and your young men shall see visions, and your old men shall dream dreams." They all were there, not only in prayer, but also in presence. They knelt and waited before the Lord.

WE ARE TO BE PRESENT TOGETHER

If the Christians in our churches would just be faithful in the worship services we would have a revival such as we've never witnessed before. God speaks in worship but we are not there to hear. Therefore we do not heed His word and do not pray. The Word becomes anemic and sterile and finally begins to vanish from the earth. O God, for an intervention from heaven!

WE ARE TO PRESENT THE GOSPEL MESSAGE TOGETHER

The Lord said, "Ye shall be witnesses unto me." The little band at Pentecost not only prayed and appeared before the Lord, but they also boldly proclaimed and preached the Good News of Jesus Christ.

I outlined the sermon Peter preached at Pentecost. There are three homiletical points and an exhortation.

First, he addressed himself to the wickedness of men which is the common ground upon which all of us stand. We are all sinners before God. We are all judgment-bound souls that some day must appear before the Almighty. In every man's bloodstream there is that black drop. In every man's heart there is sin.

Second, Peter spoke in his sermon of the mercy and grace of God extended toward us in Jesus Christ, the Son of David, whom He marked out as the Son of God by the resurrection from among the dead. This is God's atonement for our sins. This is God's mercy and grace that we might be saved.

Third, all of the future belongs to Jesus whom God raised up exalted to sit at His right hand on high until all the earth shall be made His footstool. The future lies not in the hands of a United Nations, not in the power of a tyranny or dictatorship, but it lies in the hands of Jesus the Lord. Before Christ we must some day appear.

When Peter came to the end of his third homiletical point, the followers of the Lord were cut to the heart. They were convicted in their souls and cried saying, "Men and brethren, what shall we do?" Peter said:

> Repent [turn, change your mind, change your way, change your life, change your direction], and be baptized every one of you in the name of Jesus Christ for [*eis*, "because of"] the remission of sins, and ye shall receive the gift of the Holy Ghost.
>
> And with many other words did he testify and exhort, saying, Save yourselves from this untoward generation. (Acts 2:38, 40)

There is no part of that message that is not familiar to us who live in America. Our own souls witness to the fact that we are lost in sin and that we are all sinners alike. God in His mercy has sent Jesus to save us. Some day we shall stand before Him who is the Ruler and Judge of all. The story in Acts continues:

> Then they that gladly received his word were baptized: and the same day there were added unto them about three thousand souls.
>
> And they, continuing daily with one accord in the temple, and breaking bread from house to house, did eat their meat with gladness and singleness of heart, Praising God, and having favour with all the people. (Acts 2:41, 46-47)

We are no credit to the world when we are weak, anemic, powerless, and sterile. O God, for a dynamic church!

WE WILL HAVE PRECIOUS RESULTS

Gladness and singleness of heart is always the inevitable result of a great turning to the Lord. God made this world like that. When I am in tune with Him, when I am right with Him, the whole world is singing. Peace and gladness unspeakable fill my soul and my heart.

All of the first followers of the Lord were Jews. I recently baptized a Jewish couple. They found the Lord as their personal Savior. Afterward the husband said to me: "Pastor, I have no words to describe the gladness and joy in my heart. I smoked cigarettes for thirty-three years, but now all desire to smoke has left me."

When a man gives his heart to Christ, he doesn't have to find joy or peace in a bottle. When a man finds Christ and joy immeasurable fills his soul, he doesn't have to seek for pleasure and enjoyment in the things of this world. He has Jesus, and that is all he needs.

Two Jews were speaking to each other one day in my presence. One of them had found the Lord Messiah, and he said to a distinguished leader among Jewry, "I have found my life and peace and happiness in Christ." The other Jew looked at him with a long and searching eye and said, "Sir, you do not know how much I envy you."

As we shall see in following the Book of Acts, the door was opened to the Gentiles and to all the families of the earth. The same glorious testimony follows. Whenever a man gives his heart to Jesus, there is joy, gladness, and singleness of heart. He still presides over His creation. He is still Lord of the whole world.

19

The Miracle at the Beautiful Gate

Now Peter and John went up together into the temple at the hour of prayer, being the ninth hour.

And a certain man lame from his mother's womb was carried, whom they laid daily at the gate of the temple which is called Beautiful, to ask alms of them that entered into the temple;

Who seeing Peter and John about to go into the temple asked an alms.

And Peter, fastening his eyes upon him with John, said, Look on us.

And he gave heed unto them, expecting to receive something of them.

Then Peter said, Silver and gold have I none; but such as I have give I thee: In the name of Jesus Christ of Nazareth rise up and walk.

And he took him by the right hand, and lifted him up: and immediately his feet and ankle bones received strength.

And he leaping up stood, and walked, and entered with them into the temple, walking, and leaping, and praising God.

And all the people saw him walking and praising God:

And they knew that it was he which sat for alms at the Beautiful gate of the temple: and they were filled with wonder and amazement at that which had happened unto him.

And as the lame man which was healed held Peter and John, all the people ran together unto them in the porch that is called Solomon's, greatly wondering.

And when Peter saw it, he answered unto the people, Ye men of Israel, why marvel ye at this? or why look ye so earnestly on us, as though by our own power or holiness we had made this man to walk?

The God of Abraham, and of Isaac, and of Jacob, the God of our fathers, hath glorified his Son Jesus. (Acts 3:1-13a)

Out of the many signs and wonders that were wrought by the preachers of Christ through the power of the Lord, Luke chooses one and presents his miraculous story here in the third chapter of Acts.

There must be some reason why out of all of the many wonders, miracles, and signs that were done to affirm these men as the emissaries of God, Luke chooses this one. As we look at it carefully, it will be manifest why this marvelous miracle is chosen.

First of all, the miracle in the third chapter of Acts typifies and represents the work of our Lord Christ through His church. What kind of work, to whom it is addressed, and how and why it is furthered in the earth are revealed in the wonderful position occupied by the impotent, lifelong-lame beggar. We cannot imagine anyone more wonderfully situated or marvelously positioned than that beggar. Every day he was laid at the Beautiful gate of the temple.

Before the beggar's eyes was one of the most glorious panoramas in the world. Down the fifteen steps of ascent from the Beautiful gate to the court of the Gentiles and looking east beyond, he would see the Corinthian colonnaded porch of Solomon with four rows of glistening white marble columns. The top was studded with golden spikes to keep the fowls of the air from lighting on the temple. Beyond lay the Kidron Valley and its garden of the winepress of Gethsemane. Immediately before him rose the Mount of Olives, and all around stood the hills and mountains that surround Jerusalem. What a glorious panorama he faced!

Back of him rose the temple. Flavius Josephus described the temple as breathtaking, made of solid white marble. The front of the temple was covered with gold, shining with such purity and splendor in the sun, that Josephus says the natural eye could not look upon it because the brilliance of the temple was blinding. This sanctuary rose to the crown of Mount Moriah.

Passing by the beggar every day were the most learned theologians and philosophers of his time. The rabbinical students in the school of Gamaliel, Hillel, and Shammai spoke of the revelation of God and the presence of the Lord in the world. No one was more wonderfully situated than this impotent beggar. Yet for all of this he was in no way better. He lay helpless, poor, and impotent, needing the hand of God. This is a type of humanity today. Despite our wonderful situation, we are still impotent beggars needing the ability and the power of the Lord.

THE STORY TYPIFIES HUMANITY AT LARGE

Consider the situation of humanity. The panorama around us is breathtaking: the chalice of the blue sky that arches above, the myriad stars that smile upon us at night, the sun that rises to meridian strength in the day, the vernal showers that fall on the thirsting land, and the emerald and verdant earth that is brought to life in the springtime. Even God looking upon His creation said that it was very good.

Consider those who surround us. There are legions of poets, philosophers, teachers, doctors, psychologists, psychiatrists, and political leaders who daily walk in and out before us. They speak of their hypotheses, their theories, and their speculations. They write books and say all kinds of things to and about us. Yet for all of our position and for all who surround us, humanity is still lost, impotent, and beggarly. We are magnificently positioned, but we need the presence, the hand, and the power of God. However we are placed, and however magnificently we may be surrounded, we are still as impotent and as lost as ever.

I once listened to a learned psychologist state that in years past we used to think that if we could change the environment of the man, we could change the man himself. If we would take people living in poverty and in squalor and in filth out of the environment in which they live, and build for them beautiful boulevards, sidewalks, and homes, and place them in another kind of environment, they would be a different kind of people. He said that is what we used to think and that is what we used to teach. "But," he said, "we have experimented with it." He gave an illustration.

In his own city there was a rat-infested, poverty-stricken, dirty part of town. With much money the citizens of the community cleared out the filth, built beautiful streets, planted trees, and gave the people beautiful places in which to live. After they had spent the vast amount of money and time, the people were as decadent, degraded, and as sorry as they ever were. How a man is situated has nothing to do with the character of the man himself.

I poignantly remember one of the famous trials in all legal history, the trial of Loeb and Leopold. Clarence Darrow won his case (though he admitted that the boys were murderers) on the basis that they had grown up in an affluent home. They were the sons of rich families. Being satiated with all of the gifts and affluence of life, they were pampered and petted and thus driven to a thrill in the murder of a little friend. That is hard to believe, but that was the verdict of the law.

However beautifully positioned we may be, however all of the accouterments of art or affluence may surround us, the human heart is still impotent and beggarly in the presence of the most glorious gift of life.

The truth of that came to my mind recently as I was listening to the radio in Dallas. The report stated that the police are now saying that Dallas is the focal point for the distribution of drugs, marijuana, and heroin in the United States. Couriers are bringing drugs into Dallas by the thousands of pounds, and in the case of marijuana, by the thousands of tons. Police, who had been working on the case for months, finally uncovered leads of the men who were behind a $40 million haul of drugs. And the leads pointed to some of the finest businessmen in the city of Dallas.

Who is involved in the underworld? Who lives in the gutter of life? Who seeks after all of the emoluments of this world? Is it the degraded, the decadent, the poor? There must be a mastermind back of a $40 billion drug smuggling operation. It must be someone shrewd, intelligent, and high up in the political and business world. If a man steals a dollar, he is a thief. That same man, if he has opportunity, will steal a million dollars because he is a thief. A thief is not a thief because of the amount he steals. A thief is a thief because of his heart. His position, whether he is shoplifting, or whether he is head of one of the great corporate institutions of America, is the same. The man's position makes no difference in the man himself.

That is why this miraculous story is chosen, for it typifies humanity. Man may live with the presence of God, he may see the glory of God every day and every night, yet he may be impotent, lost, beggarly, and degraded. That is humanity.

THE STORY TYPIFIES THE FACT THAT THE GOSPEL APPEAL IS TO ALL MEN

The gospel message is addressed to everyone, even to that impotent beggar. The universality of the address of the Christian message is remarkable. The Bible says, "And the common people heard him gladly." The power of the gospel message is addressed to the great throngs of mankind, not to just an elect or select group of any kind or any status. God somehow looks upon us all alike. He classifies us in just two groups: we either know the Lord in the pardon of our sins or we are lost no matter who we are. The power of the gospel has always been such in its moving through the masses of the people.

When the Anglican Church of England would not allow John Wesley and George Whitefield to preach in their churches, those mighty servants of God preached to thousands on the riverbanks, wherever men could gather to listen to the Good News of the Son of God. Baptist preachers in the pioneer days of our country pressed across the Alleghenies into the great heartland of the Midwest, finally to the prairies, and to the mountains in the Rockies, preaching wherever men gathered, wherever they would listen. They did not know where they would spend the night, fording rivers over which no bridges had been built, following trails unmarked except by Indian paths. They were full of the grace of God and eminently evangelistic, laying the foundation for the churches and the institutions that bless us today. That is the address of the Christian gospel to all men everywhere.

THE STORY TYPIFIES HEALING

The story of the beggar in Acts 3 also typifies one of the instruments through which the church has been blessed in reaching men for God—healing. The Christian message has always been associated with healing and ministering to the sick.

The passage in Acts 28:9-11 is an unusual one. In that chapter Paul and Luke are on Melita having been shipwrecked. Ministering to the people in Melita, Luke uses two words. He says that Paul *iaomai*, "heals." He, the doctor, *therapeuo*, "practices medicine." Paul, in the power of God, doing the signs of an apostle *iaomai*, heals miraculously. Dr. Luke *therapeuo*, practices medicine. Those two practices always have been close together, and they should be close together, for a man who is sick needs encouragement in his soul and in his heart as much as he needs healing in his physical frame. A man can be as sick in his mind and soul as he can be sick in his body. The chaplain praying, the pastor praying, and the beloved physician *therapeuo*, practicing medicine, go together. When someone is ill, to have the preacher stand close by to pray is in itself a great balm and a great healing. That is why medical missions are always blessed of God. That is why I think our finest hospitals will always be Christian hospitals. That is God and God's program for us.

THE STORY OCCASIONED TWO WONDERFUL TESTIMONIES

Notice the testimony of the healed beggar. That healed man, impotent from his mother's womb, praised God and told the earth what the Lord had done for him! His testimony will be discussed in the next chapter of this book.

In the testimony of Peter, he begins:

> And when Peter saw it, he answered unto the people, Ye men of Israel, why marvel ye at this? or why look ye so earnestly on us, as though by our own power or holiness we had made this man to walk?
>
> The God of Abraham, and of Isaac, and of Jacob, the God of our fathers, hath glorified his Son Jesus. (Acts 3:12-13a)

Every preacher and every teacher ought always remember: not I but Christ. There should be that self-effacement or self-denial. Every servant of Christ should manifest a humility. He is merely a voice, just an echo proclaiming what God has written in His Book. He is speaking in behalf of someone else, and he is an ambassador from the courts of heaven. Glorifying the Lord Jesus should be the spirit in any man or woman of God who speaks in the name of the Lord.

What is it that Simon Peter delivers to those wondering and expectant people? It is the rest of the third chapter of the Book of Acts. I can summarize it in a sentence. Simon Peter speaks there of the historical facts of the Lord Jesus Christ.

A True Man of God Presents
The Historical Facts of the Christian Faith

When a man preaches the gospel of Christ, what does he preach? It is never philosophy, speculation, psychology, or any other of the theorizing academic approaches. When a man preaches the gospel of Christ, what does he do? He does what Peter did. Peter proclaimed the historical facts of the Christian faith, grounded in history. He spoke of the intervention of God from heaven in human life; not a speculation, not a hypothesis, not a supposition. The faithful preacher presents the proclamation of what God has done.

The man who denies the historical facts of the Christian faith denies the faith itself, because the faith cannot exist apart from the historical facts upon which it is founded. When a man denies the virgin birth, or the resurrection of Christ, or the miracles of the apostles, or the great revelation of God in human history written here in the Book, he denies the faith. There is nothing left except the speculation, the philosophizing of the man. The Christian faith is founded upon historical fact.

When a man preaches the historical facts of Jesus, he is preaching Jesus. When he affirms the historical facts of the Christian faith, he is preaching the Christian faith. When he believes the historical facts of the Christian faith, he is believing the faith itself.

I believe that we were lost in sin. I believe that God in His pity and mercy sent His only begotten Son into this world to make atonement for our sins, just as the Bible says. I believe that the Holy Spirit formed for Him a body in the womb of a Jewish virgin named Mary in order that He might make atoning sacrifice in our behalf. I believe that He was nailed to the cross for our sins. I believe that He spilled out the crimson of His life into this world to make expiation, to bring forgiveness and payment for our wrong. I believe that the third day He was raised from the dead according to the Scriptures. I believe that He ascended into heaven, there to make intercession for us who look in faith to Him. I believe that He will keep His promise that some day He will come for His own. When I preach these historical facts of the Christian faith, I am preaching the faith itself. The Christian faith can never be separated from the historical facts upon which it is founded.

In the supreme need of life, in the supreme agony of death, judgment, or great sorrow, what comfort is it to have a preacher bring us his speculation, his hypothesis, his philosophies? It is like a broken reed.

In the supreme moment of our need, it is a great comfort to know that Jesus really died for our sins. He makes intercession for us. He stands with hands outstretched to comfort and to save and to welcome us some day into glory. That is the faith. That is the preaching of the apostles. That is the glorious gospel of the Son of God.

That is why Luke writes to Theophilus:

> It seemed good to me also, having had perfect understanding of all things from the very first, to write unto thee in order, most excellent Theophilus,
> That thou mightest know the certainty of those things, wherein thou hast been instructed. (Luke 1:3-4)

The church has a wonderful assignment, and that is to instruct our converts in the faith that they may know the certainty of those things to which they have been introduced in the Lord. We are not following some cunningly devised fable, but we are basing our heart, hopes, and destiny upon the fact of God's intervention in Jesus Christ in our lives and in the lives of lost humanity.

20

The Power of Personal Testimony

And as the lame man which was healed held Peter and John, all the people ran together unto them in the porch that is called Solomon's, greatly wondering. (Acts 3:11)

The crippled beggar had been lame all his life, having been born that way from his mother's womb. The story reads that Peter and John went up together into the temple at the hour of prayer. They saw the crippled man who was laid every day at the gate called Beautiful, *Oraion*. There he begged as the people passed by. Seeing Peter and John, the beggar extended his right hand seeking alms from them. Peter replied, "I have nothing of gold or silver to give, but what I do have, I will give you." Then Peter reached forth, and took the right hand of the lame man and by sheer strength raised him up. It would take all of the strength that I had with both of my arms to raise a man. That big fisherman with leverage at length raised him up and immediately the man's feet and ankle bones were made strong and well. The man, standing for the first time in his life, began to leap, to shout, and to praise God. The great throng in the large temple which covered twenty-six acres, saw him walking, leaping, and praising God. What a wonderful way to go to church! What a wonderful way to testify to the goodness and grace of the Lord! The people recognized the man as the one who had sat begging at the gate *Oraion* in the temple. The lame man, as he leaped and praised God, held on to John with one hand and to Peter with the other hand. He began to let the whole world know what God had done for him.

We see the contrast of testimonies in the next chapter. When Peter had finished delivering his sermon at Pentecost, three thousand souls were added to the church. When the healed beggar had finished his testifying, leaping and praising God, the number of the *andron* who believed was about five thousand. Luke does not use the word *anthropoi*, which is the word for "humanity." He uses the word *andron*, that is, "men," in contradistinction to women and children. After the testimony, the number of *andron* was about five thousand. Counting all the families there were possibly twenty-five thousand people there. It was a mind-staggering response when that man got through testifying and praising God.

Lest someone say that this experience is unique or peculiar, let me point out to you a similar occurrence in the life of our Lord. In Mark 5 the Master is in the land of the Gadarenes, in Decapolis, on the east side of the Sea of Galilee. A demented man is there who lived in the tombs and who is filled with a legion of evil spirits. The Lord wonderfully healed that man, but in the healing, the people lost their pigs. Sometimes it costs to serve the Lord.

If one had a liquor store and became a Christian, he should sell the liquor store. How could he sell something that orphans children, that makes widows out of wives, that breaks up homes, and destroys a man's life and job? How could one be in the business of breaking a man's life, a man's heart, and a man's home, and at the same time be a Christian? If he chooses to keep the store, he does not let Christ into his life. These people were guilty of this principle. It cost them some swine, so they begged Jesus to leave. The Lord left, for He does not stay where He is not invited. As He left, the man He had healed begged the Lord to let him go with Him. The Lord said, "No, but go home to your friends and neighbors and tell them what wonderful things the Lord has done for you." So the healed man went throughout Decapolis, the province on the east side of the Jordan River, and began to publish abroad what God had done for him.

Look at the eighth chapter of Mark where we read that the Lord is back in Decapolis where the formerly demented man has been testifying to His love and grace. "In those days the multitude being very great" had been with the Lord three days and nights without anything to eat. So mightily were they moved to listen to the message of the Lord Christ that they stayed without food. This is the same land where the people had begged the Master to leave. They now listened to Him attentively for three days and three nights. The Lord, having compassion upon them and being in an uninhabited area of the country, fed them. The number of people that he fed was about four thousand with only seven loaves and a few fishes. Here were the people who had begged Him to leave, now sitting at His feet, more than four thousand of them. Oh, the powerful witness of that healed Gadarene demoniac!

PERSONAL INTEREST IN WITNESSING

When we look at the Bible and turn these pages, we see the unusual ability of God to work through a man's witness and testimony. We see it all through the revelation of divine grace. It begins in the life of our Lord. That is how He started His ministry. As He walked by, John the Baptist pointed Him out and said, "Behold the Lamb of God, which taketh away the sin of the world." Two of John's disciples, Andrew and John, heard Him speak and began to follow the Lord. The Lord suddenly turned and asked, "What do you want? Whom do you seek?" They had not thought to answer and blurted out, "Lord, where are You staying?" The Lord graciously said, "Come and see." They spent the day with Him. More than sixty years later John, writing that story, says: "And I remember the exact hour. It was 10:00 in the morning." Andrew went to tell his brother, Peter, that he had found the Messiah of whom Moses and the prophets wrote. Then the Lord talked to Philip and Philip spoke to Nathanael. Then the Lord talked to Nathanael. Thus the ministry of the Savior began. It continues today in the same vein of personal witnessing.

In John 3 we read the story of Nicodemus. Nicodemus was one man and yet the Lord preached to just one man the greatest sermon on the new birth the world ever heard. In the next chapter the Lord preached another sermon, the greatest sermon on spiritual worship that ever fell from the lips of a man, and this too was to a congregation of one. She was a despicable, promiscuous outcast from Sychar, a hated and despised Samaritan woman. Why did not the Lord save that great and mighty sermon on the new birth to deliver to multitudes? Why did He not speak of that tremendous revelation of spiritual worship to a magnificent convocation of thousands of people? The Lord chose not to do it that way.

A pastor's notice announced, "It is not worth my while to prepare and deliver a sermon to a congregation of less than one hundred; therefore, we shall have no more evening services." Can you imagine that? The Lord spoke to a congregation of one and delivered His greatest sermons and His greatest messages. The whole spirit of the outreach of the Christian faith is on a one-to-one basis.

A remarkable story is that of Philip, the deacon evangelist, who was in Samaria in the midst of a great revival. The entire city was turning to the Lord. How uplifting is a marvelous revival, a great turning to God! But in the midst of that revival in Samaria the angel of the Lord said to Philip, "Arise, and go down into the desert." What an astonishing thing for the Spirit of God to do! He took the evangelist out of a tremendous revival and set him in the desert with nothing but the blue sky above him and the endless sand around him. But the Lord sent the treasurer of Ethiopia on that road and as he came near, the Spirit of God said to Philip, "Join thyself to this chariot." Philip won that one man to the Lord and baptized him in the next body of water at which they arrived.

Turn the pages of the Book of Acts and you will read about the marvelously effective ministry of the apostle Paul in the Asian capital city of Ephesus, one of the tremendous Greek cities of the world. The Temple of Artemis, one of the seven wonders of the world, was located there, and was a center of Greek pagan worship. But Paul turned that city upside down, and out of Ephesus the word went throughout all Asia Minor. The seven churches of Asia were born out of the ministry of Paul in Ephesus.

How did Paul minister? In Acts 20 speaking to the Ephesian elders who had come down to the seashore on Miletus to bid him farewell, Paul describes his ministry. He says, "Remember, that by the space of three years I ceased not to warn every one night and day with tears to repent and have faith toward the Lord Jesus Christ. What an effective way for Paul to further the gospel of Christ, from house to house! So the whole address of the Christian faith is to one man's heart, to one person's soul, to one person's life, always by the one.

OH, FOR A FAITHFUL PEOPLE TO WITNESS

It is sad whenever we come to the place in our lives when we think of people in terms of masses. The Lord does not do that. He never thinks of us in terms of multitudes, but He thinks of us as one at a time, one by one. It was the Lord who said:

> Are not two sparrows sold for a farthing? and one of them shall not fall on the ground without your Father.
> But the very hairs of your head are all numbered.
> Fear ye not therefore, ye are of more value than many sparrows. (Matt. 10:29-31)

God knows you and calls you by your name. He knows all about you. You are not just a digit and a part of an illimitable mass, but you are someone whom God knows. He was there when you were born. He gave you breath and a soul. He will be there when you die. He will send His angels for you to carry you to Abraham's bosom. He will stand by your side in the judgment as your lawyer, advocate, pleader, intercessor, and intervener. That is the way God thinks about His children, always in terms of "you."

Would it not be glorious if our people would deliver God's message to one person at a time, heart to heart, face to face, hand to hand, prayer for prayer, interest for interest? What a wonderful way that would be!

When a country boy visits the city, he has a world of revelation before him. I grew up in the country and in a little town. When I was a youth I went to New York City for the first time. You cannot imagine the effect that big city had upon a little country boy. It was overwhelming. I walked from street to street and place to place just looking. As I walked I saw an enormous building which looked like a vast Greek temple. Standing on the other side of the street from the building, I noticed that there was an enormous chiseling of words in the frieze that decorated the entire building. This is what I read: "Neither Snow Nor Rain Nor Heat Nor Gloom of Night Stays These Couriers From the Swift Completion of Their Appointed Rounds." I thought that was one of the finest sentiments I had ever read. I wondered what it was talking about, so I went back down to the other end of the block and started over and read the inscription again! "Neither Snow Nor Rain Nor Heat Nor Gloom of Night Stays These Couriers From the Swift Completion of Their Appointed Rounds." I tried to stop a New Yorker to ask him what it meant, but he walked rapidly by. I tried to stop another one to ask him what it was all about, but he also kept on walking. I thought that these were the rudest people in the world. In the little town in which I lived, if one were to ask someone something you would spend half the day talking to him. And in New York I could not even get anyone to stop. Finally I was successful, and I asked the fellow as he paused, "What is that building there and of whom are they talking?" He said: "Son, that is the United States Post Office for New York City and that is the biggest building in this town, and the biggest post office in the world. That phrase is talking about the mailman." I looked again at the impressive building. And I remember that noble tribute when I see a mailman coming to the door. Oh, what a magnificent phenomenon if that could be said about God's people delivering the message of the Lord personally! God blesses personal testimony in a powerful way.

Testimony for God Is Never Spoken in Vain

The Lord never lets personal testimony for Him fall to the ground. There is never a word spoken for Jesus but that the Lord cares for it. I may not see, but He does. The fruit of the spoken word may be even beyond my lifetime, but the Lord always prospers it. Any good and faithful word that is offered in behalf of our Lord always bears fruit.

In a little church where I pastored, a woman came to me who was the wife of a fine, good man, but a lost man. She said to me, "Would you win my husband to Christ?" I told her I would, and I told her to pray. So we set a time for me to come and eat supper with them. After the supper I was to talk to her husband about the Lord. The evening came and I went to the home with my Bible. After we had broken bread together, I sat down with him and began to talk to him about the Lord. I pleaded with him beyond midnight. After midnight, making my last appeal, he said, "No, no." I could not win that man. I went to bed defeated.

The following Sunday morning down the aisle in my little church came the twelve-year-old son of that father. He came to me and said, "I have accepted the Lord as my Savior and I want to be baptized." I said, "Son, when did you accept the Lord as your Savior?" He replied: "Last Thursday night you came to our home to speak to my father about Jesus. After supper my mother sent me to my room and to bed so that you could speak to my father alone. My mother thought that I would go to bed and to sleep, but I didn't. I went to my room and went to bed, but I kept the door open. I listened to you as you spoke to my father and as you made appeal that he accept Christ as his Savior. My father turned you down, but there that night on my bed I gave my heart to Jesus."

How I have remembered that experience a thousand times over. Lord, do not ever let me be discouraged or fall into frustration or into the spirit of despair or defeat. When I faithfully witness to the grace of God, the Lord somehow blesses it in ways maybe I do not understand, do not know, or maybe never will know this side of heaven. But God never lets a witness for Him fall to the ground.

May He bless our personal testimony. I have found in my life that when you say a good word about Jesus, the Lord does something to those who listen and He remarkably, inwardly blesses you. O, His goodness to me.

21

The Present Obligation to Be Converted

Repent ye therefore, and be converted, that your sins may be blotted out, when the times of refreshing shall come from the presence of the Lord;

And he shall send Jesus Christ, which before was preached unto you:

Whom the heaven must receive until the times of restitution of all things, which God hath spoken by the mouth of all his holy prophets since the world began. (Acts 3:19-21)

The third chapter of the Book of Acts begins with Peter and John going to the temple at three o'clock in the afternoon for prayer. In the temple at the Beautiful Gate there is a beggar who, for all his years, had been a cripple and had been laid every day at the gate to beg. Seeing Peter and John, he held out his hand hoping to receive a small coin from them. Instead of giving him a piece of money, which they could not afford to do, they said: "What we do have, we share gladly. In the name of Christ, rise up and walk." Peter took him by the right hand and lifted him up. When he did so, the man who had never walked, suddenly found his feet and ankle bones strengthened and well. He began to leap and to praise God for the wonderful miracle that had happened to him. Peter began to preach the gospel of the Son of God. He declared that the power to heal was the power of God in His Son Christ Jesus, whom they had crucified, whom God had raised from the dead. In that name not only do we have healing, but we also have forgiveness of sins. He concluded his sermon with the appeal which gave rise to the title of this chapter, "Our Present Obligation to Be Converted." Then Peter said:

Repent ye therefore, and be converted, that your sins may be blotted out, when the times of refreshing shall come from the presence of the Lord;

> And he shall send Jesus Christ, which before was preached unto you:
> Whom the heaven must receive until the times of restitution of all things,
> which God hath spoken by the mouth of all his holy prophets since the world
> began. (Acts 3:19-21)

In this passage Peter uses words that are used nowhere else in the New Testament. He says that a great renovation of the entire universe is coming. In view of that he makes an appeal for repentance and conversion. He describes the future as a time of refreshing that shall come from the presence of the Lord. Jesus is now in heaven (and must stay there until the age of consummation comes), but when He returns there is to be a great refreshing in His presence, an *anapsuxis*. An *anapsuxis* refers to "a refreshing cooling after heat." When the Lord returns there will be a time of restitution of all things, an *apokatastasis*, which means "the restoration of a thing as it originally was." The only time in the Bible that those two words are used are the instances of which I have spoken. Outside of the New Testament *apokatastasis* is used as a technical medical term referring to someone who is completely restored to health or to the healing of a joint that is dislocated. The word is found in inscriptions and in the papyri referring to the restoration of a temple that is fallen into ruins. Philo, the Jewish philosopher and theologian of Alexandria, used the word to refer to the return of the Jewish people to their homeland from the Babylonian captivity. They are restored home. Josephus uses *apokatastasis* to refer to the inheritance that is given back to those who, because of poverty, have been forced to sell their possessions. In the year of jubilee, all of their properties are restored to them. In Jewish apocalyptic literature the word is used to refer to the restoration of the universe to its primeval beauty and glory, such as described in Revelation 21, when all the heavens and all the earth are restored to their Edenic beauty and purity.

A RESTITUTION OF ALL CREATION IS COMING

The apostle says that a time is coming when in the presence of the Lord there will be a wonderful refreshing. Then he says a time is coming when there will be a restitution of all things in heaven and in earth. In view of that he uses two imperatives. *Metanoestate* is a first aorist active imperative of *metanoeo*. That is the word always translated "repentance" in the New Testament. It means "a change of mind." *Epistrepstate* is a first aorist active imperative of *epistrepho*. Translated here "converted," it literally means "to turn back," "to turn again." One can imagine the memories in the mind and heart of Peter when he used that word. That is the exact word in the exact form that the Lord Jesus said to him in Luke 22:

> And the Lord said, Simon, Simon, behold, Satan hath desired to have you, that he may sift you as wheat:
> But I have prayed for thee, that thy faith fail not: and when thou art converted, strengthen thy brethren. (vv. 31-32)

That word *epistrepho* (be converted, turn back) was deeply meaningful to Peter.

MAN IS COMMANDED TO REPENT

Man is commanded from heaven to repent of his sins and to be converted, to turn back to God. It is not optional. The Lord has a wonderful work for us. He will blot out our sins. He will regenerate our hearts. He will write our names in the Lamb's Book of Life. He will save us now and forever, but first a man must *metanoeo*, "repent." I must *epistrepho*, "turn back to God." It is not optional.

Ezekiel 18 says:

> Repent, and turn yourselves from all your transgressions, so iniquity shall not be your ruin. Cast away from you all your transgressions, whereby ye have transgressed; and make you a new heart and a new spirit: for why will ye die, O house of Israel?
> For I have no pleasure in the death of him that dieth, saith the Lord GOD: wherefore turn yourselves, and live ye. (vv. 30-32)

The obligation mandated to us from heaven is that I turn, that I confess my sins, that I ask God to forgive me, and that I be converted.

There are many things in our lives that are optional. When we go to the store to buy a shirt we can choose the color we want. It usually makes no difference what shirt we buy. It is the same when we go out to eat. Shall we eat at a cafeteria or shall we eat at an expensive restaurant? Life is filled with a thousand daily optionals.

There are some choices in life that are not optional. One of them is this mandate from heaven that I confess my sins and ask God to save me; that I be converted. That is not optional with me.

History books describe the terrible flood which destroyed Galveston, Texas in 1900. What happened was this: the federal government sent a warning to Galveston saying, "A great storm is coming; flee for your lives! Find refuge in the mainland; leave!" At that time a long, iron bridge connected the city with the mainland, and a few left the city over that bridge. But the majority of the city went out doors and looked up at the sky. There was not a cloud to be found. The ocean was calm and serene. The people went back to work and about their business.

The federal government sent them warning from the weather bureau not once or twice, but time and again: "There is a great storm coming! Flee for your lives!" The people went out and looked at the sky which was still blue, and the ocean was calm and peaceful.

Early one morning a woman awakened her husband to tell him the wind was beginning to blow and the rain was beginning to fall. He got up and checked all the windows. The rain became a deluge and the wind became a hurricane. Great tidal waves swept over the island endlessly. For months they picked up dead bodies. The entire city was destroyed.

There are some things in life that are not optional. Our mandate from the Lord to repent is exactly like that.

A time of vast judgment is coming upon this world. Death is not to reign in the earth forever. Sin is not always to be present in the sight of God. There will not always be age, sickness, disease, darkness, violence, terror, iniquity, transgression, murder, and blood. There will be a time when God will purge the earth and the heavens of all that hurts and destroys and offends. God is going to create new heavens and a new earth in which righteousness will dwell. The apostle preached that in view of the purging of this earth and the great Judgment Day of almighty God, in view of the great consummation of the age and the restoration of all things, we must repent and we must turn and we must be converted. I have no choice in that. I face death and the judgment bar of almighty God.

The Sermon on the Mount ends describing a man who built his house upon the sand. The rains fell, the winds hammered, the floods enveloped, and the house was destroyed. Another man built his house upon the rock. The same rains fell, the same floods rose, and the same winds blew, but that house stood because it was built upon a rock.

Why would a man build his house in the path of a flood and of a storm? Because there is no other way to build our house. All of us build our houses and live our lives in the path of a storm before the judgment day of almighty God. I live in this world that is ridden with disease, age, and death. I must prepare for death and dying. I must prepare for the great assize when I stand before God. That is why the imperatives *metanoeo*, "change your mind," and *epistrepho*, "come back to God," are used.

CHILDREN ARE COMMANDED TO REPENT

The mandate from the Lord reaches down to little children. What a responsibility these little children are! The day will come when they will become sensitive to sin. They will say that they need the Savior. God made them that way. Human beings are morally sensitive. We call that "the age of accountability." Little children need to be taught about Jesus and that He is their Savior. He died for them that they might have forgiveness of sins in Him. They are to trust the Lord as their Savior. When a child reaches the age of accountability, he must be brought to Jesus. It is imperative; it is not optional.

YOUNG PEOPLE ARE COMMANDED TO REPENT

Our young people are likewise mandated to repent and are as morally accountable to God as adult men and women. They also possess moral sensitivity in their souls. They also must repent and be converted. These young people may say: "But, Pastor, this is a difficult age in which we live. It is a trying time in which to be a Christian." It was difficult in the days of Daniel too. He was a teen-ager when he was taken into captivity into the king's court in Babylon. It was difficult in the days of his three friends, Shadrach, Meshach, and Abed-nego. They finally were thrown into the fiery furnace. It was difficult for them, and they were also teen-agers. It has never been easy to follow God. The world, the flesh, and the devil are against us. God commands all of us to repent of our sins and turn to the Lord and be converted.

The rich young ruler who had inherited his fortune and his place of preeminence in the community, facing a tremendous decision, lost eternal life. Think of his regret having chosen the world and its empty, sterile rewards instead of eternal salvation in Christ Jesus. The times now are difficult, but our mandate remains: yesterday, today, and until the consummation, I am to repent of my sins, I am to turn to God, and be converted.

ADULTS ARE COMMANDED TO REPENT

If that is true of children and young people, how much more is it true of us who are grown men and women? We too are commanded to repent and be converted. We have the present obligation to be converted now.

My first pastorate out of the seminary was the First Baptist Church of Chickasha, Oklahoma. When they built a new church house some years later, they invited me to preach the dedicatory sermon. As I walked through the streets of Chickasha for the first time in thirty-nine years, many memories came to my heart. One of them was this. One day the ministerial alliance, which was composed of all the preachers of the town, set aside a Saturday in which the city fathers allowed them to rope off a whole street. They were going to have a tremendous religious service on Saturday afternoon. The people were there from all over. The president of the ministerial alliance opened the service. They sang a song and had a prayer. Then all of the pastors in the city were called forward one by one and he announced who he was, of which church he was pastor, and gave a little word of invitation inviting the people to come to the service at his church the next day. After each pastor had done his part, the man who was presiding over the meeting said, "We will now have the benediction." I stood up and walked up to the pulpit and said, "Sir, are you dismissing these people now?" He said: "Yes. We are going to have the benediction." I said: "These people need preaching to. Someone ought to preach to them. We ought not to have the benediction." He turned around and said, "Anyone want to preach?" No one said he wanted to preach, so I, being the closest to him, said, "If no one will preach to them, I will." He said, "Go ahead and preach." That was second nature to me. I had been preaching on the curb at the courthouse every Saturday for three years. I stood up there with an open Bible and I preached to those people on how to be saved.

When I got through preaching, one of the pastors stood up and came to the platform. He said to them: "You go home and read your Bible. Then you will know how to be saved." My brother and sister, one can read his Bible forever and not be saved. One can preach and not be saved. One can sing about the Lord and not be saved. One can say prayers and not be saved. One can do penance and not be saved. One can write books about the Christian faith and not be saved. But a man cannot call upon the name of the Lord and not be saved. Romans 10:13 avows, "For whosoever shall call upon the name of the Lord shall be saved." A man can not achieve his salvation by doing any other thing.

When I call upon His name, when I repent of my sins, something happens. I am saved and I am saved at that moment. God does the rest. He writes my name in the Book of Life. He puts a new spirit and a new heart in this body and keeps me safe and saved forever!

22

The Matchless Ministry

Then Peter said, Silver and gold have I none; but such as I have give I thee: In the name of Jesus Christ of Nazareth rise up and walk.

And he took him by the right hand, and lifted him up: and immediately his feet and ankle bones received strength. (Acts 3:6-7)

As a background for the message today we are going to read a story in Luke 7:

And one of the Pharisees desired him that he would eat with him. And he went into the Pharisee's house, and sat down to meat.

And, behold, a woman in the city, which was a sinner, when she knew that Jesus sat at meat in the Pharisee's house, brought an alabaster box of ointment,

And stood at his feet behind him weeping, and began to wash his feet with tears, and did wipe them with the hairs of her head, and kissed his feet, and anointed them with the ointment.

Now when the Pharisee which had bidden him saw it, he spake within himself, saying, This man, if he were a prophet would have known who and what manner of woman this is that toucheth him: for she is a sinner.

And Jesus answering said unto him, Simon, I have somewhat to say unto thee. And he saith, Master, say on.

There was a certain creditor which had two debtors: the one owed five hundred pence, and the other fifty.

And when they had nothing to pay, he frankly forgave them both. Tell me therefore, which of them will love him most?

Simon answered and said, I suppose that he, to whom he forgave most. And he said unto him, Thou hast rightly judged.

And he turned to the woman, and said unto Simon, Seest thou this woman? I entered into thine house, thou gavest me no water for my feet: but she hath washed my feet with tears, and wiped them with the hairs of her head.

Thou gavest me no kiss: but this woman since the time I came in hath not ceased to kiss my feet.

My head with oil thou didst not anoint: but this woman hath anointed my feet with ointment.

Wherefore I say unto thee, Her sins, which are many, are forgiven; for she loved much: but to whom little is forgiven, the same loveth little.

And he said unto her, Thy sins are forgiven.

And they that sat at meat with him began to say within themselves, Who is this that forgiveth sins also?

And he said to the woman, Thy faith hath saved thee; go in peace. (vv. 36-50)

Then Peter said, "Silver and gold have I none; but such as I have give I thee."

We cannot help but notice the poverty of the apostles. The lame man had his hand extended not for a great sum of money but for a small coin. Holding out his hand, he thought of nothing else except a small gift from Peter and John, these men unknown to him. When Peter replies, "Silver and gold have I none," it accentuates the extreme poverty of the apostles.

Not only were the disciples poor financially, but they were hardly commendable in any other way. When Peter and John were arrested and stood before the Sanhedrin, the Sanhedrin looked upon their boldness and perceived that they were *agrammatoi kai idiotai*, translated in the King James version "unlearned and ignorant" men. They were not educated; they were not professionals. They had never been to the seminary. They had never known what it was to sit at the feet of Gamaliel as did Saul of Tarsus. They were crude, bold, unlearned, and untaught Galilean fishermen. Not only were the apostles poverty-stricken, but they did not have social standing or public acceptance as well.

But Peter adds a word: ". . . but such as I have give I thee: In the name of Jesus Christ of Nazareth rise up and walk." Peter lifted the lame man by his right hand and immediately his feet and ankle bones were strengthened. He was whole and well again. In indescribable joy he stood up, and leaped and praised God. What a gift these men of poverty possessed! "Silver and gold have I none; but such as I have give I thee." They had a dedicated heart and an immeasurable faith in Jesus Christ.

The lame man had expected a penny, but instead he received the most marvelous gift for which his heart could have asked. He was whole and well.

The world seeks after wealth, success, and fame. There are a thousand things that one can see every day of his life for which men work, search, seek, and grasp. When man acquires these possessions, they are dust and ashes in his hands. Things of this world do not satisfy the soul. They do not bless the life. A man cannot feed upon fame, fortune, or riches. They are dry husks. What we need is not what earthly riches can bring us, but it is the matchless gift that is mediated to us through the goodness, grace, healing, blessing, and forgiveness of God. Oh, that the Lord would bestow us with such ability and power to mediate that blessing to the world!

Seldom do affluent churches grow in spiritual power. They become socially conscious and they rise in the esteem of the community, but not in the power of God. An article in a magazine gave the qualifications for those who would rise in social standing in a particular city. They could not live here, they had to live there. They could not do this, they had to do that. They had to belong to certain churches in order to rise in social status in that community.

That is blasphemy! Tragically, one can find that kind of reasoning prevalent in cities throughout America.

There is a story about Duns Scotus, a mighty theologian who lived in the 1200s and died about 1305. He was visiting the Pope in Rome and the Pope was showing Duns Scotus the vast treasures of the Vatican. Running his hands through the silver and gold, he turned to the theologian and said, "No longer does the church have to say, 'Silver and gold have I none'." Duns Scotus replied, "But also no longer can she say, 'In the name of Jesus Christ of Nazareth, rise up and walk'."

Our need is never monetary. Our need is never any of the rewards or achievements acclaimed by the world. Our need is always inward, spiritual, heavenward, and Christward. We need the healing presence of the Lord. The matchless service, the matchless ministry, the matchless gift always comes from God.

THE MATCHLESS GIVER

There are golden givers and there are silver givers. There are people among us who are affluent and we praise the Lord for them; they are golden givers. There are people among us who are well-to-do; they are silver givers. In the temple in Jerusalem the Lord sat in the Court of the Women and beheld how the people gave. We read in Mark 12:

> And Jesus sat over against the treasury, and beheld how the people cast money into the treasury: and many that were rich cast in much.
>
> And there came a certain poor widow, and she threw in two mites, which makes a farthing.
>
> And he called unto him his disciples, and saith unto them, Verily I say unto

you, That this poor widow hath cast more in, than all they which have cast into the treasury:

For all they did cast in of their abundance; but she of her want did cast in all that she had, even all her living. (vv. 41-44)

Was she a washer woman? Was she a scrub woman? Whatever she was, her salary was infinitesimal. She lived on a pittance. But what she did have, she gave to the Lord. The Lord said that this is the matchless gift. The Lord looks at how much we sacrifice when we give. He judges the cost of the gift to us and how much of us is in the gift.

The Matchless Teacher

There are golden teachers. When they present the Word of God to the class, the hearers are wonderfully blessed. They are gifted and able leaders.

There are silver teachers. They may not be as gifted, nor as able, but they are blessed in their teaching ministries. Then there are others who are not endowed with a special pedagogical gift from heaven, but in a humble, sweet, and devoted way they offer themselves to teach a little class of boys or girls. These are precious and loyal people whom you never see or know. They are in the departments of the children's divisions, and Sunday by Sunday they faithfully love and minister to those little children. God honors their devoted service.

The Matchless Soul Winners

There are golden soul winners and there are silver soul winners. In America there are incomparable evangelists whose names are household words. Many evangelists are as well known and as much seen as the President of the United States. They are golden soul winners, and when they preach, people come forward by the thousands.

There are silver soul winners, men who preach in our churches and who do a wonderful task in their assignment of evangelizing the lost. Then, there are thousands of humble, God-fearing, Christ-honoring men and women who, in the open doors that are set before them, say a good word for Jesus and bring the lost to the knowledge of the Lord. We have never heard their names. They are known but to God in heaven. They never appear before great throngs, but in a gentle, humble, and Christ-like way they tell others about the Lord and pray for them, sometimes weep over them, and win them to Jesus.

A man in one of my churches would go down a street and knock at every door inquiring if the people inside were Christians and if they loved the Lord. As he went up and down the streets, every day he found people who were outside of Christ. He found people who needed prayer, comforting, and strengthening. He would go in with an open Bible and pray with them, sometimes weep with them, and time without number bring them down to me to the front of the church and say, "Pastor, here is a man who has marvelously found the Lord."

One day an affluent Pharisee had a big dinner for the Lord Jesus. The Lord was seated at the table of honor and His feet extended out as He leaned on His left arm. While He was breaking bread in that illustrious company, a woman of the street, who had been wonderfully saved, came to him. Out of the overflowing gratitude of her heart, she began to bathe His feet with her tears and to dry them with the hairs of her head and to anoint His feet with an alabaster box of ointment. The indignant Pharisee said: "This man is no prophet. If He were a man of God who had been sent from the Lord in heaven, He would know the kind of a prostitute that is bathing His feet and anointing Him with an alabaster box of ointment." Then the Lord said: "Simon, when I came, you did not wash my feet, not even with water. She has not ceased to bathe my feet with her tears and dry them with the hairs of her head. You gave me no kiss of welcome when I came. She has not ceased to kiss my feet. You did not anoint my head with oil. She has anointed my feet."

This is matchless service. It is of the heart, of the Lord. It is something on the inside of us that comes from heaven. When we dedicate that something on the inside that loves God, praises the Lord, and lifts up His marvelous name, He is pleased. The Lord looks in loving favor upon us. We give of ourselves to the Lord's service not out of our abundance, but out of our necessity. Not out of our superfluity, but out of our need do we praise His holy name with our lives. Not out of our own righteousness, but out of His forgiveness do we have eternal life.

O God, may we ever offer to Thee what we are and what we have, cheerfully and lovingly!

23

Witnessing to Modern Sadducees

And as they spake unto the people, the priests, and the captain of the temple, and the Sadducees, came upon them,

Being grieved that they taught the people, and preached through Jesus the resurrection from the dead.

And they laid hands on them, and put them in hold unto the next day: for it was now eventide.

Howbeit many of them which heard the word believed; and the number of the men was about five thousand.

And it came to pass on the morrow, that their rulers, and elders, and scribes,

And Annas the high priest, and Caiaphas, and John, and Alexander, and as many as were of the kindred of the high priest, were gathered together at Jerusalem.

And when they had set them in the midst, they asked, By what power, or by what name, have ye done this?

Then Peter, filled with the Holy Ghost, said unto them, Ye rulers of the people, and elders of Israel,

If we this day be examined of the good deed done to the impotent man, by what means he is made whole;

Be it known unto you all, and to all the people of Israel, that by the name of Jesus Christ of Nazareth, whom ye crucified, whom God raised from the dead, even by him doth this man stand here before you whole. (Acts 4:1-10)

This passage concerns witnessing, preaching, and testifying to the materialists, the rationalists, the Sadducees. Their party arose during the interbiblical period between Malachi and Matthew, a period of about four hundred years. They arose with the other parties of that day—the Pharisees, the Herodians, and the Zealots. The salient feature of the Sadducees was that they were the ruling aristocracy. The government of the Jewish state under the conquering empire was in the hands of the Sadducees. The high priest was their leader and all of his family belonged to that noble aristocracy. Every facet of the Jewish government and economy was under their direction. They were the rulers of the people. They bargained always to see that they remained rulers, whether it was in the Persian Empire, the Greek Empire, or in the Roman Empire, which is the period of the story of the Book of Acts. The Sadducees were always astute in bargaining with the conquering leaders so that they remained as head of the Jewish state. They always placed themselves first, compromising anything in order to keep their place in office.

A good illustration of their maintaining their position can be found in John 11. After the miraculous resurrection of Lazarus from the dead, the high priest said:

> Then gathered the chief priests and the Pharisees a council, and said, What do we? for this man [Jesus] doeth many miracles.
> If we let him thus alone, all men will believe on him: and the Romans shall come and take away both our place and nation. (vv. 47-48)

Wherever the Sadducees appear in history, in the Jewish state they are always bargaining, compromising, welcoming, and supporting the alien conquerors in order to keep themselves rich and affluent, and in the leadership among the nations. The Sadducees and the Pharisees opposed each other bitterly.

In A.D. 70 when the city of Jerusalem was destroyed by Titus, the Sadducees were obliterated when the nation was carried into captivity by the Romans. The Sadducees ceased to exist, and Pharisaical, Talmudic Judaism is what we know today.

WHAT THE SADDUCEES BELIEVED

Let us look at what the Sadducees believed. They were rationalists, materialists. Their interests were entirely earthly and in this world. They did not believe in a spirit world, in angels, or in the immortality of the soul. They believed that the soul died when the man died. They did not believe in heaven, they did not believe in hell, they did not believe in retribution, they did not believe in rewards good or evil, and they certainly did not believe in the resurrection of the dead. Nor did they believe in the sovereignty of God or the hand of God in human life or human affairs. They believed that all things were mortal, in our hands, and that God had nothing to do with it. One could call them practical atheists and practical infidels.

Their confrontation with the Lord Jesus is one of the most interesting studies that one could ever find in the Bible. The Lord and the Sadducees were diametrically opposite. Whatever one was, the other was not. They met in a deadly and unresolvable confrontation. The Lord Jesus believed and taught the Word of God: of heaven and the hope we have in the Resurrection, the immortality of the soul, the life beyond the grave, and the rewards of God for those who love Him. That is the very heart of the Christian faith, every syllable of which was denied by these infidel, atheistic, rational Sadducees.

We have no record, either in history or in the Bible of any Sadducee ever embracing the Christian faith. This cannot be said of the Pharisees for many became obedient to the faith. In Acts 5 we read of how Gamaliel defended the apostles:

> Then stood there up one in the council, a Pharisee named Gamaliel, a doctor of the law, had in reputation among all the people, and commanded to put the apostles forth a little space. . . .
> And now I say unto you, Refrain from these men, and let them alone: for if this counsel or this work be of men, it will come to nought:
> But if it be of God, ye cannot overthrow it; lest haply ye be found even to fight against God. (vv. 34, 38)

Saul of Tarsus, who became Paul the apostle, was a Pharisee and boasted of his lineage. He said, "I am a Pharisee and the son of a Pharisee." In Acts 23 when Saul (Paul) is tried before this same Sanhedrin, noticing that part of the council members were Sadducees and part were Pharisees, he said: "I am a Pharisee, the son of a Pharisee: of the hope and resurrection of the dead I am called in question." When he said that, a violent dissension split the group. The Sadducees wanted to condemn and destroy him, but the Pharisees defended and spoke up for him. I use this to illustrate the fact that no Sadducee ever became a follower of Christ.

The Sadducees had a reason for their bitter hatred of the Lord Jesus. It was so bitter that finally they agreed to His execution. They hated Him because of His spiritual teaching. There was nothing that the Lord taught in which the Sadducees believed. But most of all they hated Him for something else. The Sadducees had control of the temple and of the ruling clique that took care of the temple for the Jewish state. They made a lucrative profit from all of the transactions that took place there. When the Jewish people from the ends of the earth attended the festival seasons, they brought their own money with them for the ceremonies, but one could not give money to the temple from Rome, Athens,

Cappadocia, or Cairo. All foreign money had to be changed into the coin of the temple, into Judaic coins. So throughout the vast court of the Gentiles there were moneychangers, and the Sadducees received profit from each monetary change.

Not only did the Sadducees make money in each exchange of money, but those who sold sacrifices of oxen, goats, bullocks, calves, lambs, sheep, turtle doves, and pigeons were compelled to give a percentage of each sale to the Sadducees. There was not a transaction made in the temple area but that the Sadducees made a profit from it. If one went to worship at the temple and bought a sacrifice to offer to God, it was sold to him in the temple and the Sadducees profited. Our Lord's first public act in the temple was to cleanse it. He overturned the moneychangers' tables and drove out the people who sold the sacrifices, saying, "It is written, My house shall be called the house of prayer; but you have made it a den of thieves" (Matt. 21:13). They hated Jesus. He cleansed the temple again in the last week of His life after the royal entry into Jerusalem on Palm Sunday. He cleansed the temple just as He had done when He began His ministry. The Sadducees, seeing Him destroy their means of lucrative profit, counseled together how they might forever put Him away. They had a reason to despise and hate the Lord Jesus.

Throughout the Lord's ministry the Sadducees tried to trap Him. In Matthew 16 we read an instance of it:

> The Pharisees also with the Sadducees came, and tempting desired him that he would shew them a sign from heaven.
> He answered and said unto them. . . .
> A wicked and adulterous generation seeketh after a sign; and there shall no sign be given unto it, but the sign of the prophet Jonas. (vv. 1, 2a, 4)

The Sadducees did not know what the Lord was talking about. A rationalist can never know what a spiritual man is talking about nor can he ever comprehend. His mind is blinded by his own astuteness and supposed academic learning and philosophical achievement.

In Matthew 23 the Sadducees went to the Lord and told Him a story they had been using to decimate the Pharisees throughout the years. The Lord Jesus was teaching about the resurrection, heaven, and a great spiritual world and life beyond the grave. The Sadducees scoffed at such a prospect. In order to discredit the thought of the resurrection from the dead, they had an old story which they had been telling with which they continued to pulverize their enemies. A married man died without leaving a son to carry on his name. According to Mosaic law, the man's brother had to take his wife and rear children by her. The brother took this man's wife and he died leaving no sons. The third brother, the fourth, fifth, sixth, and seventh brothers died. Last of all, the woman died. In the resurrection, whose wife would she be for all seven men had her?

In the Lord's answer to those materialistic, unbelieving Sadducees, He based the doctrine of the Resurrection on the tense of a verb:

> Jesus answered and said unto them, Ye do err, not knowing the scriptures, nor the power of God.
>
> For in the resurrection they neither marry, nor are given in marriage, but are as the angels of God in heaven.
>
> But as touching the resurrection of the dead, have ye not read that which was spoken unto you by God, saying,
>
> I am the God of Abraham, and the God of Isaac, and the God of Jacob? God is not the God of the dead, but of the living. (Matt. 22:29-32)

Jesus told them that He was not the God of the dead but was the God of the living. He is the Lord God of Abraham who still lives in his presence, and He is the God of Isaac, of Jacob, and of all the saints.

THE SADDUCEES CONFRONT THE APOSTLES

The same people who encompassed the execution and death of the Lord Jesus now confront the apostles who are preaching Jesus and the Resurrection. The Sadducees confronted the disciples because they were angry that they taught the people and preached about Jesus and the hope in the world that is yet to come. That is not the first time an official legate has sought to stop the witness of a man of God. Had the disciples just healed that lame man, the Sadducees would have thought it a fine thing. But when they began to teach and preach the power of the name of the Lord, they became angry and came upon the disciples and sought to stop their teaching.

This has happened to Christian witness from its beginning to today. Through the ages, officials of government have sought to stop the witnessing and the preaching of the man of God. It was so with Stephen, with Antipas, with Ignatius, with Justin Martyr, with John Chrysostom, with Savanarola, with Balthasar Hübmaier and Felix Mantz, with John Bunyan and John Wesley, and it was so with Roger Williams. It is so today in communist nations when the heavy hand of the government seeks to prohibit the preaching of the man of God. God only knows how many preachers are in Siberia or are imprisoned in Russia today. God only is aware of how many preachers are in their graves or are languishing and rotting in dungeons in China today. People who have taught and preached the Lord Jesus and the hope that we have of the resurrection in Him always have been and even today are persecuted and killed.

So it came to pass that the council met, called its members together, and placed the disciples in the midst of the council. There were seventy members of the Sanhedrin and they always sat in a half circle. In the center of them stood the high priest who presided over the Sanhedrin. The passage in Acts 4 states that after the council assembled, they set Peter and John, unlearned and ignorant men, in the midst. That is a powerful sentence, because it is apparent what the Sadducees were seeking to do. They were proposing to outface those ignorant preachers.

The story begins in the third chapter when Simon Peter looked at the beggar and said to him, "Look upon us." The Sanhedrin said: "It will be an altogether different kind of looking when they face us. They may be able to face a poor beggar, but they will not be able to face us in the council. When we set them in the midst, they will be like the straw that the mocking wind drives away. They will stammer and stutter with nothing to say."

When Peter stood before that same Sanhedrin on a previous occasion, a little maid accosted him and asked him about his Galilean accent. Peter wilted. If Peter wilted before a little maid outside the door, what would he do now as he faced Annas and Caiaphas, John and Alexander, the kindred of the high priest, and all the members of the council?

As Peter and John stood there, they were asked by the Sanhedrin a plain and simple question. They asked, "By what power, or by what name have ye done this?" This question was a decoy, a trap. These Sadducean rationalists were smart. Had the disciples replied, "Jehovah God did it," all the Sanhedrin and the high priest would have said, "Bless His name," and the questioning would have been over. If the disciples would have answered that it was some other power, then they would have been introducing alien gods into that holy temple. One can see the high priest stand there as he had stood there in the same place months before when they were trying the Lord Jesus. We can see him prepared, when the disciples say the name of Jesus, to rend his garment and cry, saying: "What need have we for further witness? With your own ears you have heard them blaspheme. What do you think?" The Sanhedrin would reply, "They are worthy of death." That was what he had done before with the Lord, and that was what he was prepared to do here.

Whenever a person allows an infidel or a rationalist to take his religion and bog it down in the quagmire of philosophical and metaphysical disquisitions and theories and the two of them begin a discussion about the modus operandi, ways and means, how and why, and speculations, the Christian will be pulled away from the fact of the Christian faith and will be destroyed with questions and theories. The Christian faith is a fact. Its power in presenting its message to the world is ever factual. When the preacher becomes philosophical and metaphysical, trying to answer the rationalist, he is immediately lost in a world of endless questions, discussions, and minutiae.

WHAT HAPPENED WHEN PETER ANSWERED THE SANHEDRIN

The next verse says that Peter was filled with the Holy Spirit, and the flow of his language was unstoppable. The council was dumbfounded and amazed. Peter's word of testimony was like thunder. In that onrush of the language of his sermon by which he answered the high priest, Peter did two things. First, he pointed to Jesus: "Be it known unto you all . . . that by the name of Jesus Christ of Nazareth." Second, he pointed to the man who had been healed.

That is the way we should do in the world of materialism and unbelief by which we are drowned in this earth of material values. The best argument in the world is first the fact of the Christian faith. Christ was crucified for our atonement, He was buried for our sins, He was raised for our justification, and He lives in our hearts. Whenever you are in a discussion, have a saved man there. He is your Exhibit A. He is the best argument in the world. In verse 14 we read, "And beholding the man which was healed standing with them, they could say nothing against it." How could any philosopher argue against a marvelous conversion?

One of the most gifted expository preachers of our twentieth century, Dr. Harry Ironsides, was pastor of the Moody Memorial Church in Chicago. One day he was in San Francisco, standing out in the street with a band of Salvation Army people, singing the praises of the Lord and preaching the message of Christ. When he made an appeal for the Lord Jesus, a blatant infidel came up to him, and addressing all the throng who were there, said: "I challenge this preacher to a debate. I will show you how the gospel that he preaches is dust and ashes!" Dr. Ironsides replied: "Sir, I accept your challenge. We will set the date and the place. The place will be in the Salvation Army Hall. The date will be tonight. I will bring with me one hundred men who were in the depths of despair and darkness and who were lifted into the marvelous life by the Son of God. You bring one hundred men who have been saved by the gospel of infidelity and we will have our debate tonight." There is not even a song dedicated to infidelity! How would one scour the whole earth and find one hundred men who had been saved from darkness by the gospel of infidelity? Dr. Ironsides could as easily and as quickly have said, "I will bring tonight one thousand men in San Francisco who have been lifted up by the saving message of the Son of God." The living proof of a saved man is always the best argument.

The Christian faith is factual. It is never hypothetical. It is never metaphysical. It is never speculative. The state church of England pushed John Wesley out and did not allow him to preach in an Anglican church. So John Wesley, George Whitefield, and Charles Wesley conducted their services out in the streets and wherever men would gather to listen. Their heavenly efforts saved the nation from the bloody French Revolution. One day Wesley was preaching in Epworth, when the angry neighbors gathered a wagonload of his converts and took them all to the magistrate. They forgot to think through the accusation. The magistrate looked upon that wagonload of Wesleyans, turned to the angry neighbors, and asked, "What is the accusation?" There was long silence. One of them finally spoke up and said, "They think they pray better than other people." Then another long silence followed. Another one spoke up and said, "They pray all day long." A long silence followed again. Then a man spoke up and said, "They converted my wife."

The magistrate was interested and said, "How was that?" The man replied, "Well, she had a tongue that was as sharp as a razor and now she is meek as a lamb." The magistrate said, "Take these people back, and may God grant that they can convert the whole town of Epworth!"

John began his first epistle, "That . . . which we have heard, which we have seen with our eyes, which we have looked upon, and our hands have handled. . . ." (1 John 1:1). There is no greater fact in the universe, in history, or in experience than the fact of the Christian faith.

The son of a theological professor in a seminary was seated by his father one night and said to him: "Dad, today I saw the real thing down at the mission, and it is the first time I have ever seen it." You see, the boy had grown up in the home of a professor of theology. All the days of his life he had been conversant with and introduced to all of the fine theological arguments there were for the person of God, for the resurrection of Christ, and for the propagation of the faith. But the boy didn't see it in action until he went down to the mission.

Anytime the Christian faith is word, language, and argument, any time it is forensic, philosophical, and speculative, it is nothing. But when the Christian faith takes flesh and blood, the conversion of men, and the power of God to change human life, then it is real and factual. Some day the Christian faith will present us faultless in the presence of the Lord Himself where we will thank God forever and ever!

24

The Saving Name

And when they had set them in the midst, they asked, By what power, or by what name, have ye done this?

Then Peter, filled with the Holy Ghost, said unto them, Ye rulers of the people, and elders of Israel,

If we this day be examined of the good deed done to the impotent man, by what means he is made whole;

Be it known unto you all, and to all the people of Israel, that by the name of Jesus Christ of Nazareth, whom ye crucified, whom God raised from the dead, even by him doth this man stand here before you whole.

This is the stone which was set at nought of you builders, which is become the head of the corner.

Neither is there salvation in any other: for there is none other name under heaven given among men, whereby we must be saved. (Acts 4:7-12)

As you read these verses notice the use of the word "name." Verse 7 says, "And when they had set them in the midst, they asked, By what power, or by what *name*, have ye done this?" Then again verse 10 reads, "Be it known unto you all, and to all the people of Israel, that by the *name* of Jesus Christ of Nazareth, whom ye crucified, whom God raised from the dead, even by him doth this man stand here before you whole." Look at verse 12: "Neither is there salvation in any other: for there is none other *name* under heaven given among men, whereby we must be saved."

HOW THE WORD NAME IS USED

The use of the word *name* is prominent in this passage as we have just seen. Does Peter refer to a collocation of sounds and syllables in the name of Jesus Christ when he uses the word "name"? No, not at all, for

159

he is speaking to Jewish hearers who are familiar with God and *name* going together. For example, in Exodus 20 the Lord gives the Ten Commandments, and the third commandment states: "Thou shalt not take the name of the LORD thy God in vain; for the LORD will not hold him guiltless that taketh his name in vain" (v. 7). It is easy to see that the word *name* is identified with God Himself.

One of the most astonishing ecclesiastical developments in religion is this: the Old Testament name for God is lost. No man anywhere has ever been able to know the true pronunciation of the name of God. Look at the name *Jehovah*, for instance. In using the word *Jehovah* for the name of God, the translators took the four consonants of God's name and added to it the vowel pointing of the word *Adonai*, which is the word for "Lord." In using the four consonants of God's name, the closest sound is *Yahweh*. When you add to it the vowel pointing of the word *Adonai*, the result is *Jehovah*. But the name of God was so sacred and was looked upon in the holy page of the Hebrew Bible with such reverential awe that the Jewish people never pronounced it, so the pronunciation was lost. Instead of using the name of God, they just used the noun "*name*," and the word came to stand for all that God is.

In 3 John 7 the apostle writes, "Because that for his name's sake they went forth." What does John mean "for his name's sake"? He means "all that Christ is," the totality of the nature of our Lord, the personality and being of God in Himself. All that God is, is meant by that substantive "name"—the Incarnation, the life and ministry, the atoning death, the burial and Resurrection, the Ascension, His presence at the right hand of God on high, His promised coming again—all that Christ is, is summed up in the use of the word "name."

That is the way the word is used here when Peter says, "By the name of Jesus Christ of Nazareth . . . doth this man stand before you whole. . . . Neither is there salvation in any other; for there is none other name under heaven given among men, whereby we must be saved." That is, everything that God is, is given to us for our healing, for our forgiveness, for our blessing, and for our salvation.

A good illustration of that can be found in Philippians 2 in one of the greatest doctrinal statements to be found in all the Bible and in all ecclesiastical literature:

> Who, being in the form of God, thought it not robbery to be equal with God:
> But made himself of no reputation, and took upon him the form of a servant, and was made in the likeness of men:

And being found in fashion as a man, he humbled himself, and became obedient unto death, even the death of the cross.

Wherefore God also hath highly exalted him, and given him a name which is above every name:

That at the name of Jesus every knee should bow, of things in heaven, and things in earth, and things under the earth;

And that every tongue should confess that Jesus Christ is Lord, to the glory of God the Father. (vv. 2:6-11)

Look at how Paul speaks of the name of our Lord for he describes His deity. In verse 7 he describes the incarnation of our Lord coming down in human flesh, humble and obedient unto the death of the cross. Verses 9 through 11 say:

Wherefore God also hath highly exalted him, and given him a name which is above every name:

That at the name of Jesus every knee should bow, of things in heaven, and things in earth, and things under the earth;

And that every tongue should confess that Jesus Christ is Lord, to the glory of God the Father.

What a magnificent revelation! Some day every infidel, every atheist, every unbeliever, every communist, and every enemy of the Lord will bow in the presence of the Son of God. Would that they would do it now!

One can see the wonderful exaltation of the name of Christ in poetry and in song. God has given Him a name above every name, that at the name of Jesus, all men some day shall bow. Here are but a few of the beloved hymns which exalt the name of our Lord:

> I know a soul that is steeped in sin,
> That no man's art can cure;
> But I know a Name, a Name, a Name
> That can make that soul all pure.
>
> I know a life that is lost to God,
> Bound down by the things of earth;
> But I know a Name, a Name, a Name,
> That can give that soul new birth.
>
> I know of lands that are sunk in shame,
> Of hearts that faint and tire;
> But I know a Name, a Name, a Name,
> That can set those lands on fire.
>
> —Author Unknown
>
> Down at the cross where my Saviour died,
> Down where for cleansing from sin I cried,

There to my heart was the blood applied;
Glory to His name.

I am so wondrously saved from sin,
Jesus so sweetly abides within,
There at the cross where He took me in;
Glory to His name.

Come to this fountain so rich and sweet;
Cast thy poor soul at the Saviour's feet;
Plunge in today, and be made complete;
Glory to His name.

—Elisha A. Hoffman

How sweet the name of Jesus sounds
In a believer's ear!
It soothes his sorrows, heals his wounds,
And drives away his fear.

Dear name! the Rock on which I build,
My Shield and Hiding place;
My never-failing Treasury,
Filled with boundless stores of grace!

—John Newton

Take the name of Jesus with you,
Child of sorrow and of woe;
It will joy and comfort give you,
Take it, then, where'er you go.

Take the name of Jesus ever,
As a shield from every snare;
If temptations round you gather,
Breathe that holy name in prayer.

—Lydia Baxter

There is no name so sweet on earth,
No name so dear in heaven—
The name, before His wondrous birth,
To Christ the Savior given.

'Twas Gabriel first that did proclaim,
To His most blessed mother,
That name which now and evermore
We praise above all other.

And when He hung upon the tree
They wrote His name above Him,
That all might see the reason we
For evermore must love Him.

—Author Unknown

There is a name I love to hear,
I love to sing its worth;
It sounds like music in mine ear,
The sweetest name on earth.

—Frederick Whitfield

There are thousands of songs, hymns, and poems that are dedicated to the name of Jesus.

POWER IN THE NAME

The blessed name of Jesus is a name that will bring healing to our hearts and to our weary souls. For example, in Luke 10:17 we read, "And the seventy returned again with joy, saying, Lord, even the devils are subject unto us through thy name." These who afflict us (and all affliction comes from Satan and his demons) never come from God's angels or from our blessed Savior Himself. When Paul referred to his "thorn in the flesh" he called it "a messenger of Satan to afflict me." The seventy said that even the demons that afflict us and break our hearts, souls, and physical frames, and finally slay us in death are subject to us through His name. It is the healing name of the Lord Jesus.

In Acts 16:18 the apostle Paul, in the name of the Lord, heals a girl who has been used by her owner as a means of making money by telling fortunes. Paul, being grieved, turns and says to that spirit of witchcraft, "I command thee in the name of Jesus Christ to come out of her. And he came out the same hour."

In Acts 3 we read:

> And his name through faith in his name hath made this man strong, whom ye see and know: yea, the faith which is by him hath given him this perfect soundness in the presence of you all. (v. 16)

Whenever we have an affliction, we should take it to the Lord. There is no exception to that. The doctor can diagnose our illness, the surgeon can operate on us, and the pharmacist can give us chemicals and medicines, but only God can heal us. When the surgeon cuts an incision, who heals the open wound? God does. When we speak of this human frame that only God can heal, we use the body as an illustration, but all of the healing of our souls comes from Him. Take your heart to the Lord. Take your soul to the Lord. Take your frustrations and despairs. Take your disappointments and heartaches. Take your tears as well as your gladnesses and happinesses to the Lord. Ask God in the name above every name to heal, to help, and to give patience, strength, guidance, and wisdom. Satan's assignment is to cut us down, to weaken us, and to destroy us, but it is the part of the Lord to build us up, to help us, to strengthen us, and to heal us.

The name of our Lord is the name we use in prayer. We pray in His name. In Matthew 18 we read:

> Again I say unto you, That if two of you shall agree on earth as touching any thing that they shall ask, it shall be done for them of my Father which is in heaven.
> For where two or three are gathered together in my name, there am I in the midst of them. (vv. 19-20)

That does not mean that if two of you shall ask for anything, say a million dollars, you would receive it. No. That word "agree" means far more than just saying it lightly. It is an agreement of soul, an agreement of heart, an agreement in the will of God. How many times does someone say, "Pray for me." You will say, "Sure, I will pray for you." And then you don't remember to do it! That is the way most of us are in our agreeing to pray. If there is agreement like the Bible is speaking of, one gets what he asks for. There is power in the asking.

In John 14 we see how often the Lord emphasizes the fact that when we come before the throne of grace, we do so in His name:

> And whatsoever ye shall ask in my name, that will I do, that the Father may be glorified in the Son.
> If ye shall ask any thing in my name, I will do it. (vv. 13-14)

Look at John 15: ". . . whatsoever ye shall ask of the Father in my name, he may give it you" (v. 16b). Turn to John 16: ". . . Verily, verily I say unto you, Whatsoever ye shall ask the Father in my name, he will give it you" (v. 23). What an abounding reservoir is open to us when we come before God in the name of Jesus Christ! I am to come as though the Lord were praying before the Father. What would He ask for if He were I? If Jesus were in this body, for what would He ask for you? For what would he ask for me? That is praying in the name of the Lord. When I ask in the Spirit and for the sake of the Lord, just as though He were asking, God has promised He will give it to us. This is our open door in prayer.

It is in that glorious name that we are saved. We read in John 1:

> He came unto his own, and his own received him not.
> But as many as received him, to them gave he power to become the sons of God even to them that believe on his name. (vv. 11-12)

We are saved by trusting in the name of Jesus, the Son of God. Look at

John 3: "He that believeth on him is not condemned: but he that believeth not is condemned already, because he hath not believed in the name of the only begotten Son of God" (v. 18). How is a man saved? By believing in the name of Jesus Christ the Son of God and trusting in His name. Look again at the close of the Gospel of John:

> And many other signs truly did Jesus in the presence of his disciples, which are not written in this book:
> But these are written, that ye might believe that Jesus is the Christ, the Son of God; and that believing ye might have life through his name. (20:30-31)

That is the way we are saved, by trusting in the name of the Lord and believing we might have life through His name. Turn to Romans 10:

> For there is no difference between the Jew and the Greek: for the same Lord over all is rich unto all that call upon him.
> For whosoever shall call upon the name of the Lord shall be saved. (vv. 12-13)

That is an incomparable promise! Without condition, whosoever shall call upon the name of the Lord shall be saved. I can sing about the Lord and be lost. I can preach about the Lord and be lost. I can write books about the Lord and be lost. But I cannot call upon the name of the Lord and be lost, for when I ask Jesus to save me, when I open my heart to Him and invite Him into my soul, something happens to me. I am saved. "For whosoever shall call upon the name of the Lord shall be saved."

POWER TO KEEP

We are kept by the name of the Lord. John 17:11 says, "And now I am no more in the world, but these are in the world, and I come to thee. Holy Father, keep through thine own name those whom thou hast given me, that they may be one, as we are." What Jesus can do for us who have found refuge and salvation in Him!

An alcoholic had been wonderfully converted. His old cronies did everything they could to pull him back into his drunken ways, but he had been saved and he loved the Lord. One day his drinking companions were with him, and when he refused to drink, one of the men took a glass of whiskey, and to tempt him more, threw it in his face. The smell and the taste of the liquor on his lips was a tremendous trial. He lifted up his head and his voice and said, "Jesus, Jesus, Jesus." And Jesus helped him.

In reading about a cursing, volatile infidel and about the temper he had, I could not help but remember that story because right behind the house where I lived as a youth, lived the town infidel. You could hear him curse all over the town when he milked his cow in the morning. He made an impression upon me as a little boy. This infidel, who had such a violent temper, was converted and wondrously saved by the blessed Jesus. The people were interested in seeing what kind of a life he would live after he was saved. One day he was milking his cow, and, as a cow often does, she kicked over the bucket and splashed milk all over the man. The people who were watching thought he would curse and beat the cow. He got out his handkerchief, unfolded it, and began to wipe the milk off his clothes. As he did so, he sang, "'Tis so sweet to trust in Jesus, Just to take Him at His Word; Just to rest upon His promise; Just to know, 'Thus saith the Lord.'"

It's wonderful what God can do with a man's life. He does it every day. He does it for us. The sweetest experience in life is walking in the steps of the Lord!

25

Invincible Conviction

Neither is there salvation in any other: for there is none other name under heaven given among men, whereby we must be saved. (Acts 4:12)

The message of our text is an accurate reflection and description of the spirit and conviction of the church of the New Testament in the first Christian century. They did not pray that God would lessen their danger; they only asked that they might have greater boldness in presenting Jesus. For example, in the last part of this same chapter, they prayed:

And now, Lord, behold their threatenings: and grant unto thy servants, that with all boldness they may speak thy word.
And when they had prayed, the place was shaken where they were assembled together; and they were all filled with the Holy Ghost, and they spake the word of God with boldness. (Acts 4:29, 31)

Their actions corresponded to their praying. They plunged into a world of paganism, idolatry, imperialism, slavery, and depression with indescribable zeal. They were unafraid as they challenged the Roman government itself, and even the whole system of world religion. They did that under a mandate from heaven. They possessed an all-inclusive commission to go into all the world and preach the gospel to every creature. They were demanded to make disciples of all the nations of the world. Acts begins in the first chapter with a like commission:

But ye shall receive power, after that the Holy Ghost is come upon you: and ye shall be witnesses unto me both in Jerusalem, and in all Judaea, and in Samaria, and unto the uttermost part of the earth. (Acts 1:8)

167

The New Testament Church in the First Century

That intrepid little band of Christians, facing a veritable floodtide of fierce opposition, gave themselves with invincible courage to the preaching of the gospel of the Son of God. They started in Jerusalem, Acts 2; then in Samaria, Acts 8; then in Caesarea, Acts 10; then in Antioch, where for the first time heathen Greek idolators came directly out of their idolatry into the faith of Christ. They were converts who had no legal Mosaic training, but came directly out of idolatry into the church. In Acts 13 we read how they were sent to preach the gospel to the civilized world, from Antioch, to Ephesus, to Athens (the cultural center of all humanity), and finally to Rome itself. They preached that message with unswerving devotion, uncompromising conviction. Look at what Simon Peter says in the text: "Neither is there salvation in any other: for there is none other name under heaven given among men, whereby we must be saved" (Acts 4:12). Look at a like text from our Lord in John 14:

Jesus saith unto them, I am the way, the truth, and the life: no man cometh unto the Father, but by me. (v. 6)

We do not have an optional way, truth, or life, for the Lord says, "I am *the* way, *the* truth, and *the* life: no man cometh unto the Father but by me."

This little band of Christians stood before the Athenian group of philosophers who were stoic, epicurean, and the members of the Supreme Court in the very heart of the intellectual center of the world. The advancement that the Greeks made in every area of life was unsurpassed: in art, science, and in literature. We have never been able to improve upon the contributions of the Greeks to culture and life. Their architecture is the most beautiful in the world. There are no columns comparable to a Corinthian column. No temples in the world excel in beauty or compare to the simplicity of the lines and order of Greek architecture.

A like accomplishment was achieved in philosophy. There have never been philosophers that even rival the esteemed philosophers of the world of Hellas.

The same is true in literature. There is no literature that excels that of Homer, Aeschylus, Euripides, or Sophocles. The Greeks were advanced in science beyond any culture. One can read about the atomic theory in the writings of Greek scientists from the first century. Their achievements were unexcelled, and yet in the midst of that Athenian assembly, the apostle Paul says, "And the times of this *agnoeo*, [not knowing, ignorance] God winked at; but now commandeth all men everywhere to repent, because he hath appointed a day, in the which he will judge the world in righteousness by that man whom he hath . . . raised . . . from the dead." What a message!

The preaching of the gospel of Christ is to be just like that. There is no salvation in Athenian philosophy or Greek literature. There is no salvation in Roman idolatry, whatever the name of the god. There is no salvation in Talmudic legalism. There is only one way to be saved and that is through Jesus Christ the Lord. "There is none other name under heaven given among men, whereby we must be saved." This band of early Christians confronted the world with one message.

THE CHURCH CONFRONTS THE MODERN WORLD

We now look at the modern church as it confronts this twentieth-century generation in which we live. What kind of conviction and dedication can be seen in the spectrum of the whole Christian church? What kind of a world does the church face today, with what kind of conviction, and with what kind of message? What does the church do as it confronts this modern age?

The message of the modern church is so diluted with rationalism and universalism that at times it is hardly recognizable. Eaten through like a honeycomb, compromise has destroyed the thrust and the march of the modern Christian today. We face a world where dogma is decried, where conviction is discredited, and where belief is discarded. We are not to be sure about anything. The man who has a decided and firm belief is looked upon as an intellectual fossil. The man who is not sure of anything is exalted. One can see that lack of conviction and so-called "broad-mindedness" is the key to the destruction of the Christian church and the worldwide missionary movement such as was found in the first Christian century. The broad-minded liberalism of this present hour is devastating to the great truths of the Bible that our forefathers so cherished and upon which they built our first churches.

A statement from *United States News and World Report*, a weekly news magazine, said:

> It is a time of mounting pressure against missionaries—long the vanguard of Western enlightenment in Asia and in Africa.
> Countries they helped bring to nationhood now are expelling them. Christian beliefs are now diluted with an infusion of pagan customs.

At home, too, the missionary is under fire—from churchmen who say his day is "finished."

Then the article quoted one of the great modern theologians who spoke to an interfaith conference discussing missions:

The era of the foreign missionary movement is definitely over because the goals and the objectives of that movement are no longer valid. There has been a widespread assumption that the church was destined to convert the entire human race to Christianity. This must be rejected as a valid goal because it has no Biblical foundation. I suggest that the church voluntarily dismantle our present missionary organization and structure.

That is unthinkable when the whole gospel message is this: a man is lost without Christ. If one assumes the foundation upon which that theologian rests, that one religion is as good as another, then there is no reason for the preaching of the gospel in Asia, Africa, or even in heathen America. If a man can find God in Vishnu of Hinduism, in Gautama of Buddhism, in Mohammed of Islam, or in the secular, material philosophy of modern America—if a man can find God and be saved in those avenues—then there is certainly no reason to preach the gospel of the Son of God. Just let people alone; they are saved already.

But if this text is true, "Neither is there salvation in any other: for there is none other name under heaven given among men, whereby we must be saved," then men are lost and nations are lost without Christ. No matter how you say it—philosophically, sociologically, psychologically—if that text is true, then the world is lost without Jesus.

Not only does liberalism, modernism, rationalism, and broad-mindedness destroy the missionary movement, but they devastate the very preaching of the gospel itself. Theology turns to dust and ashes.

Here is a quotation from another esteemed theologian:

Much theology is projected fantasy. Religion, all religion, is nothing more than a heritage by which a community of believers share the crises of life and celebrates nature's timetable of the seasons. Man is part of the world of nature and that is all.

Written theology is a linear, typographical thing and all of that has been exploded. We live in the time of the death of God.

Against the background of the Bible, it is unbelievable what has happened to the modern Christian church.

Our Dedication to the Truth

As we face the world, truth, life, and all the gamut and spectrum of whatever we see, know, feel, and do, there are three areas in which we can either be narrow-minded or broad-minded.

First, we ought to be broad-minded as we look at the world. We ought to be broad-minded in our sympathies. Wherever people are, our hearts ought to go out to them in love, compassion, and understanding. Some of them are poor, wretched, sick, degraded; some of them are under governments that are oppressive. Wherever men are, we ought to be broad-minded in our sympathies. God so loved the *kosmos*, the whole created world, and in that sense we ought to be broad-minded in our sympathies.

Second, we ought to be broad-minded in our horizons, in our perception and relationship of truth. A man ought not base his convictions upon ignorance or upon prejudice. When we look at the world and all of its life and all that it means, we ought to take into consideration the most broad-minded understanding of which we are capable.

But third, we ought to be narrow-minded in our defense of truth, especially in God's revealed truth. In that sense we are never to be convictionless, broad-minded, or liberal. We are to be men of narrow mind, of conviction, of commitment, because all truth is narrow.

For example, mathematical truth is not subject to debate but is as narrow as truth itself. Two plus two equals four. There are thousands of numbers that two plus two do not equal. Error is broad, but truth is always narrow. A man may say: "I am not going to be a mathematical bigot. Two plus two to me equals five."

Truth gives no room for options. I heard a moving story that illustrates my point. A train was heading west across the vast, flat prairies of Kansas, during a howling blizzard. On the train was a woman with a little baby in her arms. She was going to a little town called Prairie View. Because of the blinding snowstorm, she became anxious lest she not know exactly the time and the place that she should get off the train. A kindly gentleman in the car noticed how anxious she was, and he said to her out of the goodness of his heart: "I see that you are anxious about how to know when you come to the little town of Prairie View. You cannot see through the blinding storm. I ride this train back and forth all the time and I know exactly where we are. When we come to your little station, I will tell you and you won't have to be anxious anymore." So the train sped on and finally came to a stop. The kindly gentleman said to the mother with the baby in her arms, "This is Prairie View," and he helped her off the train. The minute she was off the train, it speeded up and went down the track. After they had been traveling for miles in that blinding blizzard, the conductor came and looked around. Finally he asked "Where is that mother with the baby?" The gentleman said, "She was getting off at Prairie View, and at the last stop I helped her off the train." The conductor exclaimed, "My God, my God, then she got off the train to her death, for that stop of the train was at a switch and we are just now coming to Prairie View!" Think of the train speeding off, leaving the mother and her baby at a switch in a snowstorm in those broad and desolate prairies!

Truth is so narrow and so demanding! It is vital that we know its factuality and its reality. If truth in mathematics, in science, in history, and in geography is always narrow, do not persuade yourself that truth becomes any other thing when it pertains to God, eternity, heaven, hell, and our salvation. It is the same.

It was so in the Old Testament. For 120 years Noah pointed to the door in the ark. There was only one way to be saved, just one door, and Noah pointed to that way of escape. Most of the people laughed. Some of them may even have thought that if what Noah was preaching happened, they would climb up to a high mountain and be perfectly safe. There was only one way to be saved in the days of the deluge and that was through the door in the ark.

It was true in the days of the Passover in Egypt. God said, "Sprinkle the blood in the form of the cross on the lintel at the top of the doorposts on either side, and any person under the blood will be saved." There is no option.

Isaiah 45:22 says, "Look unto me, and be ye saved, all the ends of the earth: for I am God, and there is none else." Krishna, Mohammed, Shintu, Gautama, philosophy, and pseudo-science cannot save. The Bible plainly says, "He that believeth on the Son hath everlasting life: and he that believeth not the Son shall not see life; but the wrath of God abideth on him" (John 3:36).

Paul preached to the philosophers in Athens:

> And the times of this ignorance God winked at [overlooked]; but now commandeth all men everywhere to repent:
> Because he hath appointed a day, in the which he will judge the world in righteousness by that man whom he hath ordained; whereof he hath given assurance unto all men, in that he hath raised him from the dead. (Acts 17:30-31)

"There is none other name under heaven given among men, whereby we must be saved." In the Lord we come to know God. In Him our sins are forgiven; in Him we have the Holy Spirit of heaven, and in Him we have the assurance of the world that is to come. But outside the Lord, we are lost in conjectural speculation. We are lost in the darkness of this world.

Invincible conviction was the message of the church in its first Christian century and has been the true message of the minister of God through all the generations since. If we are true to the revelation of God, it is our message today.

> Have you been to Jesus for the cleansing power?
> Are you washed in the blood of the Lamb?
> Are you fully trusting in His grace this hour?
> Are you washed in the blood of the Lamb?

There is no other way to be saved. I am either saved in Christ or I am lost in perdition. I have found a new life in Him, or I struggle against the darkness of this world. It is that simple, it is that plain, it is that true.

26

Man's Need and God's Answer

Neither is there salvation in any other: for there is none other name under heaven given among men, whereby we must be saved. (Acts 4:12)

In our preaching through the Book of Acts we have come to the middle of the fourth chapter in which Simon Peter said to the Sanhedrin:

Be it known unto you all, and to all the people of Israel, that by the name of Jesus Christ of Nazareth, whom ye crucified, whom God raised from the dead, even by him doth this man stand here before you whole. (v. 10)

Then quoting Psalm 118:22, Peter said:

This is the stone which was set at nought of you builders, which is become the head of the corner.

Neither is there salvation in any other: for there is none other name under heaven given among men, whereby we must be saved.

Now when they [those members of the Sanhedrin—the high priest, all of the court, and the temple guard] saw the boldness of Peter and John, and perceived that they were unlearned and ignorant men, they marvelled; and they took knowledge of them, that they had been with Jesus. (vv. 11-13)

This is an unusual passage for the disciples were not accosted about the Lord nor was the original question concerning the name that saves all the families and nations of the world. The original question concerned a lame man, a man who had been born impotent. And yet these apostles are not confining themselves to any such original discussion or beginning question. They are proclaiming the saving name of Christ to the whole world. That is exactly what the apostles preached upon any occasion. It was a beginning for them to immediately proclaim the glorious gospel of Christ. "This is the stone which was set at nought of you builders, which is become the head of the corner. Neither is there salvation in any other: for there is none other name under heaven given among men, whereby we must be saved." All of that arose out of an original discussion concerning a lame man who could not walk.

The Apostles Always Preached Christ

The entire message of the apostles, whatever the occasion, however the providence, was immediately a text for the preaching of the gospel of the Son of God.

For example, in examining the construction of the Gospel of John, we notice how John closes the twentieth chapter:

> And many other signs, *semeion* [he never uses the word "miracle"] did Jesus . . . which are not written in this book:
> But these are written, that ye might believe that Jesus is the Christ, the Son of God; and that believing ye might have life through his name. (vv. 30-31)

John's Gospel is constructed like this: He chose seven of the *semeion*, the "signs" of the Lord Jesus. He says that there are so many of them that had he written them, he supposed that the world itself could not have contained the books that should be written. He chose seven signs, and each one of them is an introduction to a marvelous message about Jesus.

For example, when the Lord fed the five thousand, then immediately followed the message of the Lord portrayed as the Bread of Life, the manna from heaven, the food that angels eat. He opened the eyes of a blind man and immediately followed the message that Jesus is the Light of the world. He chose the *semeion*, the "sign" of the resurrection of Lazarus from the dead and immediately brought the message that He is the resurrection and the life. The whole message of the apostles at any time was to immediately proclaim the marvelous grace of the Son of God. We have to remember that the only Bible they held in their hand was the Old Testament. There are ministers today who have great trouble speaking out of the Old Testament concerning Christ, finding the Lord in the words of the Old Testament. Not so with the apostles. The only Bible they had was the Old Testament Scriptures, and on every page, they saw the face of Jesus Christ.

There is an incident in the life of Charles Haddon Spurgeon which I have often repeated. Someone came up to him and said, "Mr. Spurgeon, your sermons are all alike." He said: "That is right. Wherever I take a text, I immediately make a beeline to the cross and preach Jesus!"

"Now when they saw the boldness of Peter and John, and perceived that they were unlearned and ignorant men, they marvelled; and they took knowledge of them, that they had been with Jesus." They looked at Peter and John, the sons of Zebedee, and marveled at their boldness. Any time a man is filled with the Holy Spirit of Christ, he is bold in his testimony. If we are timid, reticent, and hesitant about speaking for Jesus, it is because we have backslidden and are following afar off. When a man is filled with the Spirit of God and Christ lives in power in his heart, upon any occasion, no matter where it is, he is bold to speak out for the blessed Jesus. The Sanhedrin marveled at the two disciples, and recognized the fact that they were *agrammatoi kai idiotai*, without education and training. *Agrammatoi* is translated literally, "unlettered, untaught." These men had not been to the seminary, they had not been in any school. They were rough, crude fishermen, tax gatherers, men of menial assignments and tasks—*agrammatoi*. They were not polished, educated, and scholarly. *Idiotai* is translated here "ignorant" and literally means "private men," that is, they were without status and standing.

It is a strange thing about human life. Some of the sorriest specimens of mankind that one will ever find were born in a king's court and were heirs to a magnate's fortune. Although dignity and heredity confer some standing upon men, there is no man like a man who is filled with the Spirit of God and the presence of Jesus. "And they took knowledge of them that they had been with Jesus," that is, looking at those men and hearing them speak and listening to the witness that they brought, the Sanhedrin remembered: "We know where we have seen those men. We saw them with Jesus."

What a glorious remark to be made about any group or any minister. A man is not remembered because of his degrees, his academic achievements, his scholarly background, or his ability in speaking of brilliant subjects, but he is remembered because he was filled with the Spirit of God, because he had been with the Lord.

Do you not wish that the whole world were filled with laymen and laywomen like that, and do you not wish that every pulpit had a minister who gave evidence of having been with Jesus, of having spent time in the presence of the Lord?

THE MESSAGE OF THE APOSTLES

We now look at the apostolic message they brought. The apostles talked about salvation. They saw it as something man needed.

Let us take a look at today's world. Newspapers, magazines, radio and television, all blend their voices in proclaiming that the need of the world is answered in social amelioration, in the restructuring of society, in the redistribution of wealth, and in social revolution. The universal reply to the cry of the human heart is social betterment. So look at the world. Look at Russia, look at China, look at Europe, look at South America, and especially look at seething Africa, seeking to find the answer to man's needs in social and political restructuring of its institutions. Since 1917 the Bolshevik Revolution has continued in Russia. Is there any sign that what is happening in Russia is the answer to the cry of the human heart? I have talked to many people who have escaped China. Do you think that the restructuring of the social institutions in China is the answer to man's need? Take a look at England. They have been in a socialistic experiment for several decades and they are bankrupt. Do you think that the social experiments in England have uplifted the people and have made it a better nation with greater impact upon the earth? England today is pitiful and tragic. I do not know of a country that has turned to social experiments in which man's real needs have been met. Yet the world answer to man's need is social experimentation and amelioration, the restructuring of the institutions of society.

DOES THE ANSWER LIE IN RELIGION?

You may know what I am going to say, or you think you do. You think I am going to say that the answer to man's need lies in religion. Let us look at religion honestly and fairly. According to the biblical Revelation, the masterpiece of Satan is the false prophet, religion. Look at Christianity and the institutional church. In reading the Bible and looking at our Lord, the apostles, and the message that they deliver, and then looking at the institutional church, we cannot believe what we see. What we read of the church is so contrary to the Spirit of Christ and the message of salvation preached by these apostles: the church with its hands dipped in blood, persecuting, burning at the stake, sending men into dungeons to rot their lives away. Is that the answer to man's need?

Let us look at Islam. I was once in northern Nigeria speaking at length to a Hausa merchant. In talking to him I asked, "How many wives do you have?" He said, "I can only have four at a time, but if I become weary of one of them, I just dismiss her and choose another to take her place. Just so I don't have more than four at a time." Then the merchant, talking about another young merchant nearby said, "He has only two wives, but give him time; because he is becoming affluent, he will also have four." That is Mohammedanism.

A sad story comes from the history of the Turks. They had slaughtered some Armenian Christians and a blind Turk cried out, "Bring me an Armenian Christian that I can kill, so I also might have a reward in heaven." That is the Mohammedan religion which is furthered by the sword, and propagated by coercion and force.

Let us look at Hinduism with Krishna and its 330,000,000 gods. Hinduism, an Oriental religion, is spreading over America as you would not believe. What kind of religion is it?

One day I was standing in the heart of Calcutta, which is a city far larger than Chicago. I looked up the boulevard and I saw the most impossible tangle of a traffic jam one could ever imagine. And why? Because in the center of the great city was a herd of sacred cows. No one could move, no one could drive. You couldn't do anything but watch those cows. You dare not touch them, move them, or push them along, because cows in India are sacred. When I was there the President of the Congress Party pointed to his feet and proudly said, "I have never worn shoes; I have never defaced or disgraced the hide of a sacred cow."

The Hindu doctrine of reincarnation is something to behold. If a person is bad, Hinduism says he will come back to this world as a dog. If he is worse, he will come back as a spider. If he is vile, he will come back as a serpent. If he has been indescribably wicked, he will come back as a woman! That is Hinduism.

Look at Buddhism. As there are millions of Muslims and millions of Hindus, so there are uncounted millions who for 2500 years have been worshiping at the image and idol of Buddha. You often see pictures of a fat, happy, content, Buddha in the midst of disease, disaster, despair, and death.

A Chinese correspondent was talking to an American correspondent, who happened to be a devout Christian. The Chinese correspondent said to the American: "I am a Buddhist and my religion is so much better than yours. You see, when I go to the pagoda and I bow before my god, there he is happy and smiling and affluent. I have a happy religion and I worship a happy god, but your religion is full of blood, suffering, crucifixion, and death, and when you come before your God, there He is dying in shame on a cross. I do not like your religion; I like mine much better. Mine is a happy religion." The American correspondent had never thought about it like that and he did not know how to answer.

Some time later the American saw a Chinese man, starving and dying by the side of a road. The correspondent went over to him, saw that he was dying, and called the Chinese people passing by to come and help. "This man is dying." And no one seemed to care. The American tried to find someone to help him with the dying man, but not a person would stop. They looked with contempt and disdain and passed on by. So the correspondent reached down and picked up the dying man in his arms, and as he held him in his arms and looked upon his silent face, he had his answer. Tell me, where would you take him, if you had in your arms a dying man, a victim of starvation and exhaustion? Would you take him and lay him before the fat, affluent, happy, smiling god called Gautama, the Buddha, or would you take him and tenderly, lovingly, and carefully lay him at the feet of One who knew what it was to be hungry, to be poor, to be in need and in want? The faith of the Son of God is God's answer to the need of the world.

CHRIST IS THE ANSWER TO EVERY HUMAN NEED

In Africa I stood in the midst of a church jammed on every side by half-naked people. The church was as full as it could possibly get; even the yard was filled with people listening to the Word of God. While waiting to preach, I saw on the wall in back of the pulpit a big placard. In the center was a picture of our Lord. Around the picture were these words: "Christ Is the Answer to Every Human Need." I looked at all those half-naked natives and then up to the picture. I thought that I have never been in this world where the Gospel of Christ is preached but that there we can find also a school, a hospital, an orphan's home, and also the house of the Lord, the church. Christ is the answer to every human need. For the balm of Gilead, for the healing of a heart, for the restructuring of society, for the rebirth of the man, for the remaking of all humanity—the answer is in Christ our Lord.

I knew a man, the father of three little boys, who was not a Christian. His wife suddenly died and left him with his sons. Knowing that the man was crushed and faced with an awesome responsibility, I spoke to him: "My friend, God is able to help. There is Someone, if you will invite Him into your home and into your heart, who will be an answer to every problem that you will ever face. He will be wisdom to you, a shield and a buckler, a friend in time of need who is able to see you through. Let

Jesus come into your heart. Take Jesus into your house and into your home. Love the Lord. Be a Christian. Follow Him."

The days passed and I visited with the man again. He met me at the airport and said: "You know, that first step was the hardest I ever made. I do not understand why nor can I explain it, but that first step of opening my heart to Jesus, inviting Him into my life, was the hardest decision I ever made; but having made it, having accepted the Lord, having received Him into my house and home, it has been a blessing every step of the way. I am rearing my three little boys in the love and nurture of the Lord."

There are no problems that God cannot solve, no difficulties for which Christ is not equal. There is in Him a solution for every confrontation known to the human spirit—in government, in law, in medicine, in home, in education, in business, and in every area of life. There is an ultimate answer, triumphant and glorious in Him. That is the gospel that the apostles preached, that is the message that we preach today, to come in faith, in love, in commitment to the Lord Jesus and let Him see you through.

27

Idolatry in the Church

But a certain man named Ananias, with Sapphira his wife, sold a possession,

And kept back part of the price, his wife also being privy to it, and brought a certain part, and laid it at the apostles' feet.

But Peter said, Ananias, why hath Satan filled thine heart to lie to the Holy Ghost, and to keep back part of the price of the land?

Whiles it remained, was it not thine own? and after it was sold, was it not in thine own power? why hast thou conceived this thing in thine heart? thou hast not lied unto men, but unto God.

And Ananias hearing these words fell down, and gave up the ghost: and great fear came on all them that heard these things.

And the young men arose, wound him up, and carried him out, and buried him.

And it was about the space of three hours after, when his wife, not knowing what was done, came in.

And Peter answered unto her, Tell me whether ye sold the land for so much? And she said, Yea, for so much.

Then Peter said unto her, How is it that ye have agreed together to tempt the Spirit of the Lord? behold, the feet of them which have buried thy husband are at the door, and shall carry thee out.

Then fell she down straightway at his feet, and yielded up the ghost: and the young men came in, and found her dead, and, carrying her forth, buried her by her husband.

And great fear came upon all the church, and upon as many as heard these things. (Acts 5:1-11)

In our preaching through the Book of Acts, we have come to chapter 5 in which we find a story told at great length. The Holy Spirit has a reason for guiding Dr. Luke to write the story in such meticulous detail.

Before we begin our search for the purpose of the Spirit in recounting this passage, let us define "idolatry" in New Testament terms. In the third chapter of Colossians the Holy Spirit writes these words:

> Set your affection on things above, not on things on the earth.
> Mortify therefore your members which are upon the earth . . . covetousness, which is idolatry. (vv. 2, 5a)

Covetousness, worldliness, secularism, material-mindedness is called "idolatry." Now let us look at the Book of Ephesians:

> For this ye know, that no whoremonger, nor unclean person, nor covetous man, who is an idolater, hath any inheritance in the kingdom of Christ and of God. (5:5)

When Paul names these unclean unregenerates who will have no part in heaven, he describes the covetous man as "an idolater."

Another famous New Testament description of an "idolater" is found in 1 Timothy:

> For the love of money is the root of all evil: which while some coveted after, they have erred from the faith, and pierced themselves through with many sorrows.
> But thou, O man of God, flee these things; and follow after righteousness, godliness, faith, love, patience, meekness. (6:10-11)

Having defined "idolatry" according to the New Testament as worldliness, covetousness, the love of money, let us look at this passage in the Book of Acts.

We have just finished looking at the fourth chapter and what a joy, a triumph is portrayed for us in those verses. God's people were persecuted and their preachers were placed in jail, but the more the church was persecuted, the more it grew. The more preachers were flung into dungeons, the more the church of God multipled. Men can hound, harass, condemn, persecute, and even imprison the church, but they cannot stop its almighty power. All of the fire in the world cannot burn it and all the water in the sea cannot drown the Holy assembly of God.

The Intrusion of Idolatry into the Church

In Acts 4 we rejoiced in the grace and favor of the Almighty upon His people even though they were persecuted and put in prison. But in the fifth chapter we are in another world. The chapter begins with the word "but," a black "B" in my Bible. In the fifth chapter there is death in the church. This is similar to what we read in the first chapter of the Book of Genesis, which speaks of all the emerald verdure of foliation and living things, of God's creation of the birds that fly in the air and the fish that swim in the sea, and finally the man and his wife. In the second chapter of Genesis we find the presentation of Edenic paradise, perfect, precious, and glorious. Finally we come to the third chapter, and outside the gates of the Garden of Eden is that slimy, subtle beast. That is exactly the way it is here in the Book of Acts. There is beauty, wonder, and glory in the fourth chapter, and then we come to chapter 5 with its serpentine beast.

In chapter 5 we miss the contrast that the Holy Spirit is making because of the superimposed chapter division. Actually the story of chapter 4, beginning at verse 32, belongs to chapter 5. Describing the generosity of the church, Luke writes,

> Neither said any of them that aught of the things which he possessed was his own; but they had all things common. (4:32b)

Whenever one finds great generosity in a church, this verse will always obtain:

> And with great power gave the apostles witness of the resurrection of the Lord Jesus: and great grace was upon them all. (4:33)

Whenever you find a stingy, miserly church, you will see a church that is filled with sterility and barrenness. When you find a generous-hearted people who believe that a tithe belongs to the Lord and that an offering over and beyond the tithe should also be given to the Lord, you will find grace and great power in the services of that church.

THE PERFIDIOUS PLOT

As Luke describes the church in the fourth chapter of Acts, he comes to a man named Joses, a member of the congregation in the church in Jerusalem who had property in Cyprus, an island nearby. Joses sold his property and laid the gift at the apostles' feet. The people rejoiced in the abounding generosity of Joses and they named him "Barnabas," that is, "the son of encouragement and consolation." Having seen the wonderful impression that Joses made when he sold what he had and laid it at the apostles' feet for the work and word of the Lord, Ananias, a man watching that bestowal, said to his wife, Sapphira: "Look at the nobility of that man. What a reputation he has! Let us sell what we have, and without saying anything keep back a part of the price; and let us lay it at the feet of the apostles as though we were laying before God everything that we had received for the property." Ananias and Sapphira agreed to carry out their plan in order to find recognition and reputation among the people of the Lord. This is discussed in great detail in Acts 5. That is about as sordid an act as one could conjure up, and yet it is told in great detail in the Bible.

The Holy Spirit must have some profound reason for the meticulous detail of the story. I am reminded of the story in Joshua when God commanded the children of Israel to cross over Jordan and to bring judgment and vengeance upon the Canaanites. God used them as the weapon of vengeance and judgment to carry out the mandates of heaven. Thus Israel crossed over Jordan and captured Jericho. Joshua, seeing the small size of the next town to be captured, sent just a part of his company against the little city of Ai. But the men of Ai went forth, the army of the Lord fled before them, and some of God's soldiers were slain. When the report of the defeat came to Joshua, the captain of the host of the people of God, he fell on his face prostrate before the Lord and cried, "O God, what happened? We were carrying out your mandates but our people were defeated, our army was in flight, and some of your soldiers were slain." The Lord said to Joshua, "Stand up, there is sin in the camp."

Do you remember the rest of the story? Under God's surveillance they cast lots, and one of the tribes was chosen. They cast lots and a clan was chosen. They repeated their casting of lots and a family was chosen. Finally, they cast lots and Achan was chosen. Joshua said, "Achan, what have you done?" We read his reply in the seventh chapter of Joshua:

> And Joshua said unto Achan, My son, give, I pray thee, glory to the LORD God of Israel, and make confession unto him; and tell me now what thou hast done; hide it not from me.
> And Achan answered Joshua, and said, Indeed I have sinned against the LORD God of Israel, and thus have I done:
> When I saw among the spoils a goodly Babylonish garment, and two hundred shekels of silver, and a wedge of gold of fifty shekels weight, then I coveted them, and took them; and, behold, they are hid in the earth in the midst of my tent, and the silver under it. (vv. 19-22)

Why was such a long story of Achan presented? Why this long story of Ananias and Sapphira and the judgment of God upon them? There is a reason. The Holy Spirit has a message; He points to this passage and says, "Look, will you find your name written there? Will you find your life enmeshed in that portrayal of character?" So we look in the mind of the Spirit. What is the message that God has for us?

THE ADMONITION OF THE LORD

Do you remember what the Lord said in Luke 12:15? "Take heed, and beware of covetousness: for a man's life consisteth not in the abundance of the things which he possesseth." How can one guard against covetousness?

You might say that Ananias lived 1950 years ago. No, he walks down the street of any city anywhere. You will see him when he goes to work in the morning. You see, Ananias never said anything. He just acted out the lie as though he were bringing to God his generous support for the work of the Lord. Worldliness makes liars and hypocrites of us all. You may meet some people who say, "I received from God's hand many gracious gifts and I do not fail to return thanks to Him. I have a part to contribute also to the community in which I live, from which I receive benefits and blessings." He may be assured that he is mindful of God and he has accepted his responsibilities in making the community a glorious place in which to rear his children and family. But he is a liar and a hypocrite. Here is an example.

A mother is rearing her two boys in our church. Her husband viciously seeks to stop his wife and his two children from coming to the house of the Lord. I went to see him and said: "If you do not want your wife and boys to attend church, then why would you not like to live in Russia? You would never be bothered with any Sunday school there. It is against the law to have Sunday school in Russia and the official doctrine of the state is sheer unadulterated atheism. They are anti-God, anti-Christ, and anti-church. Why do not you move to Russia?" He answered, "Not I; I could not move to Russia!" Then I said: "Why do you not move your family to a godless town where there is no church, and the women in that town are the wrong kind of women. Why do you not move to a town like that and rear your boys there?" "Oh, no, I would not live in a town where there is no church, and I would not rear my family in a place where the people were godless." You see, that man receives blessings from God and from godly people but makes no contribution to the community whatsoever, even though he acts as though he made a contribution to the godliness and sobriety of his city. Worldliness makes liars and hypocrites out of us just as it did with Ananias and Sapphira, just as it did with Achan.

THE JUDGMENT THAT INEVITABLY FOLLOWS THE SECULAR LIFE

Second, why does the Holy Spirit write that story in such infinite detail? Because there is a judgment that the worldly, secular mind carries with it that always ends in the same disastrous visitation. There is no exception. I will mention it in two ways. First, when Ananias (greedy, covetous, worldly, secular, seeking to keep things for himself) acted out this lie, the Holy Spirit withdrew His support and Ananias fell down dead. You see, when I breathe, it is God's air that I am breathing. It is God's breath, a gift from Him. He could take it away from me at any moment. The fact that I still live and that I still breathe is in God's divine choice. My eyes are a gift from God. God gave me these ears. The fact that my heart beats in my breast is a gift from God. He set that heart pulsating and at any minute He can stop it. I am dependent upon the Lord and the Lord can take my life away at any moment. Every minute men are dying who have lived a secular and worldly life, and they are plunged into eternity, lost without Christ. They cannot take any land with them, any bonds with them, any stocks, any houses with them, or any earthly possessions. What a tragedy! The secular man lives his life and centers all his energy in this world and then suddenly he leaves it all behind and faces God a pauper, lost, with no great Mediator to stand between him and the judgment that is to come. There is a judgment that goes with the secular mind that is visited upon us in this world and in this life.

We do not have to search far to find the cause and the reason for the moral disintegration of modern American life. Look how our children are educated. God, prayer, righteousness, and spiritual well-being are removed from the classroom. Instead, our children are taught the secular mind, secular values, secular ways, and their goals are material as they strive for the rewards of this world. Is it any wonder that there is corruption in moral life in America from the Supreme Court of the United States down to the lowest constable?

Why does the Holy Spirit in such detail describe the sin of worldliness? Because worldliness blinds us to the presence of God. When the world is before me, and when every vision and dream that I have is centered here in this earthly life, where does God come in? Where is there room for the Lord in my heart that is filled with carnal and worldly and earthly desire?

In the eyes of the world, Ananias's generosity is tremendous. But what

Ananias forgot was the eye of almighty God.

COVETOUSNESS LEADS TO FEARFUL CONSEQUENCES

Do you remember that in the dispensation of the law there is judgment upon sin? Did you know that in the dispensation of love it is no different? Whether it is in the Old Testament of the law or whether it is in the New Testament of grace, this truth eternally obtains: it is the fear of God that is the beginning of wisdom. Before almighty God a whole nation is as the dust in the balance. How much less a man's life! Whether in the legislature, whether in the Supreme Court or the judicial system of the land, or whether you live behind a kitchen sink or behind a clerk's desk, the beginning of wisdom is the fear of the Lord. The writer in Hebrews says:

> It is a fearful thing to fall into the hands of Almighty God.
> For our God is a consuming fire. (10:31; 12:29)

For me to live and to act as if there is no God and no world to come, is to invite personal disaster and ultimate judgment from almighty God. The Scripture says: "Set your affection on things above, not on things on the earth" (Col. 3:2).

One time I was preaching in the North Shore Baptist Church in Chicago. The superintendent of the Sunday school, who was also a deacon in the church, was James L. Kraft. He was the founder of the great Kraft Food Corporation. After the service was over I was a guest in their beautiful home. He said that as a young man he had a desire to be the most famous manufacturer and salesman of cheese in the world. He was going to be rich and famous, and he was going to do it making and selling cheese. So he started out as just a young fellow. He had a pony named Paddy and a little buggy. He would make his cheese, put it in the buggy, and drive Paddy down the streets of Chicago selling his cheese. The days and months passed, and the young man began to despair. He was not succeeding, and was not making any money. He was just working hard and long to no end and with no success. He said that one day he pulled the pony to a stop and began to talk to him. He said: "Paddy, there is something wrong. We are not doing it right. I am afraid that we have things turned around. Our priorities are not where they ought to be. Maybe we ought to serve God and place Him first in our lives; maybe that is our first priority. If we give ourselves to God, and work hard as we can, then God will open the door for us and help us, but first, Paddy, let us give ourselves to God and place Him first in our lives." Mr. Kraft said that he drove the buggy home and there made a covenant that the rest of his life he would first serve God and then he would work as God would direct. Many years later I was in a vast convocation in Washington, D. C. in which the speaker was James L. Kraft. I memorized a dramatic sentence he spoke: "I had rather be a layman in the North Shore Baptist Church in Chicago than to head the greatest corporation in America. My first job is serving Jesus."

What God could do with men and women like that! My first assignment is walking in the will of the Lord. My first obligation is to Him. My affection is set upon our Lord in heaven, and as He opens doors and blesses me I will work for Him all the days of my life. If people would live like that I believe they could change the whole course of civilization. They could swing the world on other hinges; it would be a new day and a new life.

That is what the Lord said: "Seek ye the kingdom of God; and all these things shall be added unto you" (Luke 12:31).

Is not that what the Lord did for Solomon? When the Lord gave Solomon the privilege to ask anything of Him, Solomon asked, "That I might have Your Spirit in my heart, and that I might have wisdom and the Spirit of counsel." And the Lord said to him: "Solomon, because you did not ask for riches and for fame I will not only give you wisdom from above, the Spirit of God in your heart, but I will also give you riches, fame, prosperity, affluence, and success. Moreover, if you walk in my way, I will add to you length of days."

O that there might be such a heart in us that we would follow Him all the days of our lives, and let God bless the work of our hands. That we would love Him and be good stewards of what He has given to us in heart, in mind, in life, in possession, in work, and in all to which we give our lives.

28

Shadow Ministries

And by the hands of the apostles were many signs and wonders wrought among the people; (and they were all with one accord in Solomon's porch.

And of the rest durst no man join himself to them: but the people magnified them.

And believers were the more added to the Lord, multitudes both of men and women.)

Insomuch that they brought forth the sick into the streets, and laid them on beds and couches, that at the least the shadow of Peter passing by might overshadow some of them.

There came also a multitude out of the cities round about unto Jerusalem, bringing sick folks, and them which were vexed with unclean spirits: and they were healed every one. (Acts 5:12-16)

In our study of the Book of Acts we are now in chapter 5, and the subject we would like to discuss is in verse 15, ". . . that at the least the shadow of Peter passing by might overshadow some of them."

In Jerusalem the temple area covers twenty-six acres. On the eastern side of the temple in the court of Solomon, the apostles gathered with the multitudes and preached the gospel of the grace of the Lord Jesus. The people knew that Simon Peter, the fisherman, would be passing by on his way to the temple. There would be a limited number of people he could touch out of the multitudes that thronged the temple area, so finding the way that the big fisherman had of coming up to the house of the Lord, and noticing how he came into the temple area to the porch of Solomon, they would bring their sick and lay them along the way that at least the shadow of Peter might fall upon them and they would be blessed by just the passing of the tremendous apostle of God. That gives rise to the thought of unconscious influence. We never know whom we can influence as we travel life's road.

A MAN'S INFLUENCE OUTLIVES HIS MORTAL LIFE

The president of a vast railroad system in America died. It was announced that his service of memorial would be at two o'clock on a certain afternoon. At two o'clock on the dot that afternoon, everything stopped on the vast railway system in honor and in memory of that great president. People associated with the railway system brought everything to a halt. Everything stopped except one thing, and that was the influence of the man in the casket. His influence continues on, not stopping three minutes or five minutes, or a year, or a century, but it goes on forever.

The same is true with every man's life. There is repercussion of a man's influence that never stops, even from the humblest life. Scientists tell us that if a person drops a pebble into the vast, illimitable ocean, the molecular disturbance from the dropping of that one pebble reaches out to the farthest shores of the sea. If that could be true, think how true it is in the life of a man who lives on this earth. The body dies, turning back to the dust of the ground from whence God shaped and formed it, but the personality, soul, and influence of a man never die. When I look at history and think of the long and extended shadows of men who made that history, I stand in wonder and amazement before it. There would not be volumes enough in the world to describe the influence of Alexander the Great upon human history, turning the whole world into Hellenic thinking, Hellenic architecture, and Hellenic language in which the New Testament is writen. Hellenic culture is the basis of our civilization today. The extended shadow of that young man, Alexander the Great, who conquered the world when he was twenty-two years of age, is beyond measure.

I once looked at the courses taught at Oxford University in England and I counted two hundred courses in Oxford on Aristotelian philosophy. Aristotle, the teacher of Alexander, died three hundred years before Christ, and yet today there can be something like two hundred courses in a great university teaching Aristotelian philosophy!

What could be said of the influence of men like Nietsche, Bismarck, and Hitler? And I'm afraid Germany will never get over or survive the terror, the horror, and the hurt of Nietsche, Bismarck, and Hitler.

So all of life follows a train like that. The influence that never ceases long after we are gone is a part of every man's life. We shall discuss it in two ways.

THE INFLUENCE OF THE LIFE FOR BAD

First, let us look at the influence for bad. In a sense a man does not die when he dies. The influence of his life lingers on forever to the great Judgment Day of almighty God.

In Amarillo I had a friend with whom I graduated from high school. We were in the same Sunday school class and were good personal friends. We went to Baylor University together, and to my sorrow and amazement, the young fellow turned out to be an infidel, an atheist. I went to his room one night to talk to him. He was seated under a lamp reading Thomas Paine's *Age of Reason*. Tom Paine had been dead for one hundred fifty years. But really dead? The influence of that evil-thinking man has extended through the decades after his body has turned back into the dust.

Think of the dividend for evil that wicked men will receive at the judgment bar of almighty God. We never escape the influence of evil in our lives. Nathan the prophet said to David, "The sword shall never depart from thy house." And for generations after that, the story of the household of David and the kings of Judah is written in human blood. Lives that are influenced by evil men are uncountable.

The Lord God said to Manasseh, "Because of your sins, Judah shall be destroyed, the people will be carried into captivity, and the holy house of God will be burned down with fire." How sad.

THE INFLUENCE OF THE LIFE FOR GOOD

A beautiful passage, and one of the finest theological foundational truths in the Word of God, is written in the fifth chapter of the Book of Romans:

> For if, when we were enemies, we were reconciled to God by the death of his Son, much more, being reconciled, we shall be saved by his life. (v. 10)

Interpreting this passage that reads "saved by his life," some theologians say that it refers to the days of our Lord when He lived in His flesh. No, I believe that the life of our Lord, poured out into this world, lives forever. The Lord is as much alive today as He was when He walked the shores of Galilee. The influence of the life of Jesus is a thousand times greater now than it was when He opened the eyes of the blind, when He healed the lepers, and when He raised the dead. The greatest truth I know in human history is, Jesus is alive! He is here, He is in our hearts, He guides in the way, He leads.

So it is with the life of every good man who ever lived. The repercussion of the influence of their lives is forever.

Think of how it will be when Simon Peter stands at the great Judgment Day before the great King. Think of the influence of his life through the years and the generations. What an infinite reward will be the apostle Paul's when God unravels the skein of the influence of the great apostle to the Gentiles.

Time would fail us as we could speak of these mighty men whose names are household words. On the tomb of Dwight L. Moody are written these words of truth: "He that doeth the will of God shall abide forever."

But we are not Simon Peters, we are not Pauls or even Dwight L. Moodys. What of the humble influence of that sweet disciple of Jesus whose name we never heard and of whose life we are not conscious? The humblest saint also possesses an influence that God blesses through the years.

Have you ever stood at the tomb of the Unknown Soldier in Arlington, just across the Potomac from Washington? On the sarcophagus are written these words: "Here rests in honored glory an American soldier known but to God." When you stand there and look at the monument and read those words, you think of that soldier, an American who was cut down on a foreign field of battle, who lies there, but no one knows his name. What multitudes of honors and words of appreciation and gratitude have been bestowed upon that man! But no one knows his name or who he is.

In a thousand times and in a thousand ways our lives are just like that —influential, but known only to God.

Do you remember the story in the Bible of the little maid in the household of Naaman, the captain of the host of the king of Syria? It was through the testimony of that little girl in the household of Naaman that the mighty captain of the armies of Syria was cleansed, was saved, and became a follower of the true God of heaven. What is the name of that little girl? No one knows, and we will not know until we get to heaven. But think of the repercussion of the testimony of that little child in the household of the powerful man!

Do you know the name of the little boy who was in a crowd of five thousand men who, as the day passed, were hungry, listening to the

Word of God? The Lord said that they should be fed, lest they faint by the way. The apostles exclaimed, "Feed them? Five thousand men!" "Yes," said the Lord, "feed them." Then the apostles went through the great throng to find food for the multitude. They found only a little boy's lunch. He had five little biscuits and two little fishes. The boy gave his lunch to the Lord. When the apostles placed it in the Lord's hands, He blessed it as He always did, saying grace at the table. Then the Lord broke the bread and fishes and passed out the food to the people. It was a marvelous miracle of God which was followed by one of the most magnificent sermons in the whole Bible, the message on the true manna from heaven, Christ the bread of Life. What is the name of that little boy? No one knows, and we will never know until we stand before God's great throne of grace at the judgment.

Let me ask this. Do you know the name of the woman who, in the Pacific Garden Mission in Chicago, won the famous White Sox ball player, Billy Sunday, to Jesus? I do not know her name. But think of the enormous influence of that humble woman who won that famous baseball player to the Lord.

Do you know the name of the humble layman who had in his Sunday school class a young teenager whom he won to the Lord in the stock room of a downtown Boston shoe store? That was the conversion of Dwight L. Moody. Think of what God did through that man, and yet his name is unknown.

Do you know the name of the Moravian missionary who won John Wesley and George Whitefield to the faith? I have no idea who he was. His name has been lost in the world, but think of what John Wesley and the great Wesleyan revival did for England, and think of George Whitefield who began in America the great awakening that swept into it the mighty, intellectual preaching of Jonathan Edwards.

Shadow ministries, things that humble people do for God that no one ever realizes, ever remembers, ever knows! But God knows, and He blesses that influence for good through the years.

That is the reason why, when a man dies, he does not receive his reward then. He does not receive his reward until the end of the world, until the end of time, for a man does not die when he dies. It is only God who can unravel the skein through all of human history. When men stand at the judgment bar of the Lord Jesus, without exception, they are surprised. "Why, Lord, when did I ever see You sick and ministered to You, or imprisoned and came to see You, or hungry and fed You, or naked and clothed You? When did I ever do these things?" And the Lord will say, "When you did it to one of the least of these, you were doing it to Me." God writes it down in the Book of Life, and that is why the reward is never bestowed until the end of the age. The influence goes on and on, and only in heaven will one ever know what it means.

Let me illustrate. A woman, whose name has been forgotten, gave a tract one day to a very bad man, Richard Baxter, who read it and was converted. Then Baxter wrote a book, *The Call of the Unconverted*, which brought a multitude to God, among them, Philip Doddridge, who in turn wrote a book, *The Rise and Progress of Religion*. This book brought tens of thousands into the kingdom, among them, William Wilberforce. Wilberforce wrote *A Practical View of Christianity*, which brought a multitude to Christ, among them being Leigh Richmond, who wrote a tract, "The Dairyman's Daughter," which has been the means of the conversion of uncounted multitudes. So the influence went on and on.

Look how that began. A woman whose name has been forgotten gave a tract one day to a very bad man, and the influence went on and on and extends to this day. When that woman stands at the judgment bar of Christ, and the Lord bestows upon her her reward, think of the amazement that will overwhelm her, crown her in glory, in gratitude, and in praise to God!

A man does not know what he does when he does something good for Jesus, speaking a word in His name, sowing the seed of the Word. Shadow ministries—the unconscious influence of those who love Jesus.

29

Counted Worthy to Suffer

And they departed from the presence of the council, rejoicing that they were
counted worthy to suffer shame for his name. (Acts 5:41)

The problem of human suffering is one to which the wise, the good,
and the learned have addressed themselves from the beginning of the
creation. There are two kinds of suffering. One can be in the flesh, in
the body. The other can be in the soul, in the heart, and in the spirit.
"Anguish of mind" is a common phrase in our day. I see causes of
human suffering as five, as I think through all of the afflictions that the
human race endures.

FIVE CAUSES OF SUFFERING

First, the oppression of Satan. There is an enemy of all mankind as
well as of God in this world. The story of Job is the story of the vicious
attack of Satan. In the thirteenth chapter of Luke the Lord healed a
woman who was bent completely over, and he said that she had been
oppressed by Satan for eighteen years.

When Paul referred to his thorn in the flesh, he described it as "a
messenger of Satan to buffet me."

Second, we fall into suffering sometimes because of our own sins and
derelictions. If one is afflicted with emphysema, he often is a cigarette
smoker. If a person dies with cirrhosis of the liver, it is very possible
he was an alcoholic. If he has venereal disease, he has given himself to social sin and promiscuity. These sufferings we bring on ourselves.

Third, there is a suffering that comes from our being a part of the mortal human race. An innocent child can fall into convulsions and die. A man reaches old age and finally dies. He is a part of the human race, and as such, he suffers.

Fourth, there is a suffering of self-sacrifice for others. A soldier lays down his life for his country or comes home badly wounded. A mother goes through the valley of the shadow of death in giving birth to a child, and through the years that follow after she gives her life for her child that he might advance, that he might have an opportunity.

There is last of all a suffering for the kingdom of God, a suffering in the name of the Lord. This is seen in those who, at great cost and at great sacrifice, deny the world and all of its blandishments and give themselves to the ministry of the Lord, either as a man out in the world, a businessman, or a vocational Christian leader. Sometimes we see the spirit of self-sacrifice and giving to the work of the kingdom as in the poor widow whom the Lord commended. She gave but two mites, yet it was all of her living, everything that she had. She just trusted God for daily bread, "fed by the ravens."

That is the suffering that is referred to in this fifth chapter of Acts. It is a suffering for the name of the Lord. For the most part, we read the story casually, in a cursory way. We hardly enter in to what actually happened in the life of these apostles. Let us look at the text closely.

Suffering Bodily Affliction for Jesus

"And when they [the Sanhedrin] had called the apostles, and had beaten [*dero*] them." *Dero*, translated here, "and had beaten them," actually means "to skin," such as one would skin an animal. From the term "to skin," the word came to mean "to flay," "to scourge," and even yet it does not appear to us what happened to these men. The scourge, called "a scorpion," was a whip made with leather thongs. All up and down the thongs were hooks or jagged pieces of metal. The back of the sufferer was stripped and the executioner, with all his strength, brought down the scorpion on the back of the victim. Often the first blow would bare the skin open to the bone. Remember that Paul said that he was beaten like that five times. That was the flagellation endured by our Lord before He was crucified. History records that often a felon sentenced to crucifixion died under the flagellation before there was even opportunity to nail him to the cross. We can see the apostles walking from the Sanhedrin, one of them wiping the blood away, one of them being helped because he was so cruelly hurt, and another one crippled by the awesome scourging.

When I read this story in Acts, I think of the Council of Nicaea in A.D. 325. As those pastors and bishops were brought together for the first world-wide conference, they had just gone through the terrible Diocletian persecution. I read a description of that Nicaean Council in which the servants of Christ gathered from the ends of the empire. Some of them had their tongues cut out. Some of them had their eyes gouged out. Some of them had their ears cut off. Some of them had their hands cut off. Some of them had their fingers cut off. Almost all of them were maimed, mutilated, and scarred. Think of an assembly like that!

In the fifth chapter of Acts the word "beaten," *dero*, could be translated in our English language, "skinned alive." To read that "they left the presence of the Sanhedrin rejoicing" is beyond my understanding. I have never been introduced to anything like that. The men who were wiping the blood away and crippled because of the terrible tragedy were rejoicing in the Lord. Wiping the blood and praising God, they "departed from the presence of the council, rejoicing that they were counted worthy to suffer shame for his name."

Let us look at this word once again. "They were rejoicing that they were counted worthy to suffer shame for his name." There is a Greek word, *time*, which means "of great price." The verbal form, *timao*, means "to consider with great preciousness, to reverence, to honor." In the Greek language, if one adds an "a" to the front of a word, it is a privative, it is a denial. Add "a" to the beginning of "theos" and the result is "atheist." Put an "a" in front of *time* and the meaning is "dishonor," "shame." Add an "a" to *timao*, *atimoo* (*atimazo*) and the meaning is "dishonor," "shame," "ignominy," a term that would describe a felon, a malefactor, an enemy of society. The apostles departed from the presence of the council, rejoicing that they were counted worthy to *atimoo*, "to suffer shame" for His name, and thus continued under that persecution every day in every house teaching and preaching the Lord Jesus.

Just to read the account of the devotion and selflessness of the apostles humbles us. Lord, what dilatory and poor and selfish servants we are compared to these men of God who suffered such agony and shame!

THE THEOLOGICAL MEANING OF SUFFERING

Out of that passage I am going to speak of the deep and profound theological meaning of suffering. There is far more meaning than just that the apostles bled, that they were hurt, and that they were crippled. The meaning of their suffering has infinite theological, heavenly, spiritual repercussions. Suffering has a place in the mind, the purpose, and the plan of God.

First, we are going to look at suffering in the life of the apostle Paul. In the ninth chapter of the Book of Acts the Lord said, "For he is a chosen vessel unto me. . . . For I will shew him how great things he must suffer for my name's sake" (vv. 15,16). What an amazing use of the word *nun*, "now." *Nun* almost always in Greek is an expletive, a word just added, a transitional word, "now." But not here. It is an emphatic use of the word, the first word in the sentence, "I, Paul, who now rejoice in my sufferings for You." The use of the word at the beginning of the sentence arises out of this: when the Lord said, "I will shew him how great things he must suffer for my name's sake," I would suppose that there were times of great repining in the life of the apostle. "Lord, Lord, such hurt, such blood!" I would suppose that there were times when the apostle Paul quailed under the awesome price of serving the Lord. That is the only way I can explain the emphatic "now." "In days past I trembled before the assignment of God, but now I, Paul, rejoice in my sufferings for You."

In Colossians 1:24 we read of Paul's most remarkable theological avowal of God's purpose in His sufferings: "[that I might] fill up that which is behind of the afflictions of Christ in my flesh for his body's sake, which is the church." What does Paul mean by the astonishing theological statement, "I rejoice in my suffering that I might fill up that which is behind in the sufferings of Christ"? Is the atonement not complete? Are Gethsemane and Calvary failures? Is there only partial payment of the debt of our sins in the atoning expiation of Christ?

When we look at the text it becomes apparent what the apostle meant. Christ paid for all our sins. The atonement is complete when He cried, "It is finished!" The full price for our salvation was paid. But the Lord did not exhaust the sufferings that are to be dedicated to the purposes of God in the earth. There are sufferings also for His name. A story needs a teller, the evangel needs a preacher. Thus, Paul must also suffer if the gospel is to be preached in Ephesus, in Rome, or in Corinth, as we must pay the price if the saving faith is made known to the world. There is a purpose of God in our sacrifice and in our suffering that is needed for the realization of the kingdom.

SUFFERING AS A KEY TO THE INTERPRETATION OF HUMAN HISTORY

Look at the purpose of suffering in the life of our Lord. The fifth chapter of the Book of Revelation has one of the most dramatic scenes that mind could imagine.

> And I saw in the right hand of him that sat on the throne a book. . . . sealed with seven seals.
>
> And I saw a strong angel proclaiming with a loud voice, Who is worthy to open the book, and to loose the seals thereof?
>
> And no man in heaven, nor in earth, neither under the earth, was able to open the book, neither to look thereon.
>
> And I [the apostle John] wept much, because no man was found worthy . . . to look thereon.
>
> And one of the elders saith unto me, Weep not: behold, the Lion of the tribe of Juda, the Root of David, hath prevailed to open the book, and to loose the seven seals thereof.
>
> And I beheld, and, lo, in the midst of the throne, and of the four beasts, and in the midst of the elders, stood a Lamb as it had been slain. . .
>
> And they sung a new song, saying . . . Worthy is the Lamb that was slain to receive power, and riches, and wisdom, and strength, and honour, and glory, and blessing. (vv. 1-6, 9a, 12b)

What does that mean? Here again is that same profound, theological meaning of suffering. It means this: the Lamb slain is alone able to disclose the mind and purpose of God in our suffering. With sorrow, life finds its interpretation in the Christ of the cross. It is the Lamb who has been slain who is able to take the Book and explain it to us, to open it to us for our understanding. What is the meaning of the Book?

First, it is a Book of the Scriptures. The Old Testament is meaningless apart from the cross of the Son of God. Every type, every sacrifice, every psalm, and every prophecy find their ultimate meaning and fulfillment in the atoning grace of the suffering of the Son of God.

Second, it is a Book of nature. How does one explain the strange ferocity of nature itself, like an animal gone mad? The savagery of nature is sometimes unbelievable. The havoc that it can wreak in human life! All of the old Greek and Roman poets stood before the inexplicable ferocity of nature and cried out seeking some kind of an answer before sorrow, suffering, and death. Jesus explains the answer and gives the reason for sorrow, suffering, and death in His cross. Out of death, there is life; out of suffering, there is salvation; out of the tragedies of human life, there is heaven.

Third, it is a Book of history, containing all of the sorrows written on the pages of human story. The sixth chapter of the Apocalypse depicts the record of mankind. First, there is a white horse and a conqueror. How many conquerors has the world known? These are men, the last of which was Hitler, who have offered on the altar of their ambition thousands and millions of lives. Next there is a red horseman, followed by a black horseman, followed by a pale horseman. There is no meaning, purpose, or solution to suffering apart from the Son of God who said, "All authority is given unto me." In the nineteenth chapter of the Revelation the Lord intervenes in human history in the midst of the war of the Battle of Armageddon. All sorrow and suffering but prepare for his final coronation.

Fourth, that Book is a book of our lives. How does one explain the tears and the sorrows that accompany us in our lives? We find the answers in the interpretation given to us by the suffering Christ of the cross. Our prayers, if we really pray, are to be offered in agony and in earnest supplication. The Book of Hebrews says that our Lord "in the days of his flesh . . . offered up prayers and supplications with strong crying and tears" (5:7). This is real praying, not the mere repeating of meaningless words.

Look at a passage in Colossians: "For I would that ye knew what great *agona*, conflict [agony] I have for you" (2:1).

A marvelous young man, whose life has influenced the whole Christian world, was David Brainerd. He died in his twenties in the home of Jonathan Edwards. He was engaged to Jonathan Edwards' daughter, Jerusha, who was just eighteen. As he died he said to her, "We shall spend a happy eternity together." Four months later she followed him into the world that is yet to come. Reading from David Brainerd's journal, one can still feel the hot tears of his supplications and prayers as he writes:

> I think my soul was never so drawn out in intercession for others as it has been this night. I hardly ever so longed to live to God and be altogether devoted to Him. I wanted to wear out my life for Him. I wrestled for the ingathering of souls, for multitudes of poor souls in many places. I was in such agony from sun half an hour high till near dark that I was wet all over with sweat; but O, my dear Lord did sweat blood for such poor souls. I long for more compassion.

Now that is prayer! May God forgive us for our meaningless repetition at times.

OUR SUFFERING GIVES POWER TO OUR SERVICE OF CHRIST

It is the suffering that accompanies our work that gives power to it. It is the blood in it, it is the dedication in it, it is the self-sacrifice and commitment in it that gives our service power from God.

Was it not so with our Lord, who, though He were a son, learned obedience by the things that He suffered? In John 11 we read:

> Then after that saith he to his disciples, Let us go into Judaea again.
> His disciples say unto him, Master, the Jews of late sought to stone thee; and goest thou thither again? (vv. 7-8)

Returning to Judaea and to Jerusalem to be crucified!

In the life of the apostle Paul they stoned him at Lystra and dragged him out of the city for dead, but he was spared by the grace of God and returned to Lystra, *back to the stones!* It is the blood that authenticates; it is the sacrifice in our service to God that makes it powerful.

A missionary named James Chalmers of England was sent to New Guinea to the cannibals in that big island north of Australia. Addressing the mission group that sent him, he said:

> Recall the twenty-one years. Give me back all of its experience. Give me its shipwrecks, give me its standings in the face of death, give it me; surrounded with savages with spears and clubs. Give it me back again with the spears flying about me, with a club knocking me to the ground. Give it me back, and I will still be your missionary!

He returned to New Guinea and was slain. He laid down his life, murdered by those same, vicious cannibals. Yet those were the people who, when our American airmen were shot down in the Pacific in World War II and were washed upon the shores of the South Pacific islands helped them. Instead of killing and boiling the American servicemen for food, these former cannibals won them to the Lord. God's purposes for us are known only in the sufferings of Him who is the Lamb slain from before the foundation of the earth. It is the Christ of the cross who alone is able to interpret the meaning of our suffering.

30

Men Moved by the Spirit

And in those days, when the number of the disciples was multiplied, there arose a murmuring of the Grecians against the Hebrews, because their widows were neglected in the daily ministration.

Then the twelve called the multitude of the disciples unto them, and said, It is not reason that we should leave the word of God, and serve tables.

Wherefore, brethren, look ye out among you seven men of honest report, full of the Holy Ghost and wisdom, whom we may appoint over this business.

But we will give ourselves continually to prayer, and to the ministry of the word.

And the saying pleased the whole multitude: and they chose Stephen, a man full of faith and of the Holy Ghost, and Philip, and Prochorus, and Nicanor, and Timon, and Parmenas, and Nicolas a proselyte of Antioch:

Whom they set before the apostles: and when they had prayed, they laid their hands on them.

And the word of God increased; and the number of the disciples multiplied in Jerusalem greatly; and a great company of the priests were obedient to the faith. (Acts 6:1-7)

The occasion that gave rise to the choice of these men in our text was trouble in the mother church in Jerusalem. It was trouble by human frailty, infirmity, and altercation. These were the men who had been taught by the Lord Himself. This is the church upon which God had poured out the ascension gift of the Holy Spirit. This is the church where the preaching of the Word was confirmed by signs and wonders, and yet it is torn by human infirmity. Why would God allow a development such as that? Why would the Holy Spirit not gloss over such altercation and difficulty as are exhibited on these holy pages?

TWO QUESTIONS THAT WE MUST FACE

In order to answer this, two questions must be faced. One, why does God write of trouble in the church in the Bible? Why does He not hide it? The reason lies in the character of the Word. The Word of God is true and infallible, and God records events exactly as they occurred. For example, the story in the beginning of the church as presented in the New Testament is one of internal problems in the church. The problems are presented just as they happened, faithfully and truly, hiding nothing. The first chapter of Acts describes the suicide of one of the twelve apostles. The fifth chapter opens up to us the hypocrisy and the lying of Ananias and Sapphira in their jealousy of Barnabas, the son of consolation. In Acts 6 we find the story of the trouble in the church arising between the *Hellenestes*, the Greek-speaking Jews, and the *Hebraios*, the Aramaic-speaking Jews, surfacing in the house of the Lord, that eternal conflict between Hellenistic culture and philosophy and Hebrew revelation.

As one examines the New Testament, he finds all of it to be an honest and forthright presentation of events just as they happened, good and bad. The dissimulation of Peter is meticulously outlined. This chief apostle quailed before a little maid, cursing and swearing that he did not even know the Lord nor had he ever seen Him. Another difficulty that is recorded is the fierce confrontation between Paul and Barnabas arguing over John Mark, a kinsman of Barnabas, and so violent was the altercation between them (the Greek word that is used is *paroxysm*; there was such a paroxysm between Paul and Barnabas), that they went their separate ways. As though that were not enough, the Word of God also mentions the fierce confrontation between Paul and Peter in Antioch. In the second chapter of the Book of Galatians Paul accosts Peter "to his face" and calls him a hypocrite. All of these stories of animosity and ugly behavior of the men of God are recorded in the Bible. That is because God faithfully and truly writes down what happened, and glosses over none of it. The infallible Word of God leaves out nothing.

The same true reporting is found in the Old Testament. The bad as well as the good in the life of Abraham is recorded; all of the supplanting and hyprocrisy of Jacob, called "Israel," and the stories of Samson, of Judah, and of David are recorded in the Word of God, omitting nothing.

An organization of atheists, called "The Free Thinkers," published a book entitled, *The Bible Exposed*. They wrote the negative facts of the

Bible in their book as though they were discrediting the Word of God. Such behavior reveals the mentality of an atheist. He thinks just so far but no farther. What the book actually did was to authenticate the truth of the revelation of the Almighty. The Bible is the infallible Word of God and it paints a true picture of its characters. God writes it down just as people are and do, and with infinite confidence we can open the sacred Book and read its holy words.

A second question: Why would God allow trouble in the church, of all places? Why does He not keep the world out of the church and why does He not keep the church away from the world? Why does He not separate them from each other? Why place the church in a position where all kinds of troubles that afflict this world also afflict the congregation of God?

If men were running the church, it would be carefully kept away from the world with its sin, shame, and iniquity. Men have tried to keep the world out of the church by building high walls around their monastaries, and on the inside of the monastaries they have placed priests, monks, and nuns in order to separate them from the world.

That is man, but not God. God never built any high walls around His church. God placed His Church next door to hell itself, and wherever there is sin, wrong, shame, violence, corruption, and blood, there ought to be the church of the living God in the very heart of it.

Think of how Paul began his second letter to the church at Corinth: "Paul, an apostle of Jesus Christ . . . unto the church of God which is at Corinth" (2 Cor. 1:1). Corinth was one of the most wicked cities that ever existed. The corruption, the vice, and the sin in Corinth reached to heaven like that of Sodom and Gomorrah, and yet God placed His church in the midst of the city.

Look again. In the second chapter of the Apocalypse the Lord addressed the church at Pergamos and says, "And to the angel of the church in Pergamos . . . I know . . . where thou dwellest, even where Satan's seat is." It was found in the very heart of the political, cultural debauchery and corruption of the kingdom of Pergamos. Where should the church be? Right where Satan has his throne, right in the heart and the core of human life.

Frequently people have said to me, "When are you going to sell your property downtown and move out to the green pastures, where it is easier for people to attend the services?" For forty-seven years my great predecessor, Dr. George W. Truett said, "We will never move out; we are staying right here." For thirty-three years I have avowed the same thing. Where Satan has his throne, in the very heart of the life of the city, there ought to be the lighthouse for Jesus Christ, the church of the living God. That is why God does not shield the world from His church. What the Lord said, can be found in the high priestly prayer of John 17: "I pray not that thou shouldest take them out of the world, but that thou shouldest keep them from the evil" (v. 15).

THE WISDOM OF THE APOSTLES

Now let us look at the wisdom of these apostles. A confrontation had taken place between the *Hellenestes*, the Greek-speaking Jews who were foreigners born outside of Palestine, and the *Hebraios*, the Aramaic-speaking Jews of Palestine. The apostles were wise with the wisdom of God because they saw in that division the possibility of infinite hurt, anger, bitterness, and rupture. Did they hide their eyes from it? No. Whenever trouble begins to rise in the church, the man of God ought to sense it, and he ought to meet it head on right then and settle it. It is much better to settle any kind of a problem or difficulty that arises in the church than to let it breed, multiply, and finally destroy so many. That is what the apostles did. Seeing the possibility of ruin and rupture in the church, they courageously and boldly faced the problem. They called together the multitude of the people.

We are sometimes amazed at how some people will react to certain situations. It amazes us how right and how just the verdict of some people can be. They have sensitivities that we do not give them credit for, and they have wisdom that comes from God. In this situation the apostles let these people make their own decisions and solve their own problems. They appointed the men upon the counsel and admonition of the people and they settled the problem beautifully. The apostles divided the assignments and said, "The laymen and laywomen will take care of all of the business of the church while we pray and study God's Word and deliver His message."

Let us look at that decision. First, the apostles never divided up the work among them in such a way that some of the apostles would do one task and the rest would do another task. All of the apostles were going to give themselves to prayer and to the ministry of the Word, and then the businesses of the church would lie in the responsibility and assignment of the lay members of the church. The apostles said they were going to give themselves to prayer and to the ministry of the Word, and we heard them pray because their prayers are written on the holy page. We have read them, and oh, what praying! The building shook where those men of God were praying and talking to the Almighty. We have read their sermons, and what sermons! They were filled with the convicting power of the Spirit and people were saved by the thousands under the preaching of these dedicated apostles.

The depth of their praying is a rebuke to we ministers. Our praying is so often peripheral and mechanical without power, feeling, or passion. They are just words and syllables. But think of the power and unction from heaven in the apostles' delivery of the message of God!

A definition of preachers and preaching that I once heard was this: "Preaching is a mild-mannered man speaking to a mild-mannered congregation upon how to be more mild-mannered."

An effective preacher is the preacher who prays in the power of God and delivers the message of God with unction from heaven and with conviction of the Holy Spirit.

Then to assist the preacher are the dedicated laymen and laywomen who, like Aaron and Hur holding up the hands of Moses, help the pastor do a great and mighty work for God. A preacher who preaches out of all the frustations and businesses of life and all of the worryings of the church will have a weak message and a weak ministry of the Word. When the preacher stands up he should preach a message from heaven itself, having prayed, studied, and listened to the voice and mind of God.

Often young ministers have come to me and asked, "If you have just one thing to say to a young preacher, what would you say?" I always have the same reply: "If I have just one thing to say to you it is this: Keep the morning for God. However busy you may be, keep the morning for God, and out of the praying, out of the Bible studying, out of the meditation, out of the baring of your soul before God, stand in the pulpit with unction and with power and deliver a message from heaven." Parishoners will grow in grace if a preacher will do that. It will be like manna to their hungry souls, it will be like drinking at the fountain of the water of life. The congregation will come to know God more because the preacher knows Him and has taken time in His presence.

As for lay people, they ought to assume the responsibilities for all of the business of the church. Is there financial need? That is a wonderful way for laymen to serve Jesus. Are there buildings to be built? Are there maintenance crews to be hired? Are there a thousand things that enter into the life of the church? The laymen have that assignment to care for the church, to see that it runs beautifully and well, and that it is adequately provided for. Then when the preacher stands up to preach, he is not trying to squeeze money out of miserly and stingy people. The laymen have taken care of all of the financial needs of the church, and when the preacher stands up to preach, he is to take the Bible and open it, and where he leaves off Sunday morning, he begins Sunday night and ministers to the people the living Word of almighty God.

Here is a Criswellian translation of a Greek text: "Let every one of you lay by him in store as God hath prospered him, that there be no ding-dongin' for money when I stand up to preach!" That is exactly what that text means. When a preacher has to preach so that it sounds like he is trying to raise money, the people come to church and say, "All they are interested in is just money; all they want is what they can get out of me." That is not pleasing to God. The pastor is to give himself to prayer and to the ministry of the Word and let the laymen make appeal for money. God will build a great church when the preacher, a man who knows God and calls Him by name, works together with the laymen and laywomen who do the work of the Lord building Sunday schools and Training Unions, caring for the stewardship program, erecting buildings, and carrying the financial program.

There is one thing that I must remind myself about the team of a pastor and the laymen. It is found in the Book of Joshua. When the men of Israel came before Joshua who was standing in the stead of Moses, they said:

> . . . All that thou commandest us we will do, and whithersoever thou sendest us, we will go.
> . . . only the LORD thy God be with thee, as he was with Moses. (1:16-17)

The pastor and his God is an unbeatable team.

THE CHOSEN MEN

Look at the seven men who were chosen and their qualifications. They were "men of honest report"; they could be trusted. They were not men who were not one way to your face and another way behind your back. They were men who could be counted upon, men with whom one could entrust the destiny of the church.

They were also men of *sophia*, "wisdom," that is, men who combined love and zeal with good common sense. The Lord is pleased when His church is run by men who have good common sense. There are men of the world who understand things in the world. Our Lord one time said that "the children of this generation are wiser than the children of light." There are men working in tremendous skycrapers running big corporations who are most gifted and astute. The same gifts, astuteness, and shrewdness should be found in running the church and the institutions of the Lord. That is exactly what the Bible says. The chosen men had good judgment and good sense.

Did you notice the middle characteristic listed about these men? They were men who were "full of the Holy Ghost." Now some think that the Holy Spirit was poured out upon the apostles, and He is the gift for the preacher and the pastor, but the Holy Spirit is not expected to be poured out upon the laymen and the laywomen of the church.

Listen to what the Bible says. In the second chapter of Acts, when Simon Peter stood up to speak his great Pentecostal message, he quoted from the second chapter of Joel, in which Joel said that the Lord would pour out His Spirit upon all flesh and that the old men would dream dreams, and the young men would prophesy. Every man and woman can be filled with the Holy Spirit of God. Just think of that! There is a way for a man to open a door that will glorify God. There is a word that we can say when we shake someone's hand that magnifies Jesus. There is a way that we can park the car for someone that will make him glad to come to the house of the Lord. Every phase of God's work is to be filled by the moving of the Spirit of the Lord. Those who teach and train, those who sing and play, all can be filled with the Spirit of the Lord to make for a glorious house of worship.

THE RESULT

Look at the conclusion: "And the word of God increased; and the number of the disciples multiplied . . . greatly." When people are filled with the Spirit of the Lord such things will always happen in the church. When what we do has the unction and blessing of God upon it, people will come to Jesus, they will walk down the aisles, they will be baptized, they will go out witnessing and testifying. Their homes and families will all be in the house of the Lord when they are filled with the Spirit of the Lord.

We will never win the world to Jesus by a paid preacher and a paid missionary. What God intended was that all of His people should say good things about Jesus. He intends that all of the people magnify and praise the Lord inviting, teaching, training, praying, and winning souls—all of us sharing in the ministry alike. When that comes to pass, the glory of the presence of the Lord will move in His house. When our people are burdened in prayer and come with great expectation, a preacher can stand in the pulpit and feel the presence of God in everyone's souls. The Lord will always crown the service with a sweet harvest when cooperative efforts are shared by the pastor and his people.

31

The Smiting of God's Glory

And Stephen, full of faith and power, did great wonders and miracles among the people.

Then there arose certain of the synagogue, which is called the synagogue of the Libertines, and Cyrenians, and Alexandrians, and of them of Cilicia and of Asia, disputing with Stephen.

And they were not able to resist the wisdom and the spirit by which he spake.

Then they suborned men, which said, We have heard him speak blasphemous words against Moses, and against God.

And they stirred up the people, and the elders, and the scribes, and came upon him, and caught him, and brought him to the council,

And set up false witnesses, which said, This man ceaseth not to speak blasphemous words against this holy place, and the law:

For we have heard him say, that this Jesus of Nazareth shall destroy this place, and shall change the customs which Moses delivered us.

And all that sat in the council, looking stedfastly on him, saw his face as it had been the face of an angel.

When they heard these things, they were cut to the heart, and they gnashed on him with their teeth.

But he, being full of the Holy Ghost, looked up stedfastly into heaven, and saw the glory of God, and Jesus standing on the right hand of God,

And said, Behold, I see the heavens opened, and the Son of man standing on the right hand of God.

Then they cried out with a loud voice, and stopped their ears, and ran upon him with one accord,

And cast him out of the city, and stoned him: and the witnesses laid down their clothes at a young man's feet, whose name was Saul.

And they stoned Stephen, calling upon God, and saying, Lord Jesus, receive my spirit.

And he kneeled down, and cried with a loud voice, Lord, lay not this sin to their charge. And when he had said this, he fell asleep. (Acts 6:8-15; 7:54-60)

In our discussion of the Book of Acts we have come to the eighth verse of the sixth chapter where we are standing at a great divide in the kingdom of our Lord. It is similar to the division at the end of the eleventh chapter of Genesis and the beginning of chapter twelve, which starts with the story of Abraham. So it is in this important transitional period in which Stephen stands before the presence of the Lord as God's mighty witness. When we come to Acts 6:8, we change from Peter to Paul.

THE DEACON-MARTYR STEPHEN

Stephen has a beautiful and meaningful name. His name in Greek is *Stephanos* which means "a crown," "a garland." The word refers to the reward that was given to a civic leader of the state and to the crown of glory that was received by one who ran and won in the Olympic Greek games. It is meaningful that this man with the name *Stephanos* should be the first Christian martyr, and the first one to receive the martyr's crown.

A long record of his death and martyrdom is presented in both the sixth and seventh chapters of Acts. Next to the life of our Lord, this is the longest account of any death in the Bible. The Holy Spirit saw fit to single out this man's life and martyrdom for such detailed portrayal on the sacred page. Have you ever thought how briefly, if at all, mention is made of the death of the apostles or of those first Christian leaders? Herod Agrippa II beheaded James, the brother of the Lord. His death is mentioned only parenthetically and in just a few words. The only reference made to the martyrdom of Peter is when the Lord in the twenty-first chapter of John prophesied that he should die by crucifixion. It is only in tradition that we learn that Paul was martyred. We have no idea how the rest of the apostles died, outside of Judas. Only a brief reference is made to the death of anyone in this great company of martyrs, but the martyrdom and the death of Stephen are meticulously delineated in the Bible. The last day of his life is presented in detail in Acts 6 and 7.

Let us look at the man himself. First of all, Stephen was a *Helleneste*, a Hellenist. He was a new type of preacher. The apostles were Galileans, and were crude, uneducated men. In the fourth chapter of the Book of Acts, Peter and John were called *agrammatoi kai idiotai*, translated "ignorant and unlearned men," as they appeared before the Sanhedrin. But Stephen was from an altogether different world; he was a man of reputation and culture. He was foreign-born and spoke Greek. Beginning with him, the whole spectrum of the Christian faith took on a different color and hue. Beginning with Stephen the gospel message of Christ was thrust into the cultural, political, social, economic, and academic life of the world just as it is today.

Stephen possessed tremendous conviction that was as deep as the earth beneath and as high as the heaven above. He was a man of vast commitment and persuasion. How different that is from the society in which we live today. In our day the agnostic and cynic are the men who are admired and exalted in the academic world. They do not believe anything and they make "conviction" a word that is opprobrious, full of antipathy. The man who is accpeted in the academic community today is to be eclectically broadminded. To him, life is without purpose, without plan, and without meaning. He stands as an existentialist looking at the whole creation of God and recognizing no part of the hand of the Almighty in it.

If Christianity is any one thing above everything else, it is dogmatic. All truth is dogmatic. In poetry and in fiction we can be fanciful, but in mathematics we have to be actual, real, and truthful. Mathematics is an exact science. So is the truth of the Christian faith. Christianity is not a speculation, it is a revelation. The Christian faith is not a puzzle or an enigma; it is an oracle of almighty God and is of all things dogmatic. It has great propositional truth. This is the truth of God and therefore it can have no parley with infidelity, atheism, agnosticism, rejection, or denial. In God's sight and in the Christian faith an act is right or it is wrong.

Lately we have seen an extensive effort exerted by homosexuals and lesbians who are organizing for their rights, privileges, and status before the law. The publicity about their activities has dominated magazines and newspapers for quite some time. Does the Christian faith have anything to say about that? Just as the judgment of God fell upon Sodom and Gomorrah and just as the first chapter of the Book of Romans is in the Bible, so also the homosexual and the lesbian are an affront to God and a disgrace to the human race and shame to the nation. Why do not all of the murderers, thieves, and violent people who have broken the law get together and say, "We demand status and we demand our right before the law." Christianity, as long as there is a Christian faith, says that some things are right and some things are wrong and God says that sodomy is wrong.

STEPHEN'S TRUTH AROUSED A FURY OF OPPOSITION

Stephen is an interesting man. He stood as an emissary of the Lord God, preaching the truth of the Almighty. What kind of a response did he have? It was vicious and violent in the extreme. Stephen was speaking in the synagogue of the Cilicians. We must remember that Saul was from Tarsus, the capital of the Roman province of Cilicia. Foreign-born Jews had their own synagogues in Jerusalem, and in one of them, in the synagogue of the Cilicians, Stephen stood proclaiming the message of Jesus Christ, and Saul of Cilicia was there. Saul and all of the men with him were unable to stand before the power, the wisdom, and the truth by which Stephen was mightily delivering a defense of the Christian faith. So they suborned men, they hired witnesses and haled Stephen before the Sanhedrin. Would you not think that all it would take to win the hearts of the people would be to tell the truth of God? But the opposite often takes place. Truth creates a repercussion of violence and viciousness in the hearts of those who hear and see it.

An illustration of that is found in a great university that belongs to a Christian denomination. A theological seminary is located on the campus. It was decided one day in that university that there would be a debate between those who believed that God created us and those who believed that we evolved from a cell. Men searched the university to find one who would defend the creationist belief that God made us. They could not find one person on the faculty or entire campus to defend the creationist position. Then they searched the seminary and could not find one professor or one student who believed that God made us. Out of desperation they went to another seminary in the city and chose a professor to speak in defense of the truth of almighty God. Can you believe that? It is only in evolution that a river rises higher than its source, that there are effects without causes, and that something was created out of nothing. It is only in evolution that life is born out of dead, inert stones and that there is purpose and plan of life without intelligence. Yet when one stands up to defend the presence of almighty God in human life and the creative hand of God in the universe, he is scoffed and scorned as though he were an affront to our academic intelligence. One would think that truth would immediately be seized and loved by people, but it seems as though it is just the opposite. As we go on in life and look at it more closely, we will find that same tragic response and repercussion in every area of human life.

The angry crowd dragged Stephen out of their city and stoned him to death, even though capital punishment had been taken out of the hands of the Jews and was now lodged in the office of the Roman procurator. In the story of the crucifixion of our Lord, His Jewish brethren wanted to crucify Him, but they did not have the power to put Him to death. Capital punishment was in the hands of Pontius Pilate, the governor, so to carry out the death of Jesus, the Lord has to be condemned by the Roman governor. Did the crowd take Stephen to the Roman governor? No. So furious was their reply to the truth Stephen preached that they seized him, and without consulting the governor or the Roman law or a Roman soldier, they haled him out of the city and stoned him to death. We might raise the question, Why did God not deliver him? Why did God let Stephen be the merciless, ruthless victim of that implacable anger? Why does God not deliver us from the many troubles that afflict us and why does He not deliver us from the problems that seemingly to us are insoluble? Why does God allow us to fall into tears, sorrow, heartache, disappointment, frustration, and all of the ills that afflict the human frame? Why did God not deliver Stephen?

REASONS FOR STEPHEN'S MARTYRDOM

There are two answers. First, God, through Stephen, brought to pass before the eyes of the world both in that day and in ours a moral miracle. When a man praises God in the day of sorrow, as the psalmist says, "When we can sing songs in the night"; when a man can name the name of the Lord as Job did, "The Lord gave, the Lord hath taken away; blessed be the name of the Lord"; that is a moral miracle. Look at Stephen's response to the angry mob who were stoning him to death:

> And he kneeled down, and cried out with a loud voice, Lord, lay not this sin to their charge. And when he had said this, he fell asleep. (Acts 7:60)

Looking into the murderous faces of the furious crowd as he was crushed to the ground beneath a hail of stones, Stephen lifted up his face to heaven and said: "Lord, lay not this sin to their charge. Forgive them." His response shook heaven itself, and it plummets us into humility as we think of the littleness of our own muttering, griping, and fault-finding with the insignificant matters that plague us in our lives when we ought to be Christians glorifying God in our distresses, in our sorrows, in our hurts, in our ills, and finally in our death.

Second, why did God allow Stephen to die? Because it is only in the crises of our lives that we ever achieve a real vision of God. I can tell you truly, both by experience and by reading the Word of God, that when everything is flowing along beautifully, we may verbally say, "O Lord, I thank Thee," but we have not had a real experience with God until the day of trouble comes. It is then in the hour of crisis that we see the vision of heaven. Stephen said, "Behold, I see the heavens opened, and the Son of man standing on the right hand of God" (Acts 7:56). In the hour of crisis he cried, saying, "I see!" The cry of every true Christian in the hour of trouble is: "I see. I see the hand of God. I see the presence of the Lord. I see the face of Jesus. I see the plan, purpose, and blessing, and finally, my brethren, I see the farther shore. I can see heaven itself. I can see the beautiful and holy city!" God's Christian people have died saying: "I see, I see." That is when we really see in the crises and in the sorrows and tears of our lives.

It is in that hour of sorrow and tragedy that we shine for Jesus. "And all that sat in the council, looking stedfastly on him, saw his face as it had been the face of an angel" (Acts 6:15). "His face shone and he wist not that he shined like an angel."

Alfred Lord Tennyson penned these lines about Stephen:

> He heeded not reviling tones
> Nor sold his heart to idle moans,
> Tho' cursed and scorned and bruised with stones.
>
> But looking upward, full of grace,
> He prayed, and from a happy place
> God's glory smote him on the face.

"Looking stedfastly on him, [they] saw his face as it had been the face of an angel." O Lord, how I am rebuked in my own life and encouraged to lift up my spirit unto You!

"Behold, I see the heavens opened, and the Son of man standing on the right hand of God." Did you know that everywhere else in the Bible Jesus is seated on the right hand of the Majesty on high, at the right hand of the Father? He is always seated, except on one occasion, and that is when Stephen saw Him. The Lord arose to welcome His first Christian martyr home to heaven. He stood up to receive the soul of Stephen. Stephen said, "Behold, I see . . . the Son of man." The Son of man is the name of the Lord in the days of His flesh. How did Stephen recognize Jesus for he was born abroad? I do not think that Stephen had ever seen Jesus before this, so how did he know Him? Just by spiritual intuition. On the Mount of Transfiguration how did Peter, James, and John know Moses and how did they know Elijah? There is an intuitive knowledge just as certainly as there is an empirical, practical knowledge. It is with the eyes of the soul and the heart that we see God and it is with the understanding of our inward spirit that we know the things of God. Stephen knew the Lord, looking upon His face, and the Lord knew Stephen and stood up to receive his soul. Oh, when glory smites our face!

Did you ever read this poem? How true it describes the triumph in the home-going of Stephen!

I SEE JESUS

Once a man named Stephen,
   preached about the Lord,
Folks were saved and folks were healed,
   As they heard his word;
Satan did not like it,
   soon he had his crowd,
And as he was tried
   they heard Stephen cry aloud.

"I see Jesus, standing at the
   Father's right hand,
I see Jesus, yonder in the promised land;
Work is over, Now I'm coming to Thee,
I see Jesus, standing, waiting for me."

As the stones fell on him,
   beating out his life,
Stephen knew he'd soon be thro',
   with all toil and strife;
So much like the Master,
   with a heart so true,
He prayed, "Lord, forgive,
   for they know not what they do."

Thro' the gates of glory,
   down the streets of gold
Marched a hero of the Lord,
   Into heaven's fold;
When he met the Saviour,
   at the great white throne,
I believe He smiled and said,
   "Stephen, welcome home."

32

Stephen's Defense of the Gospel

The defense of Stephen is one of the mountain peaks in the ongoing, redemptive ministry of the Holy Spirit through Jesus Christ. Stephen defended the gospel in the seventh chapter of Acts, but as a background let us read beginning with the eighth verse of Acts 6:

> And Stephen, full of faith and power, did great wonders and miracles among the people.
>
> Then there arose certain of the synagogue, which is called the synagogue of the Libertines, and Cyrenians, and Alexandrians, and of them of Cilicia and of Asia, disputing with Stephen.
>
> And they were not able to resist the wisdom and the spirit by which he spake.
>
> Then they suborned men, which said, We have heard him speak blasphemous words against Moses, and against God.
>
> And they stirred up the people, and the elders, and the scribes, and came upon him, and caught him, and brought him to the council,
>
> And set up false witnesses, which said, This man ceaseth not to speak blasphemous words against this holy place, and the law:
>
> For we have heard him say, that this Jesus of Nazareth shall destroy this place, and shall change the customs which Moses delivered us.
>
> And all that sat in the council, looking stedfastly on him, saw his face as it had been the face of an angel.
>
> Then said the high priest, Are these things so?
>
> And he said . . . (vv. 6:8-7:2a)

Stephen is so much a martyr that we forget that he was anything else. He was the first man to lay down his life for the Lord. His life ended in such a blaze of glory that we do not remember the virtues that kindled the flame. He is so much in our minds the martyr that we look upon the long address, his *apologia*, he delivered as being a wearisome and tiresome repetition of Old Testament history. The mind of God saw it as something else.

Dr. Luke, who recorded this dramatic story in the Book of Acts, and the Holy Spirit who inspired him to write it out, looked upon this address as one of the high watermarks of redemption. Vitally important to Luke, Stephen is the transition from Aramaean, Galilean, Palestinian, Judaistic Christianity represented by Simon Peter, to the universal Christian faith represented by the Hellenistic, Greek-speaking Saul of Tarsus, Paul the apostle. There is a new way and a new approach to the story of the early Christian church when we come to the Hellenistic layman, Stephen.

He did not create the confrontation between Judaism and Christianity. The conflict was inevitable. Stephen but precipitated it.

Stephen sounds the keynote of foundational Christian freedom. When he recounts the story of God's dealings with the Jewish race, we are startled by his new interpretation. He is as familiar with the Scriptures as an Alexandrian theologian and he speaks of them with a philosopher's insight and understanding. He has a caustic criticism of materialistic religion like that of a Platonic Greek philosopher and under his hands the truth of redemption, salvation, and forgiveness in Christ Jesus is doubly and trebly Christian. His address is the answer to Acts 7:1: "Then said the high priest, Are these things so?" He discusses in his defense the castigations that were made against him.

STEPHEN'S ACCUSERS CLAIM THAT HE SPOKE AGAINST "THIS HOLY PLACE"

First, his accusers said that he spoke against "this holy place" referring to the temple and to Jerusalem where the people came to worship God. Stephen then addresses himself to that accusation.

What is the relation between a locality and the worship of God? Stephen said that there is no relation whatsoever, that anywhere is a good place to call upon the name of the Lord. Anytime is a good time to worship Jehovah God. Stephen said in his address that the externals, the paraphernalia of religion have nothing to do with its spiritual nature. In his apology he states that in the beginning of Jewish worship, locality and place had nothing to do with the worship of God. Abraham lived in the land of promise but owned no part of it except a small burying place to put his dead away. His altars were here, there, and yonder, and his worship was acceptable to God wherever he called upon the name of the Lord.

Stephen said that Moses was not in Canaan when the Lord appeared to him. He was on the backside of a Midian-Sinaitic desert and the Lord said to Moses, "Put off thy shoes from thy feet: for the place where thou standest is holy ground" (Acts 7:33). It was holy ground, though it was not in Jerusalem or on the temple site.

Then Stephen spoke of David who captured Jerusalem but was not allowed to build a temple. Until the temple was built, the tabernacle was cast in different places throughout Israel, and the children of Israel called upon the name of the Lord in that place.

Stephen said that when Solomon built the temple he closed his beautiful and magnificent dedicatory prayer with the word: "But will God indeed dwell on the earth? behold, the heaven and heaven of heavens cannot contain thee; how much less this house that I have builded?" (1 Kings 8:27). Then Stephen quotes from the sixty-sixth chapter of Isaiah:

> Thus saith the LORD, The heaven is my throne, and the earth is my footstool: where is the house that ye build unto me? and where is the place of my rest?
> For all those things hath mine hand made. (vv. 1-2a)

Structures on the earth cannot contain the great and mighty God. A kitchen corner is as good as a cathedral. A tiny tepee is as acceptable as the tallest temple. The poorest of suppliants is as welcome as the robed, gorgeously-arrayed priest. Stephen in this apology is striking the death knell of the root of the privilege claimed for the temple and the priesthood. His emphasis upon spiritual religion made his listeners' pharisaical pretenses sterile, empty, and barren. God does not need a human priest and a suppliant does not need a temple in order to come into the presence of God. A man can go to God anywhere, can pray in the name of the Lord, and can be accepted by the Almighty. In a sense Stephen is reproducing the marvelous message of the Savior in the fourth chapter of the Gospel of John when the Lord said to the Samaritan woman:

> Woman, believe me, the hour cometh, when ye shall neither in this mountain [Mount Gerizim], nor yet at Jerusalem, worship the Father.
> Ye worship ye know not what: we know what we worship: for salvation is of the Jews.
> But the hour cometh, and now is, when the true worshippers shall worship the Father in spirit and in truth: for the Father seeketh such to worship him.
> God is a Spirit: and they that worship him must worship him in spirit and in truth. (vv. 21-24)

STEPHEN'S ACCUSERS SAY THAT HE "SPOKE AGAINST MOSES"

The accusers of Stephen then said that he blasphemed by speaking against Moses. What relation does Moses have to the promises and the revelation of God? Did God's promises terminate in him? Is Moses the great end and consummation of God's purposes of grace? Stephen in his apology said no. He said that following Moses there were kings, and to David the promise was made that he would have a greater son who would sit upon his throne forever. Then Stephen said that beyond Moses and beyond the kings there were the prophets of the Coming One:

> Rejoice greatly, O daughter of Zion; shout, O Daughter of Jerusalem: behold, thy King cometh unto thee: he is just, and having salvation: lowly, and riding upon an ass, and upon a colt the foal of an ass. (Zech. 9:9)

By no means does the consummation of the revelation of God end in the words of the great lawgiver, Moses. Then Stephen quoted from Moses himself. In Deuteronomy 18 we read:

> The LORD thy God will raise up unto thee a Prophet from the midst of thee, of thy brethren, like unto me; unto him ye shall hearken.
> I will raise them up a Prophet from among their brethren, like unto thee, and will put my words in his mouth; and he shall speak unto them all that I shall command him.
> And it shall come to pass, that whosoever will not hearken unto my words which he shall speak in my name, I will require it of him. (vv. 18-19)

Moses did not look upon himself as the final consummation of the redemptive purpose of God in the earth but he pointed to someone else who was yet to come.

Sometimes I think of the unusual interpretation that the apostle Paul gives to Moses in 2 Corinthians 3. In speaking of the descent of the great lawgiver from the top of Mount Sinai, the Bible says that "Moses wist not that his face shone." After forty days and nights in the presence of God, Moses reflected the shekinah glory of the Lord, and when he came down from the top of Mount Sinai his face shined. Then Paul says that Moses placed a veil over his face so that the children of Israel would not see that which was fading away. For a moment the light shined in the face of Moses, but it was a temporary and transitory shining. Moses put the veil over his face so that Israel might not see the fading glory as it passed away. The law was a schoolmaster to bring us to Jesus. Moses was a great teacher who pointed to Him who was yet to come. His ministry was temporal and transitory. For the people of the Jewish faith in Jerusalem to say that the great revelation of God found its consummation in Moses was to deny what Moses himself said, and to deny the history of the race.

STEPHEN'S ACCUSERS CLAIM THAT HE SPOKE "AGAINST GOD AND THE CUSTOMS" OF THE JEWISH PEOPLE

Third, the people accused Stephen of blasphemy because he spoke "against God and the *ethos* which Moses delivered unto us." The word *ethos* has been taken directly from Greek into English and refers to "the peculiar traits" of the people, to the "usages," "mores," and "customs" of a people. Out of all the nations and peoples of the earth, there was no race, tribe, or people who had an ethos, or custom in approaching God as uniquely as did the Jewish people. So the angry crowd accused Stephen of saying that God was going to change their rites and rituals.

Was that true? What relation do the customs of worship of the people have with the true worship of God? The apology of Stephen was that the rituals of Jewish worship were but types and pictures of the great truth of redemption that God would one day reveal in Christ Jesus. They were transitory and temporal and were given to the people that they might be taught the faith that was yet to be revealed in the Lord. Consequently, all of the sacrifices were pictures of the great sacrifice when Jesus died for our sins on the cross. These sacrifices in the temple could not suffice to wash away sins. They had to be repeated again and again because they were ineffectual. Their purpose was to point to Him who was the Lamb of God, who takes away the sin of the world. All of the feasts of the Jewish people such as the Passover were but pictures of Him who was offered for our sin in our stead; they were not an end in themselves.

The sanctuary itself was but a beautiful picture of God, teaching us about Him. The seven-branched lampstand depicted Jesus as the light of the world. The table of shewbread was but a picture of Jesus who is the manna, the bread of heaven. The veil between was but a picture of the Lord's flesh. When it was rent, when He was torn, through His death we were given access into the sanctuary of God.

Finally, these subject citizens were, if they refused the Lord, not even to belong to the kingdom of God. The kingdom would be taken from them and given to the Gentiles and would become a worldwide faith and a worldwide Christianity. Stephen had an astonishing intuition into the purposes of God in the Old Testament covenant.

Then Stephen came to his final allegation and accusation. He said to the people, "You make much of the rite of circumcision given to Abraham, but you yourselves are uncircumcised in heart and in soul. You make much of the Mosaic legislation, but you denied Him of whom Moses spake and you crucified Him, the Just One, the Son of heaven. You make much of the prophets, but you yourselves bear witness that you are children of the fathers who slew the prophets as you persecute God's witnesses today."

THE ACCUSERS' IMPLACABLE ANGER

When Stephen finished his defense, the Jews were infuriated. In bitterness and hatred, they violently seized him.

We are reminded of the like violent death of Savanarola, a man of tremendous unction, spirit, and prophecy. Threatened by the papal legate, he continued to announce the truth of almighty God. Then he was excommunicated. The messenger of excommunication read the fatal decree to Savanarola, closing it with the words, "I separate thee this day from the church militant and from the church triumphant." Savanarola replied, "From the church militant, yes, but from the church triumphant, never, because it is not in thy power to do so." Savanarola was seized, tortured, hanged on a gallows, and his body burned with fire.

So they did with Stephen. The angry crowd seized him and cast him out, but they could not separate him from God. They stoned him to death but they could not blot out his vision of heaven. They took away his life, but they could not take away his fellowship in the Lord Jesus, whose glorious face he saw as he was stoned. Stephen died in defense of the faith.

When I read Second Corinthians 4, I remembered that the people who stoned Stephen laid their garments down at the feet of a young man named Saul. He was a Cilician who had been in the synagogue disputing with Stephen and was humiliated because he was unable to resist the power and the wisdom by which Stephen spoke. How did the complete, long address of Stephen find its way into the Bible? Saul remembered every syllable and word of it and told it to Luke who wrote it down. Saul was there and saw the face of Stephen like the face of an angel and he was there when Stephen, dying on the ground, lifted up his face and saw Jesus standing at the right hand of the Majesty on high. I have often thought that it was out of that experience that he wrote this incomparable passage in the fourth chapter of 2 Corinthians:

> For God, who commanded the light to shine out of darkness, hath shined in our hearts, to give the light of the knowledge of the glory of God in the face of Jesus Christ.
>
> But we have this treasure in earthen vessels, that the excellency of the power may be of God, and not of us.
>
> We are troubled on every side, yet not distressed; we are perplexed, but not in despair;
>
> Persecuted, but not forsaken; cast down, but not destroyed;
>
> Always bearing about in the body the dying of the Lord Jesus, that the life also of Jesus might be made manifest in body.
>
> For which cause we faint not; but though our outward man perish, yet the inward man is renewed day by day.
>
> For our light affliction, which is but for a moment, worketh for us a far more exceeding and eternal weight of glory;
>
> While we look not at the things which are seen, but at the things which are not seen: for the things which are seen are temporal; but the things which are not seen are eternal. (4:6-11, 16-18)

The words of Stephen were hammers on Paul's heart. The vision that Stephen had of the Lord was one that Saul could never forget. Nor can we.

As Luke recounts this part of the Book of Acts, the apostles are not mentioned. But Stephen and his marvelous defense of the faith are carefully delineated. He was not an apostle; he was not a pastor, nor an ordained minister. Stephen was a layman, a deacon. He represented the great laity that won the Greco-Roman world to the Lord. For us to persuade ourselves that the kingdom of God is dependent upon the paid servant of Christ, the preacher, the pastor, the staff, or the missionary, is tragic indeed. The kingdom of God moves in the spirit of the laymen and the laywomen who make up the kingdom of our Lord. These mighty witnesses avow the truth of Christ as beautifully, powerfully, and gloriously as can be found in the ministry. I see a deep and everlasting meaning that the first martyr, the first man to lay down his life for Christ, was not Peter, nor James, nor John, nor any other apostle, but he was a layman defending the faith and sealing his defense with his blood. Such a witness will make any church great and any ministry strong. By the side of the minister stands a godly man witnessing to the truth.

O Master, that there might be an unconscious witness to the Lord in our living, our walking, our working, our coming, our going, our speaking, our uprising, and our downsitting, all of it flowing in a beautiful and wonderful way to the truths of Jesus!

33

The Blood of the Martyr Stephen

When they heard these things, they were cut to the heart, and they gnashed on him with their teeth.

But he, being full of the Holy Ghost, looked up stedfastly into heaven, and saw the glory of God, and Jesus standing on the right hand of God,

And said, Behold, I see the heavens opened, and the Son of man standing on the right hand of God.

Then they cried out with a loud voice, and stopped their ears, and ran upon him with one accord,

And cast him out of the city, and stoned him: and the witnesses laid down their clothes at a young man's feet, whose name was Saul.

And they stoned Stephen, calling upon God, and saying, Lord Jesus, receive my spirit.

And he kneeled down, and cried with a loud voice, Lord, lay not this sin to their charge. And when he had said this, he fell asleep. (Acts 7:54-60)

How beautiful was the providence that gave Stephen the name of *Stephanos*, the Greek word for "garland" or "crown," since this layman-deacon was the first one to receive from the hand of our Savior the martyr's crown!

STEPHEN TESTIFIED AS A CHRISTIAN OUGHT TO TESTIFY

Stephen testified as a Christian ought to testify—fearlessly, boldly, courageously, unflinchingly. He stood before the Sanhedrin and all of the leaders of the temple worship—the scribes, Pharisees, Sadduccees, officers, and leaders of the Jewish religion—and addressed himself to a subject that of all things in their minds was obnoxious and opprobrious. He was speaking in his defense of the temporary character

224

of all Jewish worship. To the Jewish people the Levitical law with its Mosaic legislation was forever. To the Jews their temple would stand until the end of the ages. It was *the* place in all the world that God had chosen for worship. The institutions that had been given to them by Moses were eternal and unchanging institutions. For Stephen to stand in the presence of the council and speak of the temporary and intermediate character of all of the Jewish ritual and worship in the temple was to their ears unthinkable blasphemy. Stephen stated that Moses himself was not the final word from God, but that Moses had pointed to Someone who should follow after him to whom the people were to listen. All of what Stephen said was, in the ears of his hearers, blasphemy.

Not only did Stephen fearlessly and courageously speak the truth of God regarding the temporary character of all the Mosaic legislation and the temporary character of the temple at Jerusalem, but he also confronted them with the same kind of castigation and condemnation John the Baptist did when he was preaching along the river Jordon. John called the people who came out to listen to his message "a generation of vipers," warning them to flee from the wrath to come, saying that the axe had already been laid at the root of the tree. If a person did not repent and find redemption in the coming Messiah, whom John said was in their midst, they also would be as lost as the heathen. In his preaching, John cast the entire race of Israel outside of the covenant of God, saying that, of these stones, God could raise up children to Abraham, and that they had to repent, get right with God, or they had no part in the kingdom. That was an astonishing doctrine to the Jew in that day as it is an astonishing doctrine to the Jew of today.

One time I listened to a learned rabbi in New York City who said, "The great difference between the Jew and the Christian is this: to us there is no need of salvation. Since we are the children of Abraham, we are saved. There is no such thing as having to be saved." But the preaching of John the Baptist and all those who followed after him was this: we all are sinners, Jew and Gentile, bond and free, male and female, and we must repent of our sins and find forgiveness in Christ Jesus. That was the preaching of Jesus Himself. Our Lord once addressed such words to these same people: "whited sepulchres, which indeed appear beautiful outward, but are within full of dead men's bones, and of all uncleanness" (Matt. 23:27). These are the men to whom Stephen addresses his climactic castigation:

> Ye stiffnecked and uncircumcised in heart and ears, ye do always resist the
> Holy Ghost: as your fathers did, so do ye.
>
> Which of the prophets have not your fathers persecuted? and they have slain
> them which shewed before of the coming of the Just One; of whom ye have been
> now the betrayers and murderers:
>
> Who have received the law by the disposition of angels, and have not kept it.
> (Acts 7:51-53)

Those are awesome words of condemnation and judgment! Should a man speak like that? Should a Christian tell the truth like that? You see, the reason that it is startling to us is that we do not do that. We don't seem to have the fearless courage in us today to stand before a sinful, gainsaying, and Christ-rejecting world. We mollify our witness and we compromise with the evil in the world. It is a rare man who will stand up and say the truth at a price. It is so much easier for us to say sweet, complimentary, and compromising words rather than oppose evil, unbelief, rejection, sin, wrong, and iniquity. The Lord said, "Woe unto you when all men speak well of you," when everyone has a tendency to praise you. The reason they do that is because you are not opposing their sin. You are not standing up for what is right and you are not presenting the truth of God as it is in Christ Jesus. It is almost unusual to hear someone stand up and say, "If you do not believe in the Lord Jesus Christ for the forgiveness of your sins, and if you do not repent and turn to Him, you will be damned in hell forever." Yet the Bible witnesses to that eternal truth from the beginning of the first verse in the Book of Matthew to the end of the benedictory prayer in the Revelation. It says that outside of Christ there is no salvation, that He alone is the Way, the Truth, and the Life. But Stephen wasn't afraid. He testified as a Christian ought to testify—boldly, courageously, and unflinchingly.

I often think how it characterizes the modern pulpit to be soft and compromising. I once heard an unusual story. A great service was being held in a church in which a number of visitors were present. A deacon was with the preacher of the evening just before the service began and he opened the door a bit to see who was seated in the congregation. He looked over the people and said to the speaker: "I see some Presbyterians here. Do not say anything about the Presbyterians." Then he saw some Methodists and said, "Do not say anything about the Methodists." Then he said, "I see a few Catholics. Do not say anything about the Catholics." Then he scanned the audience carefully and said: "I do not see a Mormon. Preacher, give 'em fits!"

What an insult to the truth of almighty God that we shape our message according to the response of the people who might be present to listen! God bless the man anywhere in the earth who declares the whole truth and the whole counsel of God!

STEPHEN DIED AS A CHRISTIAN OUGHT TO DIE

Second, Stephen died as a Christian ought to die—with a vision of heaven in his heart. He was executed according to Jewish custom. They deliberately planned the execution of the Lord Jesus because the Jews took it to the Roman procurator, since they did not have the power to use capital punishment. The Roman government had removed the power of capital punishment from Judaean hands. The death of Stephen was murder because the Jews took that power into their own hands. They never bothered to say anything one way or another to the officers of the Roman legion, much less to the Roman procurator, Pontius Pilate. This was something they did out of the bitterness of their hearts.

A Jewish execution was conducted like this. First, the witnesses went before the culprit and proclaimed aloud the crime of the victim. In the execution of Naboth when Jezebel suborned witnesses, they came together and cried in the city of Jezreel: "Naboth has blasphemed God! Naboth has cursed God!" Following those suborned witnesses and their testimony, the angry crowd stoned Naboth to death. This is what happened to Stephen. The witnesses angrily stated the charges before the criminal as they led him out of what in Jerusalem today is called St. Stephen's Gate, which leads on the east side down to the rocky bed of the Kidron Valley. After they arrived at the place of execution, the two main witnesses took the victim and hurled him down violently from the height of at least twelve feet, then they cast two great stones upon him, at which they paused for the culprit to confess his sin to God. Then the multitudes picked up the rocks and stoned the criminal. They paused for him once more to have opportunity to confess his crime to God before he died. Then they killed him summarily with heavy, hurled stones. Thus it was with Stephen. One can follow the outline of that execution exactly in the seventh chapter of Acts.

First, Stephen stood before the Sanhedrin. He suddenly beheld the council and all of the officers, guards, and leaders of the temple, all of the temple with its sturdiness and tremendous structure, and the Levites, the priests, the scribes, and the leaders all fade away as a part of the material world. Looking up into heaven, Stephen saw it open wide, rolled back like a scroll, and there at the throne of glory stood the Lord

Jesus Christ. "Behold," he cried, "I see the heavens opened, and the Son of man standing on the right hand of God." What a glorious vision when this world faded away and there before Stephen was the exalted and living Lord! Then the crowd seized Stephen and cast him out of the city, down to the Kidron Valley on the east side. There the witnesses went before Stephen, saying, "He has defamed Moses, he has cursed God, and he has blasphemed this holy place." The Bible says, "And the witnesses laid down their clothes at a young man's feet, whose name was Saul" (Acts 7:58b). They girded themselves to lift up Stephen and to hurl him down from the height and then to cast the two great stones upon him. As they did they paused for his confession before God, and this was Stephen's confession: "And they stoned Stephen, calling upon God, and saying, Lord Jesus, receive my spirit." Then the multitudes picked up stones, hurled them against him, and beat him down to his knees. He looked up and saw their murderous faces. Knowing that he soon would die, Stephen cried the prayer, "Lord, lay not this sin to their charge." And Stephen "fell asleep."

To "fall asleep" is the Christian way of describing the death of a sainted child of the Lord. We do not die and men cannot kill us. We fall asleep in Jesus. Let me show you how completely that has entered into our language.

The Greek word for "to fall asleep" is *koimao* and the Greek word for "a sleeping place" is *koimeterion*. When one takes the word for "sleeping place" and spells it in English the result is "cemetery." A cemetery is a Christian word invented by the Christian faith and message. We place our sainted dead not in a graveyard. We place them in a *koimeterion*, "a sleeping place." They have fallen asleep in the Lord and are awaiting the day when God will raise them up, awaken them. Stephen died as a Christian ought to die—with a vision of heaven in his heart.

STEPHEN'S INFLUENCE ENDURED AS A CHRISTIAN'S OUGHT TO ENDURE, MIGHTILY FOR GOD

Last, Stephen's life and influence endured as a Christian's life and influence always endure. The Christian life never fails, never fades, never falls into uselessness, vanity, futility, or frustration. God sees to that. Hebrews 11:4 says: ". . . he being dead yet speaketh." No word for Christ ever falls to the ground. It has its repercussion in the purposes of God and no life ever laid down for Christ was ever laid down in vain. God blesses that life.

It seemed as if Stephen's life was lost, stoned to death. But look what God did with it! Those who were crying the defamation and condemnation of Stephen laid down their clothes at the feet of a young man named Saul, a man from Cilicia. He was in the synagogue disputing with Stephen, and was unable to stand before the wisdom, the heavenly unction by which Stephen witnessed to the grace of God in Christ Jesus. Saul was the one who reported to Luke every syllable of this long address. Stephen's words burned like fire in his memory. Saul had presided over the martyrdom of Stephen.

Then a strange thing happened. It is often true that when a man is convicted, when he sees a truth that he does not like, he doubly wars against it. The truth is doubly hateful and bitter to him. Saul of Tarsus consented to Stephen's death and breathed out threatening and slaughter against the church. He haled into prison men and women; he persecuted the Christians in strange cities. Saul said that "he was exceedingly mad against them." Why? When the Lord appeared to Saul on the road to Damascus the Lord said, "Saul, Saul, it is hard for thee to kick against the pricks." What the Lord meant was this: Every time Saul got quiet, every time he was alone with just his soul and God, he relived that day in which he presided over the execution of Stephen. Saul never saw a man die like that man died with the light of heaven on his face. He never heard a man pray like that man prayed, asking God to forgive those who were stoning him to death, nor had he ever heard a man speak in the wisdom and unction of heaven as Stephen spoke in the Cilician synagogue. Saul, in the quiet of his life and in the nakedness of his soul, said to himself: "That which Stephen said was not true; it was blasphemy. Jesus is not the Son of God. What he said was a lie!" And then Saul's heart would say "But I remember Stephen's face. I remember how he died. I remember the words he said and the great apology he delivered from God's Holy Word!" Finally, when the Lord appeared to Saul, he said, "Lord, what will thou have me to do?"

In Acts 22, where Saul is standing before these same people years later recounting his conversion, he says, "I wanted to go back to Jerusalem and lay down my life in the place where I executed Stephen so that my blood could stain the same ground that his blood stained." You see, God never lets a faithful witness fail, or fall into futility to the ground. God blesses it forever as He did the testimony of Stephen.

You might ask me if I really believed that? Yes! No missionary has ever sacrificed for Christ on a foreign field but that God has seen and watched over him. There is not a missionary grave but that God has marked the spot. He saw him die and recorded the spot, though to us it is vain and futile how men lay down their lives in a nation like China or Angola. God blesses the sacrifice ultimately, and in ways we never know or realize.

A young man was told by the doctors that he could not go to the mission field. He was warned that if he were to go to the mission field he would immediately die. The young fellow replied, "But I am going." The doctors asked: "Why? You are not physically able to face the hardships of those assignments. You will certainly die. Why do you insist on going?" The young fellow answered: "Doctor, did you ever see a great bridge over a broad river? The reason the bridge is there and the reason it stands is because hidden in the earth below are large stones buried which no one sees. They are the foundation stones upon which the bridge rests. I am going to be one of those hidden, buried foundation stones." The boy went on into the mission field and he died as the doctors had warned, but God saw him and He marked the place.

A friend with whom I attended the seminary, and who was later president of our Southern Baptist Convention, recounted a story about a friend of his in college who gave his life to be a missionary. The young man trained in another country and was later appointed to the Belgian Congo. All during the time that his friend was training, the two corresponded regularly. Then, when the one went to the Congo, his letters stopped. My friend wondered what had happened. He learned that as his friend was going up to his mission station in the Belgian Congo, he contracted a jungle fever and died before he reached his destination. The natives buried him under a large spreading tree on the banks of the Congo River. My friend said to me, "When word came back to our school of what had happened to him, more than sixty men and women volunteered to take his place." Then he added, "When word came back to his home church that the man had died on the way to his mission station, thirteen boys and girls volunteered to prepare themselves to take his place."

God sees to it that any witness, any sacrifice, any word that we may offer to God never falls to the ground. God blesses and multiplies the witness forever.

O Lord, that there might be in us that faithful witness to what Jesus means to us and through us to a lost and judgment-bound world! The saving message of Christ has come to us at great cost. Men and women have laid down their lives that we might know the truth of the grace of God through Christ Jesus. Our Lord Himself died for our sins according to the Scriptures, was raised for our justification, and He waits in heaven for our obedience, love, worship, repentance, and faith in Him. O God, may we not disappoint You by not being there when the roll is called. Master, may it be that the sacrifice of the Son of God finds repercussion in my heart. May these who have brought the message of the grace of God find in us a willingness to answer with our lives.

34

Everywhere Preaching the Word

> Therefore they that were scattered abroad went every where preaching the word.
>
> Then Philip went down to the city of Samaria, and preached Christ unto them.
>
> And the people with one accord gave heed unto those things which Philip spake, hearing and seeing the miracles which he did.
>
> For unclean spirits, crying with loud voice, came out of many that were possessed with them: and many taken with palsies, and that were lame, were healed.
>
> And, there was great joy in the city. (Acts 8:4-8)

"They that were scattered abroad went every where preaching the word," in other words, the entire Christian community witnessed. They all were preachers, ministers, and missionaries testifying for the grace of God in Christ Jesus.

A young fellow was talking to a friend, trying to persuade him to be a witness for Christ. The one to whom appeal was being made belonged to a church which was called "hard-shell." They were not missionary-minded and did not engage in soul-winning. The young evangelist testified to the grace of God, and used the passage in Acts 8: "They that were scattered abroad went every where preaching the word." All of us are to be ministers of Christ, witnessing for the Lord. The young fellow being approached argued, "But that refers to the apostles. The Great Commission was given to the apostles. They were to go into all the world and preach the gospel to every creature, and they faithfully carried it out in their lifetime." Then the young evangelist said, "Would you read the first verse?" Acts 8:1 reads, "At that time there was a great persecution against the church which was at Jerusalem; and they were all scattered abroad throughout the regions of Judaea and Samaria, *except the apostles.*" The Aramaic-speaking, Palestinian Jews were not bothered. It was the foreign-born, Greek-speaking Jews who were harrowed out of the land, one of whom was Stephen, and who were bitterly and outrageously stoned to death.

All of us, not just the apostles, are to be witnesses to the grace of God in Christ Jesus. Do not ever persuade yourself that we will win the world to Christ by paid preachers and paid missionaries. It was never so, it is not so now, and it never will be so. The most dynamic and powerful period in the story of the Christian church is encompassed in the first three Christian centuries. That little band of believers, facing a world of idolatry and heathenism, won the entire civilized Greco-Roman empire to the Christian faith. How did they do that? They succeeded because all of the community of Christians were ministers, missionaries, and witnesses, such as Lydia of Thyatira. She was at Philippi, across the Hellespont. She is described as a "seller of purple." She was a drummer. In Thyatira they used beautiful dyes to make piece goods. I remember when I was a small boy that drummers used to come to our house, laying out their goods before my mother, a gifted seamstress, who would buy the piece goods and make pretty dresses. Lydia was like that. She was a seller of beautiful silks and piece goods and wherever she went in her journey she was a missionary, a witness to the grace of God.

Christian witnessing was especially well done by the soldiers. They accomplished far more than any one group to spread the knowledge of Christ and the Christian faith. A good example is Cornelius, who was the centurion of the Italian band located in Caesarea, the capital of the Roman province of Judaea. Wherever they went, the soldiers scattered the gospel message of Christ. They were all witnesses; and that is God's purpose for us. It is not just the paid preacher or the paid missionary, but all of us who are to be soul-winners and witnesses to the Lord Jesus.

An attorney was asked: "What do you do for a living? What is your job?" He replied, "I am an Attorney at Law to pay expenses, but my business is witnessing to and serving the Lord Jesus." That is the purpose of God in the lives of all in the Christian community.

THE PAID CLERGY ARE AT EASE IN ZION

There is something about the paid ministry that has a tendency to clothe itself in velvet and purple and to live inside a beautiful sanctuary behind stained glass windows and let the world outside of the four walls of the beautiful church die.

As a young man I remember the pastor of the First Baptist Church in Amarillo, a gifted and marvelous minister of the Word of God, resigning that affluent pulpit and going north to accept an assignment. The reason he resigned was that a survey had been made in the northern part of the United States and the official report was this: "There are seven thousand churches with seven thousand pastors who [that year] preached five hundred twenty-six thousand sermons without a single convert and without a single baptism." Can you imagine a harsher endictment against the clergy than that? The Amarillo pastor described a church which had a multi-million dollar plant, a large staff, and one of the most famous preachers in America, and the year before they had only two people come for baptism. Paid preachers and missionaries will never alone win the world to Christ. According to the Word of God, all Christians are to be missionaries, preachers, ministers, and witnesses to the truth of God in Christ Jesus. "They that were scattered abroad went every where preaching the word."

THE BLESSING OF TRAGEDY

God has a purpose in all suffering and tragedy. What is the tragedy in the story of Stephen? Is there purpose in the sadness and the horror that accompanied his death? In Acts 8:2 we read: "And devout men carried Stephen to his burial, and made great lamentation over him." The layman Stephen must have been a tremendous man of God. He was not an apostle nor a preacher; he was a deacon, but he spoke with such unction and power that his hearers were not able to withstand the wisdom by which he testified. He spoke in the synagogue of the Cilicians, and Saul was from the capital city of Cilicia, Tarsus. That is what burned the young man Saul; he was a theolog, a student in the school of Gamaliel, but under the power and unction of Stephen, Saul withered like burning grass. When Stephen was stoned to death in the fury of the rage of the people, Saul consented to his death. Stephen's fellow Christians made great lamentation over him as they buried him.

We read in the third verse, "As for Saul, he made havoc of the church, entering into every house, and haling men and women committed them to prison." This tragedy occurred a long time ago but two-thirds of the population of the world today would still not hesitate to do something like that. There are countless pastors and missionaries who are rotting in dungeons today behind the iron and bamboo curtains. I have heard men describe that knock at the door at two or three o'clock in the morning. This is what was happening in the church in Stephen's day, when men and women were committed to prison for their faith.

Look at this tragedy. "And at that time there was a great persecution against the church which was at Jerusalem . . . and they were all scattered abroad." God has a reason for every tear that is shed, every heartache that is felt, and every sorrow that overwhelms a man's life. There is no disappointment, no frustration, no despair, and no sadness in a man's life that does not have a purpose in it from the hand of God. In all sorrow and sadness God is speaking to us. Our happinesses? We praise God for them. Our joys? We thank the Lord for them. Our blessings that enrich and sustain our lives? We praise His name for them But it is in sadness, sickness, sorrow, and tragedy that God speaks to us. We need to listen to His voice. There is no tear that falls but the reason for it lies in some purpose of God for us.

One can easily see the purpose of God in the tragedy of Stephen unfolding in the Book of Acts. The church in Jerusalem must have been like heaven. They numbered already more than fifty thousand. The congregation had the apostles minister to them. Just think of listening to Peter preach in the power of the Holy Spirit. Imagine talking to John, the sainted apostle, who leaned on the breast of the Lord at the Lord's table at the Last Supper. Think of looking and listening to the apostles and seeing the wonders they did. Even the shadow of Peter falling upon the sick could heal them and raise them up. Imagine a church like that! It was as though the Lord had poured out upon them the greatest blessing that even God could bestow. But the Lord sent trouble and tragedy, martyrdom and death, persecution and havoc, and the church was scattered abroad.

In the next verse we read that in the scattering of the first church, "Philip went down to the city of Samaria, and preached Christ unto them" (Acts 8:5). Then he went down into Gaza and preached Jesus to the Ethiopian eunuch, the treasurer of the nation of Ethiopia. He was probably the first member of the Coptic church. In the next chapter we read of the conversion of Saul of Tarsus. He could not forget how Stephen spoke, how he prayed, and how he fell asleep in Jesus.

In the following chapters we read the story of the Hellenists as they scattered over the Roman empire, and finally came to Antioch preaching the Gospel. They were called *Christians* first in Antioch because of the tremendous effect they had upon that heathen Greek city. In Acts 13 we read of the beginning of the worldwide missionary movement under Paul (Saul) and Barnabas, the son of consolation; all of it arising out of the tragedy of the martyrdom of Stephen and the havoc and persecution that scattered that church in Jerusalem.

TRAGEDY SPEAKS TO US TODAY

I once stood before the baptistry of the William Carey Memorial Baptist Church in Calcutta, India. Beside the baptistry was a large, white marble plaque which bore an inscription stating that this was the place where Adoniram Judson, Ann Hasseltine Judson, and Luther Rice were baptized into the Baptist communion. They had been sent out by the Congregational Board of Missions as missionaries, but by the time they arrived in Calcutta, they said, "We are Baptists," and they were baptized in that church. Their being baptized in that manner cut them off from missionary support from the Congregational Board. The Baptists churches in America were little, feuding, fighting, debating groups up and down the eastern seaboard. It was agreed that Adoniram Judson and his wife would stay in India, finally in Burma, but Luther Rice would return to America with the story that God had given the Baptist communion missionaries to spread the gospel of Christ. Luther Rice organized the first convention of churches, the Triennial Convention, and he organized the first missionary support pulling those churches together in a great worldwide commitment. As I stood there thinking through the great commitment into which God led our Baptist people, I also went back in memory to the man, Adoniram Judson, whose father was pastor of the Congregational Church in Malden, Massachusetts.

The Judsons had sent their eldest son, Adoniram, to Providence College in Providence, Rhode Island, which is presently known as Brown University, our oldest Baptist university. During his college days Adoniram returned home and announced to his father and mother: "I am an infidel. I do not believe in God and I certainly do not believe in Christ, and less do I believe in the church. I have come to tell you that I renounce the faith." What had happened was that a brilliant infidel, Elbert Winthrop, had persuaded Adoniram to give up the faith and to renounce the Lord. The announcement shocked his father, pastor of the church, and broke the heart of his mother. His father pleaded with him and his mother cried. But he announced to them as an infidel: "I am leaving home. I am going to see the world."

So Adoniram Judson left home feeling in his heart: "I can answer every argument of my father. I am an infidel." Then he had to admit that the tears of his mother bothered him. He braced himself and thought, "What would Elbert Winthrop think of me if he knew of my sentimental weakness in that my mother's tears were heavy on my heart?" So he went out from his father's house, from the faith, from the church, and from God, and lived a prodigal and debauched life as he said, "seeing the world."

As he journeyed through the northern states, he came one evening to a country inn and asked the landlord if he might stay there for the night. The landlord said: "Yes, I have a room, but in the room next to it a man is dying. Would it bother you?" Judson replied: "Ha! Bother me? I am not afraid of death. All I feel is pity for the poor creature who is dying. I will take the room."

Through the hours of the night he listened to the agony, the cries, and the convulsions of the man in the next room. Try as hard as he could, he was unable to get that man out of his heart and out of his mind. "Is he ready to die, is he ready to meet God? Who is he? Is he a Christian?" Then Judson caught himself and thought, "What would Elbert Winthrop think about me if he knew that I was thinking these thoughts?"

The next morning when Judson dressed, the first thing he did was to seek out the landlord and ask, "The man in the next room, how is he?" The landlord replied, "Sir, he is dead." Judson asked, "Did you know who he was?" "Yes," said the landlord, "he was a young fellow from Providence College." Judson cried, "Providence College? What was his name?" The landlord answered, "His name was Elbert Winthrop."

It took Adoniram Judson an hour to think connectedly, to get his thoughts in order. He was astonished and awestruck. He fell on his face and asked God to forgive him. Then he went back to his mother and father. He made a confession of faith in the church and was received into membership. He enrolled in Andover Theological Seminary, was appointed our first missionary, and in Calcutta, India was baptized into the Baptist communion.

Out of sorrow, agony, tears, crying, and death God speaks to us. There is always a message in every memorial service that we attend. There is a message in every funeral procession going down the city streets. There is a message in every illness that one endures and in every tear that falls from one's eyes. God is speaking, and there is a purpose and meaning in God's hand moving in the tragedies that we see and sustain in our lives. Blessed is he who, like Adoniram Judson, falls before Jesus, saying: "Lord God, forgive me. I am not an infidel. I may have thought I was; it may have been suggested to me. I may have listened to arguments on infidelity, but I am no infidel. I believe in God, I believe in Jesus Christ who died for my soul, and I believe that some day I will see His face." That is what it is to be a Christian and accept the Lord as Savior.

35

In Memoriam (Christian Grief)

And devout men carried Stephen to his burial, and made great lamentation over him. (Acts 8:2)

First, let us look at the different reactions to the martyrdom of Stephen. There were those who looked upon his stoning as a measure and an achievement of triumph. His executioners congratulated themselves. They could not stand in the presence of the wisdom and power by which Stephen witnessed to the grace of God in Christ Jesus. So, unable to answer him, the angry crowd carried him violently outside the city wall and stoned him to death. They were proud of what they had done, triumphant in their attitude, and glad for their achievement. An example of that gloating attitude can be seen in Saul at whose feet the furious mob laid down their garments when they rained their stones against Stephen. Saul was even more bitter against Stephen, the Lord, and the church, having seen the blood of the martyr taken up by the ground. "He made havoc of the church, entering into every house, and haling men and women committed them to prison" (Acts 8:3). Saul says that when they were put to death, he cast his vote against them. Having martyred, slain, and stoned him to death, the death of Stephen was to the crowd like blood to a hungry wolf. The anger of the Jews toward their own brethren who were embracing Christianity became all-consuming. An example of that spreading bitterness can be seen in the twelfth chapter of Acts. We read that when Herod saw that the Jews were pleased when he killed James the brother of John, he proceeded further to take Peter also. This was one reaction to the martyrdom of Stephen.

But here is another reaction. In the text of our message today we read, "And devout men carried Stephen to his burial, and made great lamentation over him" (Acts 8:2). These who cried over the death of Stephen were the children of God. They are those who were redeemed by the blood of Christ, had been baptized into the faith, and belonged to the church of Jerusalem. "They made great lamentation over him." The word translated as "lamentation" is an impressive and intense word. There is a New Testament word *kopto*, which means "to cut off" or "to cut down like a tree." The word came to be applied to those who in great agony cut themselves and beat their breasts. The substantive form of the verb is *kopitos* which is a descriptive word of deep intensity describing grief that is immeasurable. *Kopitos* refers to "beating the breast"; wailing, lamenting, and crying before the Lord. The word *kopitos* is preceeded by the word *megale* which means "intense," "great." "And devout men carried Stephen to his burial, and made intense lamentation, grieving in an immeasurable sorrow over him." When a person dies he may mean nothing to some people, and yet to others he may be like life and breath itself.

For example, suppose that in a battle only one soldier was killed. That would be a marvelous victory, an incomparable triumph! But think about the mother of that slain boy. Think of the sweetheart or the wife of that boy. To us it would be a victory because only one life was lost. But to a mother, what a tragedy!

In World War II, I remember a comment made when a boy who belonged to our church was killed in the Pacific. The comment was this: "For that mother, the war is over." What is nothing or less than nothing to one person may, to someone else, be prized and dear beyond any way that one could describe it. When Mary Magdalene saw the sepulchre empty, she turned to a man thinking him to be the gardener and said: "Where have you laid His body? Tell me and I will take it away." To others, He was just dust and ashes, but to Mary Magdalene, He was a Savior most precious.

The executioners of Stephen congratulated themselves for such a triumph in encompassing his death, but other devout men carried him to his burial and made great lamentation over him. That leads me to speak about Christian grief, the tears that come to our hearts in sorrow over those who have passed away.

IS IT CHRISTIAN TO GRIEVE?

Is it all right for a Christian to weep, be grieved and in sorrow over the death of those we have loved and lost for awhile? Is it Christian to grieve or to cry? Many people would say: "Absolutely not. Under no condition is the Christian ever to grieve, to shed tears over those who have passed away."

I well remember as a boy, a family who belonged to a fellowship that does not believe that a Christian should grieve. The husband in the family died suddenly of a heart attack. His wife wept uncontrollably and those of the communion to which she belonged gathered around her and said: "Dry your tears. There is no such thing as death. That is in your mind, like sickness." As a little boy I watched in amazement as they persuaded her not to cry. She dried her tears, pranced around the house, and the death of her husband from then until he was buried in the ground was flippantly accepted. What a profound impression that experience made upon me as a boy!

What about Christian grief? Does it advance our faith when we cry and lament over these who have passed away? Let us look at the tears of Jesus.

In the story of Jesus standing at the tomb of Lazarus we find the shortest verse in the Bible, literally translated, "Jesus burst into tears." In the King James version the translation is, "Jesus wept." He was sorrowing at the grave of Lazarus even though He knew He was to raise him from the dead.

When Jesus came to the brow of Olivet, seeing Jerusalem before Him, He wept over the city, saying:

> O Jerusalem, Jerusalem, . . . how often would I have gathered thy children together, as a hen doth gather her brood under her wings, and ye would not! Behold, your house is left unto you desolate . . . . (Luke 13:34-35)

Our Lord wept one other time in Gethsemane, ". . . with strong crying and tears unto him that was able to save him from death" (Heb. 5:7). Jesus wept and lamented.

We can speak of the tears of Paul. Three times in his address to the Ephesian elders, recounted in Acts 12, Paul said that he cried, that he wept many tears. In 2 Corinthians 2 Paul said, "For out of much affliction and anguish of heart I wrote unto you with many tears" (2 Cor. 2:4). In the last letter Paul ever wrote, the second letter to Timothy, he says to his son in the ministry, ". . . being mindful of thy tears" (1:4).

And then there were the tears of Simon Peter. While he was cursing the Lord, denying that he ever saw or knew Him, the Lord turned and looked upon Peter, and the Bible says, "And Peter went out, and wept bitterly" (Luke 22:62). The look of Jesus crushed him.

We also read of the tears of the sainted apostle John in the fifth chapter of the Apocalypse when search was made in heaven, in earth, beneath the earth, and in the nether world for someone able to break the seals and to open the book and look on it. John writes, "And I wept much, because no man was found worthy to open and to read the book, neither to look thereon" (v. 4). Then one of the elders speaks to him and says, "Weep not: behold, the Lion of the tribe of Juda, the Root of David, hath prevailed to open the book, and to loose the seven seals thereof" (v. 5). Christian tears.

TEARS AND GRIEF IN THE BIBLE

Notice also in the Bible how those who loved God grieved over those who had been translated. In 2 Samuel 18, David cried and said, "O my son Absalom, my son, my son Absalom! would God I had died for thee, O Absalom, my son, my son!" (v. 33). He wept over the death of his son.

Naomi wept over the death of her husband. When she returned to Bethlehem-judah, having lost in death her husband Elimelech and her two sons in Moab, the town was stirred, saying, "Is not this Naomi, who has been gone so many years?" In the first chapter of Ruth we read: "And she said unto them, Call me not Naomi ["pleasantness, happiness"], call me Mara ["bitterness"]: for the Almighty hath dealt very bitterly with me" (v. 20).

And Jacob wept because of the death of his wife. We read in the Book of Genesis that the midwife said to Rachel, "Fear not; thou shalt have this son also" (35:17). But Rachel died in giving birth to that little boy, and as she died she named him *Ben-oni*, that is, "the son of my sorrow." But Jacob said, "He shall not be called *Ben-oni*; he shall be called *Benjamin*, the son of my right hand," and Jacob built there a pillar over the grave of Rachel.

Jeremiah wept for a nation. Jeremiah 9:1 begins: "Oh that my head were waters, and mine eyes a fountain of tears, that I might weep day and night for the slain of the daughter of my people!" In the second chapter of Lamentations we read: "Their heart cried unto the Lord, O wall of the daughter of Zion, let tears run down like a river day and night" (v. 18). There are Christian tears of grief and suffering.

That is why God's people do so many things in memory of those whom we have loved and lost for awhile, and whom we believe in Christ we shall see again.

Alfred Lord Tennyson wrote his incomparably great poem and entitled it "In Memoriam to A. H. H." It was written in memory of Arthur Henry Hallam, a friend who had suddenly died.

In our church we have a Hall of Memories in which are seen hundreds of plaques in memory of those whom we have loved and who are now in heaven. I placed the first plaque in the Hall of Memories in memory of my father. Next to it the church placed a plaque in memory of its great pastor, Dr. George W. Truett. Along with those plaques there are scores of other plaques given in memory of those who have preceded us to heaven.

Is it right for the Christian to weep? Is it right for the Christian to grieve? Is it right for the Christian to be sad because of a separation from those who have been taken away from us?

The answer is yes. It is right. Christ cried those tears. Paul cried those tears. Peter wept those tears. John wept those tears. The saints of the Bible wept those tears, and we weep them, too. The only thing is this: Paul admonishes us, "that ye sorrow not, even as others which have no hope" (1 Thess. 4:13). Beyond our tears is the triumphant grace of God extended to us in Christ Jesus. He is more than life, He is resurrection itself, He is heaven itself to us. These memorials are to bring to us the promise that we have in Him. The Lord's Supper is a memorial of His death, of His compassion, of His atonement for our sins on the cross, bringing back to our hearts the memory of His sobs, His tears, His blood, and His death. "For as oft as you eat this bread and drink this cup, ye do memorialize the death of our Lord."

God has provided some better thing for us. There is the day of resurrection, the day of the coming of our Lord, the day of the opening of the sky, the day of the gates of glory, the day of the rendezvous of God's redeemed in heaven. Beyond our tears, our sorrow, and our lamentation there is triumph, glory, and resurrection. This is the Christian faith. We may cry now, we may weep now in sorrow over those who have been taken away, but beyond our tears is the glorious restoration, the resurrection which will give back again those whom we have loved and lost for awhile. It is Christian to love, to remember, to dedicate ourselves to God in a new way, to treasure in heart forever the memory of those who have preceded us into heaven.

36

Philip the Evangelist

Then Philip went down to the city of Samaria, and preached Christ unto them.

And the people with one accord gave heed unto those things which Philip spake, hearing and seeing the miracles which he did.

For unclean spirits, crying with loud voice, came out of many that were possessed with them: and many taken with palsies, and that were lame, were healed.

And there was great joy in that city. (Acts 8:5-8)

There was a reason why Philip went down to Samaria. A tremendous and tragic persecution arose against the church in Jerusalem and the Hellenistic Christians, the Greek-speaking Jews, were scattered abroad. Saul led that persecution bringing havoc to the church.

We read in verse 5, "Then Philip went down to the city of Samaria." There are two reasons for the successful ministry of Philip in Samaria. First, the Samaritans looked with contempt and hatred on the Jew, so the high priest in Jerusalem had no jurisdiction in Samaria. When Philip went down to Samaria, he had an open opportunity to preach Christ to the Samaritans. Another reason why the revival led by this deacon in Samaria was so successful was because of the previous ministry of our Lord there. We read in John 4, "And he must needs go through Samaria" (v. 4). There our Lord spoke to the Samaritan woman and the whole city of Sychar came out to see Him and believed in Him. Therefore, Philip had a wonderful open door to proclaim the message of Christ in Samaria.

THE MESSAGE HE PREACHED—JESUS

Notice the message that Philip preached. "Then Philip went down to the city of Samaria, and preached Christ unto them." Later when the Holy Spirit sent Philip down into the desert, he was standing along the road when the chariot of the treasurer of Ethiopia passed by. God said to Philip, "Join thyself to this chariot" (v. 29). The Ethiopian eunuch was reading aloud the fifty-third chapter of Isaiah. We read in Acts 8:

> And the eunuch . . . said,
> I pray thee, of whom speaketh the prophet this? of himself, or of some other man?
> Then Philip opened his mouth, and began at the same scripture, and preached unto him Jesus. (vv. 34-35)

Is that not a wonderful description of the assignment given to the man who stands in a pulpit, who witnesses by the wayside, or who speaks to a friend? "Philip went down to the city of Samaria, and preached Christ unto them." What should be the content of the message of a man who is sent from God? He may speak about many things of passing interest—book reviews, current events, all sorts of subjects. If a minister wants to preach about contemporary events all he needs to do is to subscribe to *Reader's Digest* or *U. S. News and World Report* and he can have his sermons Sunday after Sunday.

But who wants to go to church to hear a rehashing of all of the things that are discussed by the commentators on radio and television, by all the current magazines, and by the editorial pages and the headlines of the newspapers every day? What we long for and seek is a word from God. Does the Lord have anything to say? Is there a message from heaven?

This was the substance of the preaching of the men in the New Testament. "And he preached unto him Jesus." They preached Jesus born of a virgin; Jesus in His ministry in Galilee and Judaea, Jesus dying for our sins on the cross; Jesus buried and raised the third day from the dead; Jesus ascending into heaven; Jesus in His intercession at the throne of grace; Jesus coming again to judge the living and the dead. The message always is Jesus.

There is something marvelous about a man who preaches the Lord Jesus. If he were to stand in a pulpit and preach about economics, politics, cultural revolution, book reviews, or any other thing of passing and current events, his people might attend once. A few of them might return a second time, but it wouldn't be long and there would be no one

present. The church would be empty. But when a man preaches Jesus
the people return again and again. The preaching of Jesus is manna for
our hungry souls and water of life for our thirsting spirits. The marvel of
the Spirit of God that works in the preached message of the Lord Jesus is
a phenomenon to behold.

John Newton is a marvelous example of this. He was born in 1725.
He was a friend of William Cowper, the great English poet who wrote
such marvelous hymns as "There Is a Fountain Filled With Blood."
They both lived in a little English town called Olney. Together they
published a book of Christian hymns, one of which, written by John
Newton, is "Amazing Grace, How Sweet the Sound."

John Newton was an orphan. His mother died when he was a small
boy, and his father was a sea captain. Newton, likewise, went to sea, and
fell into the most prodigal and profligate of all lives. He was finally
impressed into the British navy, was a deserter, and flayed. He eventu-
ally sold himself to a slave trader in Africa and fell the lowest a man
could descend. There was nothing more debauched, nothing more
iniquitous, nothing more vile and wicked than the life into which John
Newton fell. Then he found the incomparable grace of God in Christ
Jesus. Here is a poem that he wrote of his marvelous conversion:

> I saw One hanging on a tree
>   In agony and blood;
> He fixed His languid eyes on me
>   As near His cross I stood.
>
> Sure, never, till my latest breath,
>   Can I forget that look:
> It seemed to charge me with His death,
>   Tho' not a word He spoke.
>
> My conscience felt and owned the guilt,
>   And plunged me in despair;
> I saw my sins His blood had spilt
>   And helped to nail Him there.
>
> Alas! I knew not what I did—
>   But now my tears are vain:
> Where shall my trembling soul be hid?
>   For I the Lord have slain.
>
> A second look He gave, which said,
>   "I freely all forgive:
> This blood is for thy ransom paid,
>   I die that thou may'st live."

> Oh, can it be, upon a tree
> The Savior died for me?
> My soul is thrilled, my heart is filled,
> To think He died for me.

What a sweet testimony!

The inscription on John Newton's grave in the little town of Olney in England reads: "John Newton; once an infidel and libertine, a servant of slaves in Africa, was by the rich mercy of our Lord and Saviour Jesus Christ preserved, restored, pardoned, and appointed to preach the faith he had long labored to destroy." Is that not like heaven? No wonder a man like that could write "Amazing Grace, how sweet the sound that saved a wretch like me." There is power in the gospel. There is converting ableness of God in the name of Jesus our Lord. That is the message that the deacon-layman Philip preached.

THE ORDINANCE HE CALLED HIS PEOPLE TO OBEY

Now let us look at the ordinance that Philip called his people to obey. We read in verse 12: "But when they believed Philip preaching the things concerning the kingdom of God, and the name of Jesus Christ, they were baptized, both men and women." Now we begin reading at verse 36:

> And as they went on their way, they came unto a certain water: and the eunuch said, See, here is water; what doth hinder me to be baptized?
> And Philip said, If thou believest with all thine heart, thou mayest. And he answered and said, I believe that Jesus Christ is the Son of God.
> And he commanded the chariot to stand still: and they went down both into the water, both Philip and the eunuch; and he baptized him.
> And when they were come up out of the water, the Spirit of the Lord caught away Philip, that the eunuch saw him no more: and he went on his way rejoicing. (Acts 8:36-39)

The ordinance that Philip called his converts to obey was baptism. "See, here is water; what doth hinder me to be baptized?"

After fifty years of being a pastor, I believe that if a person is truly converted he will say: "I have found the Lord. I want to be baptized." John said that he received the ordinance from heaven. It is God who invented baptism. The first time anyone saw a man take another man and baptize him was when *Ioannes ho Baptistes*, "John, the one who baptizes," did it. There were as many Johns in that day as there are Johns today, but this is the John who did something the world had never seen before. He baptized men. The Jews had many ablutions; they washed their feet, hands, heads, and bodies; they washed their pots and pans.

But they did it themselves. The first time the world ever saw a man take another man and baptize him was when John did it. John said he received the pattern from Heaven. Jesus said John's baptism was from heaven, and He incorporated it into the Great Commission: "Go ye therefore, and teach all nations, baptizing them in the name of the Father, and of the Son, and of the Holy Ghost" (Matt. 28:19). The apostles faithfully carried out that commission. There is no instance in the Bible but that those who accepted the Lord were baptized. When the Jewish people cried at Pentecost, "What shall we do?" we read:

> Then Peter said unto them, Repent, and be baptized every one of you in the name of Jesus Christ [eis, because of] the remission of sins, and ye shall receive the gift of the Holy Ghost. (v. 38).

This was the first response of the Ethiopian treasurer. "See, here is water; what doth hinder me to be baptized?" "I have accepted the Lord as my Savior; I want to be baptized just as God has commanded in the Book."

FAITHFULNESS TO GOD'S COMMAND IN BEING BAPTIZED

Sometimes the Holy Spirit will lead a person to do some unusual things, that when one looks at them theologically, they would be quite hard to defend. Yet, under the circumstances, that action is most blessed of God.

In one of my village churches there was a man who owned the general store. He was not a Christian. I visited and prayed with him, read the Bible, and made an appeal to his heart. One Sunday he came down the aisle. He stood at the end of the first pew. I went over to him and he gave me his hand, saying: "I receive the Lord Jesus as my Savior. I ask Him to forgive my sins, and I want to be a Christian." I replied: "Wonderful! Come and be seated here." He said, "No, I have said all my life that I will not sit on that front pew as a penitent and I will not be baptized." I said to him, "Then you cannot be saved."

Theologically, that is not true. Is it sitting on the front row that saves a man? Is it the water baptism that washes our sins away? No, it is Christ and He alone who saves us. It is the blood that washes us from our sins. And yet I said to that man: "If you do not come down here and sit on the front row, and if you do not receive the ordinance of baptism, you cannot be saved. If you turn around and go back, you will go back a lost sinner."

The man was astonished at that word, especially since he was much older than I. He stood at the end of the front pew, and I could see in his face the war in his soul. I think that had he gone back, he would have been a lost man. If a man is right in his soul and he has really given his heart to Jesus, he will be glad to come down before men and angels anywhere in the world and confess his faith. To receive the ordinance of baptism is something that his heart longs for.

That man fought the battle in his heart that day and he won it, praise God! He came all the way with me and sat down and we prayed together. Then I introduced him to the church as a new convert and as a candidate for baptism, and I baptized him. The last time I saw him, he was superintendent of the Sunday school in the church and he was a leader of the Brotherhood in that part of the state.

What I told that man would be hard to defend theologically, but empirically, it is God's truth. When a man is really saved, he is happy to confess the name of the Lord Jesus. "I have found Him dear and precious to my soul, and I want to be baptized."

THE SPIRIT OF PHILIP'S CONVERTS

Look at the spirit of Philip's converts. We read in Acts 8:39: "And when they were come up out of the water, the Spirit of the Lord caught away Philip, that the eunuch saw him no more: and he went on his way rejoicing."

> Then Philip went down to the city of Samaria, and preached Christ unto them.
> And the people with one accord gave heed unto those things which Philip spake, hearing and seeing the miracles which he did.
> And there was great joy in that city. (Acts 8:5-6, 8)

There is no one who has the ability to deceive us like Satan. I marvel at his astute genius of misrepresentation. Satan will take a young person and he will whisper in his or her ear: "Do not give your heart to Jesus. Think of all the good times you are going to miss. Think of all the wonderful things in the world that you will never enjoy if you give your heart to Jesus and if you become a Christian. There are many things in the world that are fun, happy, experiential, and wonderful."

There was never a bolder lie or a deeper deception than that. There is no gladness in the world like life in Christ. There is no bitter aftertaste. There is no dark hangover. There is no remorse. There is no "Would to God I were dead." If I were looking for people who were candidates for suicide, I would look in the world that is given to the glitter of the sin and the debauchery that the world could afford. One need not look in the church at God's people. The happiest people in the world are God's people. These are the people who have found life and found it abundantly. The good life is the happy life, the Christian life. "And he went on his way rejoicing."

One of the songs that we sing in Vacation Bible School goes like this:

> On Sunday I am happy,
> On Monday full of joy,
> On Tuesday I have peace within
> That nothing can destroy;
>
> On Wednesday and on Thursday
> I'm walking in the light,
> O Friday is a heaven below,
> And Saturday's always bright.
>
> O glory, glory, glory,
> O glory to the Lamb!
> O Hallelujah! I am saved
> And I'm so glad I am!
>
> O glory, glory, glory,
> O glory to the Lamb!
> O Hallelujah! I am saved
> And bound for the happy land.

As I look at the little boys and girls as they sing that song, I think in my heart, "Would to God I could keep them all in the faith and they would never know sin and the seamy side of life, but that all of their days would be happy, bright, and full of joy."

O God, before I am translated to heaven, I importune that I could see a great, moving revival. I have seen a city that is simply caught up in the fever of a great athletic contest, such as a football game. The whole population is moved by it. I have seen a city caught up in a political campaign, simply ablaze with interest. Lord, may the day come when a great revival will sweep thousands and hundreds of thousands into the kingdom of God, when people will rejoice down every street, speak about Jesus in every home, talk about the Lord in every business transaction. May a real revival come that the people may always be happy and rejoice in the Lord.

37

The Joyful Way

Then Philip went down to the city of Samaria, and preached Christ unto them.

And the people with one accord gave heed unto those things which Philip spake, hearing and seeing the miracles which he did.

For unclean spirits, crying with loud voice, came out of many that were possessed with them: and many taken with palsies, and that were lame, were healed.

And there was great joy in that city. (Acts. 8:5-8)

In this chapter we shall look at Philip the soul-winner, Philip the evangelist, as it is recorded for us in the eighth chapter of Acts. There is more in that passage in its wording than at first we might suppose. We shall first look at what the Holy Spirit has written down on the sacred page.

"And the people with one accord gave heed unto those things which Philip spake, hearing and seeing" the *semeia*, "signs," translated here "miracles," which is an acceptable translation, but *semeia* literally means "signs." These were signs of God confirming the truth of the Word. Any time a sign is needed to confirm God's message and messenger, God will always provide that sign.

"For," and then the passage describes some of those signs: "unclean spirits, crying with loud voice." This possibly refers to the cry of those who were delivered just as the spirit in agony was dismissed from the person who was oppressed by an unclean demon. But I feel there might be another interpretation as I study the text. Look at the passage which says "hearing and seeing the miracles [signs] which he did." Is that not an unusual construction? "Hearing the signs." One does not hear a sign;

251

he usually *sees* a miracle. But the Holy Spirit writes, "hearing the signs which he did." "For unclean spirits, crying with loud voice." Let us put those words together.

The word used here for crying, *boao*, can mean "a cry of agony," but the first meaning is "a shout of joy and deliverance." "With a loud voice" in Greek is *megale*, "a great, intense" voice. When one combines all of those words the meaning is this: Philip preached Jesus to those who were possessed with unclean spirits (lust, hatred, iniquity, sinful ways), and as they were delivered they shouted their joy of salvation (crying, *boao*, "shouting for joy"). That is why the Holy Spirit writes "the people *heard* the signs." There was a great exaltation as those who were possessed were delivered, saved, and brought into the life and glory of the Lord. "And there was great joy, *kara*." There is a little family of words in the Greek New Testament that are similar—*kara*, "joy"; *karis*, "grace"; *karisma*, "a grace gift"; and *karismata*, the plural form. The name Karen is the accusative form of *karis*; "grace, joy." One of the meanings of *kara* is "an exalted gladness in the Lord." One of the meanings of *karis*, "grace," which is one of the most beautiful words in both Greek and English, is "a beautiful spirit and attitude," "a marvelous overflowing heart." "And there was *megale*, intense joy [gladness of deliverance and salvation], in that city." The whole story is one of marvelous visitation, heavenly intervention, and revival.

Our Scripture passage speaks of the preaching of Philip and the casting out of the unclean spirits of those who were possessed. They were delivered by the regenerating power of the Spirit of Jesus. They cried out for joy when they were delivered: "And there was great joy in that city."

Satan has his minions who are just like him. According to the Bible, "Satan turns into an angel of light." The fallen angels, the demons, the evil and unclean spirits, are just like their master, Satan. They purport to be angels of light and they come to us and say to us: "Did God say there were certain things you shouldn't do and certain things you should do? Did he say that if you disobey Him judgment would follow? Ha! God's way is a dead, dreary way. Come, follow me!" So we are tempted, led astray, and deceived by what the Bible calls "unclean spirits," these little angels of light who dance lightly before us.

It looks that way, doesn't it? The world is so interesting and its glamour and light so wooingly enticing. But God's way is that judgment always follows Satan's deceptions and devices. God created life so that when we follow in His will and way we are happy, we have peace and blessing, but when we violate His will, and when we fall into sin and iniquity, a judgment of agony and ultimate death goes with it.

It is like Rudyard Kipling's great poem, *The Jungle.*

> This is the law of the jungle,
> As old and as true as the sky.
> The wolf that shall keep it may prosper,
> But the wolf that shall break it shall die.

God put this world together in a certain way and when we violate that way, when unclean spirits entice and deceive us from it, agony and judgmental death follows, but when we keep God's way, we are delivered, we are at peace, and we are happy in Him.

We now shall choose some things in which vile and evil spirits deceive us. First, we will look at what God says, second, at what Satan says and what these evil spirits entice us to do; third, the agony that follows when we are deceived; and fourth, the glory of it when we are delivered, when we follow in the way of the Lord. We shall examine four things in which Satan seeks to deceive us.

SATAN DECEIVES US IN COURTSHIP AND MARRIAGE

First, Satan deceives us in courtship and marriage. There is nothing in life in which the unclean spirits present themselves as messengers of light, fun, and happiness in such a deceiving manner as in courtship and marriage. As young people enter young manhood and young womanhood they become interested in someone else, and this interest comes from God. The Lord says, "Therefore shall a man leave his father and mother, and shall cleave unto his wife; and they two shall be one flesh" (Gen. 2:24). The Lord affirmed that in the nineteenth chapter of Matthew.

> And he answered and said unto them, Have ye not read, that he which made them at the beginning made them male and female,
> And said, For this cause shall a man leave father and mother, and shall cleave to his wife: and they twain shall be one flesh. (vv. 4-5)

The unclean spirits scornfully reply: "Ha, did God say that? Look at the fun you are missing. There is nothing more interesting than to play with sex. To be pure and virtuous is to miss all the fun of life. Come now! Don't be prudish and square. If God said that, he was giving you a dull, drear, drab way of life!"

So the girl is used and prostituted, and the boy is faithless and an adulterer. God's judgment that follows is inevitable because God put this world together a certain way, and when we violate His law, that violation always brings agony and death.

One could say: "Look at the saints in the Old Testament. They had more than one husband or wife." But the Lord said that was permitted because of the "hardness of your hearts." Still it violated the will of God. And the result was trouble and agony.

Abraham loved Sarah and Sarah loved Abraham, but out of an unusual situation Hagar was given to Abraham, and out of that union Ishmael was born. To this day the world confronts the judgment of that terrible sin, the confrontation between the Jew, the children of Isaac, and the Arab, the children of Ishmael.

David, the man after God's own heart, looked upon Bathsheba and committed adultery with her. The Lord's prophet Nathan told David that the sword would never depart from his house, and thereafter the story of David is written in blood to this present day.

Solomon with his many wives divided the kingdom, gave to his successor a divided kingdom which was never again united. God said to Solomon, "If you will obey Me, I will give you length of days." But Solomon was cut down in the strength of his manhood and of his kingdom.

You see, these evil spirits entice us, woo us, and they purport to be angels of light in showing us a happier way. There is no happy way but the Christian way. If that is not true, then there is no God and one need not worry about anything. People can live like dogs. But there is a God, and He has fashioned life in such a way that by following His way and will there is gladness, peace, blessedness, and joy. "For unclean spirits, crying with loud voice, came out of many that were possessed with them. . . . And there was great joy in that city" (Acts 8:7a-8).

There is nothing finer in the world than to see a pure young man fall in love with a virtuous girl and stand in the presence of the pastor and pledge to one another a covenant of love that shall bind them as one forever. That is God's way, and it is a happy and a beautiful way.

Satan Deceives Us in Our Bodies

Second, what does God say about the body? He says that the body is the temple of the Holy Spirit; it is God's house. The Holy Spirit of Jesus dwells in this house. Paul said, "I beseech you therefore, brethren, by the mercies of God, that ye present your bodies a living sacrifice, holy, acceptable unto God, which is your reasonable service" (Rom. 12:1).

This is the finest discipline a man can observe. What do these evil spirits purporting to be the angels of light say? "Ha, so God says you are to keep your body clean, strong, and healthy and you are not to take into it things that weaken and destroy it. Look at the fun you miss!" So the pusher comes and you take pot, and the liquor dealer comes and you drink liquid pot. Then the house of the Lord is debauched. Does God follow it with a judgment? Inevitably, as certain as the sun shines, as certain as God lives, there is a following judgment when we do violence to the house of the Spirit of the Lord.

Dr. W. F. Powell, when he was pastor of the First Baptist Church of Nashville, Tennessee, called me one day and said: "I am sending to you a young man by the name of John Clifford who is the most promising young preacher I have ever seen in my life. He has just held a revival meeting for us at the First Church of Nashville and God has poured out His Spirit upon the meeting. I am sending him to you."

John Clifford came to see me and I was amazed. He was one of the handsomest young men I ever saw. He was about six feet four inches tall and had beautiful curly hair. He was a magnificent specimen, and he was a man of God. I said to him, "We shall arrange for your coming here to the First Baptist Church in Dallas and to lead our people in a glorious revival meeting."

He came. Some time later, unknown to me, he was seated at the back of the auditorium. After the service was over, when everyone had left, one of the most desheveled, dirty-looking, unkempt men I ever saw came and spoke to me. He said, "Pastor, do you know who I am?" I answered, "No, I never saw you before." He said, "I am John Clifford." He died a young man, diseased, and in delirium tremens from alcohol. Being careless with our bodies is a way of agony, judgment, and death.

Satan Encourages Dishonesty

What does God say about being honest? The ninth commandment says that we are not to lie; we are not to bear false witness. Paul wrote, "Provide things honest in the sight of all men" (Rom. 12:17b). In Acts 6 the qualifications for a deacon are presented, and the first one is that he be of honest report, a man of integrity. Again evil spirits of Satan come to us and say: "Ha, tell the truth? Why, if it is to your advantage, anywhere, anytime, to deceive and lie to advantage, do it; you gain by it!" Then the judgment and the agony always follows.

A rich man, whom God had blessed, had a brother who was a poor construction worker. The rich brother said to his poor brother, "I want you to build me a house and I want you to make it the finest that money can buy—spacious, large, and beautiful." The poor brother was delighted, so he started to build the house that his rich brother had requested. But he said to himself, "This is a chance for me to make money." So he took out of the foundation the good material that should have gone into it and he put in a cheap foundation and put the difference in the money in his pocket. Instead of placing fine lumber in the building, he used cheaper lumber and pocketed the difference. Instead of installing superior plumbing in the house, he chose cheaper plumbing. Throughout the house he used cheaper materials to deceive his own brother.

When the house was finished, his rich brother came to him and said, "Let us go see the beautiful house." They stood and looked at it and the rich brother said to his poor brother: "Brother, it is yours. This is a gift of my heart to you."

That is as true a parable of life as I know. The man who cheats, deceives, and lies destroys himself. God sees to that.

In my first pastorate I had a young man who was marvelously converted. His wife was already in the church, but was not a Christian. The young man had been very worldly and compromising, and was a representative of a large company, but he had been wonderfully saved.

After he had been a Christian about four or five months he came to see me and said: "I do not know what to do. Since I have become a Christian, all of those things that I did before do not seem right to me and I have quit them. It does not seem right to me to gamble at poker or to drink with my clients. But now I have lost my customers because they do not like me anymore. Since I do not drink with them, they do not want to talk to me or buy from me anymore. I am becoming destitute and I do not know where to turn or what to do." I said to him: "My friend, if God does not do some great and marvelous thing for you, He does not live. If you live as a Christian and God does not do something wonderful for you, then there is no blessing in the Christian way of life."

The months passed, and one day that young fellow came back to me and said: "Pastor, God has done a miraculous thing for me. It became known that I was a child of God, that I belonged to the church. My customers said one to the other: 'He is a Christian; he will tell you the truth; you can count on what he says; his word is his bond; he will not misrepresent what he sells.' They began to send for me and to call for me because they knew I would tell them the truth. Now I have more business that I know what to do with. God has wonderfully blessed me and helped me."

THE JOYFUL WAY AND THE CHURCH

Fourth, let us apply the joyful way to the church. What does God say about His church? Ephesians 5:25 reveals to us that Christ "loved the church, and gave himself for it." Hebrews 10:25 admonishes us that we are not to forsake the assembling of ourselves together. Isaiah 30:21 quotes the Lord as saying, "This is the way; walk ye in it."

Unclean spirits now attack the Word of the Lord and scornfully ask, "Did God say *that?*" The spirits of deception point to the boat, to the lodge, to the car, to the open road, and we are soon enticed to forget the Lord's day and the Lord's house and to make the day of worship not a holy day but a holiday. We become convinced that it is a waste of time to go to church, so our children grow up worldly-minded. But in church there is manna from heaven to feed our souls. There is water of life for our thirsting spirits. If I don't eat and if I don't drink, my soul shrivels and dies. The children grow up without the knowledge of the Lord and the fullness of His Spirit in their hearts.

O God, how I thank You that I grew up in a home in which every Sunday was a sacred day with us. We put on our finest clothes (even though we were poor), the best we had, and we appeared before the Lord every Sunday.

There is no joy like spiritual joy, no happiness like godly happiness, and no uplift in the human heart like that experienced in the house of Jesus. This is the happy way, this is the heavenly way, this is God's way; walk in it. His way finally leads straight into the gates of glory, down the golden streets to the throne of God's own holy and heavenly presence. Do not let these minions of Satan rob you of the dearest life in the world, of being happy in the Lord. Build your house upon the rock, upon Christ, and see it stand forever!

38

Receiving the Holy Spirit

> Now when the apostles which were at Jerusalem heard that Samaria had received the word of God, they sent unto them Peter and John:
>
> Who, when they were come down, prayed for them, that they might receive the Holy Ghost:
>
> (For as yet he was fallen upon none of them: only they were baptized in the name of the Lord Jesus.)
>
> Then laid they their hands on them, and they received the Holy Ghost. (Acts 8:14-17)

This passage in Acts 8 is one of the most difficult of all the passages one will ever read in the Bible, but it contains a marvelous, precious, and beautiful message.

THE NARRATIVE

The story briefly is this: In the persecution of the church in Jerusalem that arose around the martyrdom of Stephen, we see Saul making havoc of the church. As a result the Christians were scattered abroad, and as they went everywhere, they witnessed to the grace of God in Christ Jesus. They preached the Word. Then a deacon-layman, named Philip, went down to a city in Samaria to preach Christ unto the Samaritans, who were half-Jewish. With one accord they turned to the Lord, they accepted Him as their Savior, and were baptized in the name of the Lord Jesus. When tidings of the conversion of the Samaritans to Christianity reached the ears of the church at Jerusalem, they were astonished and amazed. The despised and outcast Samaritans believed the gospel and received the Word of truth preached by Philip. Even John had said to the Lord when a city in Samaria had not received him, "Lord, let me call fire down from heaven and consume them even as Elijah did in years gone by." An amazing turn of events had happened, for these Samaritans received the Word of God and had been baptized.

So the astonished church at Jerusalem sent Peter and John to Samaria to see what happened. They rejoiced in the open heart of the despised, outcast Samaritans because they had turned and received Jesus as their Savior. But they had not received the Holy Spirit. He had come upon none of them. They had just believed in the gospel and been baptized. So Peter and John prayed and laid their hands upon the heads of the Samaritans who had accepted the Lord, and when they did so, the Holy Spirit was poured out on them. What an amazing event! How does one interpret and explain it? Out of a multitude of interpretations, I choose five to summarize briefly.

The Many and Various Interpretations

One interpretation is that of the Roman church which says the passage teaches the superiority of the bishops over the pastors, and especially do they emphasize the primacy of Peter.

The Anglican church, the Church of England, says that the passage illustrates the validity of ordination. Only in the laying on of hands of the apostles and their successors is there validity of ordination. All other ordinations are of men. The only valid ordination is that of the apostles and their successors.

The interpretation of the passage by practically all of the liturgical churches is that this is the beginning of what they called "confirmation." In their churches a baby is sprinkled, baptized, christened, and then later on, when the child is twelve or thirteen years of age, he is "confirmed" in the faith. The basis of their doctrine of confirmation is found in this passage.

The Holiness people look upon this passage as an illustration of the second work of grace. The first work would be our regeneration, our salvation, but they say that there is a second work of grace and that is our sanctification, what they call the "second blessing." They use this passage as a definite confirmation of that theological persuasion.

A fifth group of people, the charismatics, say that in the sign of speaking in tongues, the Holy Spirit enters into the individual life. There is no speaking of tongues here, but they say there must have been just the same. They believe that the sign of speaking in tongues is the sign of the descending of the Holy Spirit into the individual's life.

Men study this passage in the eighth chapter of Acts, and from their study evolve such divergent interpretations. What has happened here? The Samaritans believed, received the Word of God, were baptized in the name of the Lord Jesus, but did not receive the gift of the Holy Spirit until the coming of Peter and John. What was God doing?

I would like to tell you what I believe this passage means.

THE SCRIPTURAL PRESENTATION AND MEANING

One of the observations that we make of the way God works is that He always does His work according to purpose and plan. There is never disorder or chaos in God. God makes the flower according to an exact plan. He makes the butterfly according to a precise specification. I think of the billions of snowflakes that have fallen in the earth, and every one of them is made according to a meticulous and beautiful plan of the Lord. Even the planets that swing in their orbits through the universe move according to a definite plan of God.

Whenever one reads the Book of God in nature or in revelation, he finds the same. What He does He does according to a set plan. In our passage of Scripture we have come to a change of dispensations. We have come to a new era and a new age and God is moving according to a foreordained and preannounced plan.

Let us look for a moment at the change in dispensations. In Matthew 10 we read how the Lord chose His twelve apostles. Beginning at verse 5 we read:

> These twelve Jesus sent forth, and commanded them, saying, Go not into the way of the Gentiles, and into any city of the Samaritans enter ye not:
> But go rather to the lost sheep of the house of Israel.
> And as ye go, preach, saying, The kingdom of heaven is at hand (vv. 5-7)

The Lord's word is plain. "Do not go to the Gentiles and do not go into any city of the Samaritans, but go only to the Jew, to Israel." That is the old dispensation.

In Acts 1:8 we come to a new era, a new dispensation, "But ye shall receive power, after that the Holy Ghost is come upon you: and ye shall be witnesses unto me both in Jerusalem, and in all Judaea, and in Samaria, and unto the uttermost part of the earth." This begins a new dispensation, a new age. The Book of Acts is a book of introduction to the new dispensation. It is a book of transition from the Jew to the Gentile, from Judaism to Christianity, from Judaea to the uttermost parts of the earth, and from law to grace. If one does not study the Bible according to its dispensational truth, he will never understand it, and the Bible will become a chaotic conglomerate to him.

For example, in the old dispensation, in the Old Testament, whenever a person sinned, he was to take a bullock, or a lamb, or if he was poor, a turtle dove, or a pigeon, and he was to come before the Lord and sacrifice its blood and make expiation and atonement for his sins. But we do not live in that dispensation. We do not live in that age and that government. We live in the age and dispensation of the atoning sacrifice of Christ who was once offered for the sacrifice of sin, and to those who look for Him, He will appear the second time apart from sin to salvation. We take our sins now and plead the blood of Jesus and He makes expiation, propitiation, and atonement for us; and we are forgiven in His suffering, in His blood, and in His cross. We live in this age. When we read the Bible we must always remember the age, the government, the dispensation in which God said what He did.

So in the old dispensation it was: "You are not to go to the Samaritan and you are not to go to the Gentiles, preaching the kingdom of heaven. Go only to the Jew, to the lost sheep of the house of Israel." But now we see a new day, a new dispensation, revealed here in the Book of Acts.

Whenever God moves, He moves purposefully. He moves according to a plan, a foreordained and revealed outline. And God always moves; He never stays. His creation is followed by redemption. His redemption is followed by sanctification. His sanctification is followed by glorification. God is moving in the story of our text.

God also uses a foreordained plan in moving from the old covenant to the new covenant. He announced His plan to Peter in the passage in the sixteenth chapter of Matthew:

> And I say also unto thee, That thou art Peter, and upon this rock I will build my church; and the gates of hell shall not prevail against it.
> And I will give unto thee the keys of the kingdom of heaven: and whatsoever thou shalt bind on earth shall be bound in heaven: and whatsoever thou shalt loose on earth shall be loosed in heaven. (vv. 18-19)

God is saying: "Peter, I give to you the keys of the kingdom, and when you act according to My will and purpose, the door that you open shall have been the door that by sovereign, elective purpose was to be opened in heaven, and the door that you close shall have been closed according to My elective Purpose in heaven. I give to you, Simon, the keys of the kingdom."

In Matthew 18 God said that same thing to the apostles, "Verily I say unto you, Whatsoever ye shall bind on earth shall be bound in heaven: and whatsoever ye shall loose on earth shall be loosed in heaven" (v. 18). This was given to both Peter and the apostles. The keys of the kingdom were not given to Philip, the deacon-layman. They were not given to the seven in Jerusalem. They were not given to Saul of Tarsus who later became Paul the apostle. The keys of the kingdom to open the door of the new age and the new dispensation of grace and the Holy Spirit were given to Peter, to the apostles, and to them alone.

So, in the Book of Acts, the book of transition which enters into a new era and a new dispensation, look how the Lord divides these ethnic groups. "Ye shall receive power, after that the Holy Ghost is come upon you: and ye shall be witnesses unto me both in Jerusalem, and in all Judaea [the Jew], and in Samaria [the half-breed Jew], and unto the uttermost part of the earth [the Gentiles]" (Acts 1:8). How does one get the word "both" to apply to Jerusalem, Judaea, Samaria, and the uttermost parts of the earth? "Both" always refers to two, never to three, never to four as it is here. What did the Lord mean when He said "*both* in Jerusalem, in all Judaea, and in Samaria, and unto the uttermost part of the earth"?

The word is surely "both" in Greek. *Te* is a conjuctive annexation, it is a conjunctive of addition. So the Lord in the passage says, "You are to be My witnesses in the new age of the Holy Spirit *both* in Jerusalem and in Judaea." He puts them together as one. Jerusalem and Judaea refer to the ethnic group of the Jew. "And in Samaria," to the half-breed Jew. The third ethnic group is "and to the uttermost part of the earth," the Gentiles. When one turns to the Book of Acts he sees that God has done exactly what He announced. The opening of the new dispensation, the keys of the kingdom of heaven, this new age of the Holy Spirit and the grace of Jesus, is given to Peter and to the apostles. According to the Word of the Lord, they opened those doors exactly as God outlined.

First, to the Jew in Jerusalem and Judaea; second, to the Samaritans in Samaria; and third, to the Gentiles to the ends of the earth. As one goes through the Book of Acts following this outline, plan, and purpose of the Lord, he finds it exactly as God said it would be.

In Acts 2, Peter uses the keys of the kingdom for the first time and he addresses that pentecostal audience in exactly this way. He says, "Ye men of Jueaea, and all ye that dwell at Jerusalem," using the keys of the kingdom and opening the new dispensation for the Jew.

Second, the Lord said "and in Samaria." When we turn to the eighth chapter of Acts we find Philip, a deacon and a layman who is preaching the gospel of the grace of God in Christ Jesus to the Samaritans.

But the Lord had said, "It is Peter and the apostles who are to use the keys of the kingdom and open the new dispensation for the Samaritans." So it was only when Simon Peter and his friend John went down to Samaria that the Samaritans received the Holy Spirit. This is the second time the keys of the kingdom were used by Peter, and the new dispensation of grace and the fullness of the Spirit were granted to the Samaritans through the hands and the praying of Peter.

But there is another ethnic group, not only "to the Jew in Jerusalem and Judaea," and not only "to the Samaritans," but God said, "and to the uttermost part of the earth," to the Gentiles. We read in Acts 10 and 11 that God had sent Simon Peter: "I give unto thee the keys of the kingdom of heaven, and whatsoever thou shalt bind on earth [the doors that you close on earth] shall have been closed in heaven; whatsoever you open on earth shall have been opened in heaven." And Peter uses the keys of the kingdom of heaven the third time and the new dispensation is opened for the Gentiles. The angel tells Cornelius, a Roman centurion, to send to Joppa for Peter who will bring the message of salvation to his Gentile household. This same Philip of Acts 8 lived just across the way from Cornelius in Caesarea. Why did the angel not tell Cornelius to invite Philip to open the door to the Gentiles? Because God ordained that the new dispensation for the Gentiles should be introduced by Peter, not by Philip or any other. The Holy Spirit came upon the household of Cornelius in the preaching of the message by Peter.

God is following that program, that outline, and that purpose meticulously as He said in His Book. Just as God makes everything according to a plan, so God introduced His dispensation according to a plan, and the plan was placed by God into the hands of Peter. This glorious opening of the new dispensation was to be made first to the Jew, where we find the pentecostal Jerusalem; second, to the Samaritan, and there occurred the pentecost of Samaria; and third, to the Gentiles, and Peter opened the door according to the will and purpose of God to the whole Gentile world, and that includes us.

THE TRANSITION MADE, NOW WE HAVE THE HOLY SPIRIT

These are the purposes of grace as the Lord worked them out in this beautiful, incomparable book called the Book of Acts. Now we have the Holy Spirit without measure. No longer do we go back to that transitional period. It would be strange to have the beginning again and again. The transition has been made from law to grace, from Judaism to Christianity, and from Jerusalem to the Gentiles and the ends of the earth. The keys of the kingdom have been used by Peter, the door is open, and the Holy Spirit has been given in all of His fullness. It is just for us to possess Him and for Him to possess us.

We may ask that if that is true, what does it mean in Acts 19:2 where Paul said to the twelve disciples at Ephesus, "Have ye received the Holy Ghost since ye believed?" That seems to negate what I said about the new dispensation being introduced by Peter, and yet the apostle Paul asked these men who were supposed to have been baptized into the faith, "Have ye received the Holy Ghost since ye believed?" Is this a second work of grace?

No, for the Greek word that is used is an aorist verb, *pisteusantes*, and the exact translation of the passage is, "Did you receive the Holy Spirit *when* you believed?"

They had never heard of the Holy Spirit so they were not genuine converts. Then Paul preached the gospel to them and they were marvelously saved, and upon their salvation, upon their repentance and acceptance of Christ, they were filled with the Holy Spirit of God, which had already been introduced to the Gentiles by Peter.

In the fifteenth chapter of Acts we read that the first Jerusalem conference was held. They discussed the Gentiles who came into the Christian faith without being Jews. The Gentile converts did not observe the Mosaic legislation, they were not circumcised, and they were heathen Gentiles who came directly into the faith out of their Greek idolatry. Look at the passage:

> And when there had been much disputing, Peter rose up, and said unto them, Men and brethren, ye know how that a good while ago God made choice among us, that the Gentiles by my mouth should hear the word of the gospel, and believe.
> And God, which knoweth the hearts, bare them witness, giving them the Holy Ghost, even as he did unto us. (Acts 15:7-8)

Do you see what Peter said? God chose him out of everyone on earth to be the instrument through whom the new dispensation should be introduced to the world.

RECEIVING THE HOLY SPIRIT TODAY

What is it to receive the Holy Spirit of God? I am convinced that we receive the Holy Spirit when we receive Jesus in our hearts. The great message of the gospel now is summarized in Acts 2:38. When Peter was asked, "What shall we do?" he replied, "Repent, and be baptized every one of you in the name of Jesus Christ *eis* (the Greek word) [because] of the remission of sins, and ye shall receive the gift of the Holy Ghost." Now we receive the gift of the Holy Spirit when we turn and when we believe. When we receive the Lord Jesus, His Spirit comes into our hearts. When we accept the Lord, we have all of Him. He is a person. The Spirit of Jesus and Jesus are one. So when I receive Him, I receive all of Him.

The only problem is that He does not have all of me. The problem is not in the Lord; it is in me. I keep back from Him and reserve from Him areas of my life and secret chambers of my heart. I deny Him access into those secret areas and I deny Him possession of certain things in my life, but when I yield to the Holy Spirit, I receive a blessing. When I yield further, I receive a second blessing, and when I yield still further, I receive a third blessing, and when I yield still more, I receive a fourth blessing and a fifth and a sixth and a seventh and an eighth and an ad infinitum of God's goodness and glory. I am filled with the Holy Spirit as I give my life to Him and yield Him my members, my thoughts, my mind, my heart, and my way. It is like the saying that we so often quote, "That there might be less and less of me, and more and more of God until there is nothing of me and everything of the Lord." What a wonderful way to live—more and more the Holy Spirit guiding us, leading us, and possessing us in our life and in our work.

Do you have a business? Let God be a partner with you in it. Turn its decisions over to the Holy Spirit. He is yours without measure and God will work with you and guide you in your business.

Do you have children? Are there little ones growing up in your home? Let God guide you in their direction and in their teaching. Give them to the Spirit of Jesus and let the Lord possess them. Let the Spirit of God in infinite wisdom and presence help you make the decisions concerning your children.

Do you have trouble and turmoil in your life? Take it to the Lord. Let Him give you the peace that passes understanding.

Are you sick? Are you crushed because of a disastrous illness? Take it to God. Let the Holy Spirit speak to you and let Him heal, or let Him use the illness, the tragedy, and the sorrow for His glory. There is nothing in life that the Holy Spirit cannot sanctify, hallow, and bless if we will just leave it in His care. "Lord, possess my heart, possess my life, and possess my downsitting and my uprising. Possess my walking, my coming, and my going out. Bless the work of my hands. O Jesus, come into my soul."

When the Lord comes into your soul, there is a blessing, there is a fullness of the Spirit of wisdom, counsel, guidance, strength, comfort, and healing.

This is the dispensation in which we live. This is the age in which God has cast our life and lot and it was introduced to us in the Book of Acts as Peter used the keys of the kingdom in Jerusalem for the Jew, in Samaria for the Samaritans, and in Caesarea for the Gentiles who inhabit the ends of the earth.

39

Simony in the Sanctuary

But there was a certain man, called Simon, which beforetime in the same city used sorcery, and bewitched the people of Samaria, giving out that himself was some great one:

To whom they all gave heed, from the least to the greatest, saying, This man is the great power of God.

And to him they had regard, because that of long time he had bewitched them with sorceries.

But when they believed Philip preaching the things concerning the kingdom of God, and the name of Jesus Christ, they were baptized, both men and women.

Then Simon himself believed also: and when he was baptized, he continued with Philip, and wondered, beholding the miracles and signs which were done.

And when Simon saw that through laying on of the apostles' hands the Holy Ghost was given, he offered them money,

Saying, Give me also this power, that on whomsoever I lay hands, he may receive the Holy Ghost.

But Peter said unto him, Thy money perish with thee, because thou hast thought that the gift of God may be purchased with money.

Thou hast neither part nor lot in this matter: for thy heart is not right in the sight of God.

Repent therefore of this thy wickedness, and pray God, if perhaps the thought of thine heart may be forgiven thee.

For I perceive that thou art in the gall of bitterness, and in the bond of iniquity.

Then answered Simon, and said, Pray ye to the Lord for me, that none of these things which ye have spoken come upon me. (Acts 8:9-13, 18-24)

In this passage of Scripture we meet Simon the sorcerer. We're surprised how extensive a roll this man plays in postapostolic Christian literature. In the writings of the Apocrypha of the New Testament and in the writings of the church fathers, Simon plays a most impressive part.

267

He appears in Justin Martyr's *Apology*; in Irenaeus' great work, *Against Heresies*, in which he is thought to be the founder of Gnosticism; he appears in the *Acts of Peter*, and especially in the pseudo-Clementine *Recognitions and Homilies*.

Here are some of the fantastic fables concerning Simon Magus: he was born at Gittom, in Samaria. He was educated at Alexandria where he picked up the language of a mystic gnosticism from Dositheus. He was for a short time, so it has been said, a disciple of John the Baptist. He murdered a boy so that the soul of his victim might become his familiar spirit, and might give him insight into the future. He had as a companion a prostitute of great beauty by the name of Helena, whom he represented as the incarnation of the Wisdom and Thought of God, and the mother of all angelic orders. He identified himself as the promised Paraclete and the Christ, and took the name of "He who stands," indicating his divine power. He boasted that he could turn himself and others into brute beasts, and also that he could cause statues to speak. His life was one of ostentatious luxury. He was accompanied by the two sons of the Syrophoenician woman of Mark 7:26. After this episode in Acts 8, he went down to Caesarea and Peter was sent there by James, pastor of the church in Jerusalem, to confront him and to hold disputations with him on various forms of doctrine. From Caesarea he made his way to Tyre and Tripoli and from there to Rome, and there was worshiped by his followers. Justin Martyr writes that he saw there an altar dedicated to Simon Magus. Peter followed him to Rome, and in the reign of Claudius the two engaged in doctrinal confrontations in the imperial city. Hippolytus and Epiphanius write of the extravagant claims of Simon, and Jerome quotes him as saying: "I am the Word of God, I am the Comforter, I am the Almighty, I am all there is of God." Simon Magus evolved his own trinitarian formula. He revealed himself in Samaria as the Father Jehovah Almighty; among the Jews he revealed himself as the Son; and among the Gentiles he revealed himself as the Holy Spirit.

Withal, Simon is portrayed in postapostolic literature as the heretic of all heretics. Eusebius, the great Christian historian, in his ecclesiatical history sums it up by declaring Simon Magus to be the author of all heresy.

How did he die? One account found in "The Apostolic Constitutions" says that he offered to prove his divinity by flying in the air, trusting that the demons would support him, but that, through the power of the prayer of Peter, the demons he employed failed him. He fell, all his bones were broken, and thereupon he committed suicide.

If you visit St. Peter's Basilica in Rome, you will see a large painting of Simon Magus falling to death upon the prayers of Peter.

Another account of Irenaeus says that Simon Magus was buried alive at his own request in order that he might show his power by rising on the third day from the dead, and so met his death.

That is just a little of all the fantastic, fabulous fables that have been written about Simon Magus. We see an interesting development in the passage before us. Such a disposition lingers throughout the history of the church, and the word simony, named after Simon Magus, refers to the desire to buy the presence of the Holy Spirit with money.

SIMON'S ECLIPSE IN THE PREACHING OF THE GOSPEL

First, we are going to look at the eclipse of the preaching of Simon Magus. He had a vast influence, Luke says, over the small and the great. He had a vast influence over all Samaria. He presented himself as the great power of God and the entire nation was bewitched by him. So Philip went down to Samaria to preach the gospel and he ignored Simon Magus. Philip just proclaimed the truth of Christ.

Is that not a lesson for us? We should not send out missionaries to argue with infidels, and Christianity is under no obligation to go to Samaria to do battle with Simon Magus. Philip went down to Samaria and paid no attention to Simon Magus whatsoever and just declared the truth of God in Christ Jesus. The record says that he preached the gospel and the hand of the Lord was with him, and as he preached, God visited the Samaritans with a great revival.

Is not that just as it ought to be? Philip's gospel superseded that of Simon Magus, who preached himself and presented himself as a great power of God. But Philip, this deacon-evangelist-layman just preached Jesus, and Simon was eclipsed by the truth of God revealed in our Lord.

That is always true. To do otherwise would be as foolish as a light bulb arguing with the sun as to who was going to rule the light of the world. The sun continues to shine, but a little light will flicker and finally go out. So it is with the message of the preaching of the Son of God. Just declare it! Do not worry about an infidel, an agnostic, a blasphemer, and an unbeliever. Just make known the truth of God in the revelation of the Lord in Christ Jesus, and God will bless it and He will bless you.

SIMON'S ATTEMPT TO COME BACK

Second, we are going to look at the attempt of Simon Magus to come back. Overshadowed and eclipsed as he was by the preaching of Philip, he picked an avenue to come back in order to regain that bewitching sorcery by which he held all Samaria in the palm of his hand. When Peter and John came down from Jerusalem, they prayed, and as they laid their hands upon the heads of the Samaritans, the fullness and the unction of the Holy Spirit came upon those Samaritans. When Simon Magus looked at what had happened, he was overwhelmed by what he saw. He observed that Peter and John waved no magic wand over the people, nor were they dumbstruck, nor did they fall down before the dazzling dignity of these two apostles from Jerusalem. All those two men did was pray and lay their hands upon the heads of the Samaritans and they were infused with the power, wisdom, and glory of the presence of the Lord.

When Simon Magus saw that, he said: "If I could buy that power I would have all these people back in my hands again. Think of the money I could make if I could just have that power!" So he went to Peter and John and said, "I will give you a great sum of money if you will sell to me this power, so that on whom I lay my hands they may receive this gift and presence of the Holy Spirit." And that is simony.

What about that? What about money and what it can buy? Money has a negative value and that is all. There is nothing beyond it. Money has always a negative power, that is, if one does not have money, he does not have what it takes to buy food, shelter, and clothing. But beyond that, money makes no contribution to a man's life at all.

Money will buy luxuries, but it will not buy spiritual power. Money will buy advancement and preferment, but it will not buy the recognition of God. Money will buy sycophantic, fawning favor and accolades, but it will not buy soul-respect. Money will buy libraries, but it will not buy poetic fire or insight or wisdom. Money will buy a prostitute, but it cannot buy love. Money can buy diamonds, but it cannot buy the sparkle and light in the eye. Money can buy pleasure and entertainment, but it cannot buy happiness. Money can buy a suit, but it cannot buy a physique. Money can buy medicine, but it cannot buy health. Money can buy a house, but it cannot buy a home. Money has value only in a negative sense and beyond that it has no contribution to make at all.

So Simon Magus came before Peter and John and asked for spiritual power. That request gave birth to a curse in the church that has continued to this present day, and that is seeking to buy spiritual power and spiritual preferment with money.

Peter was horrified at the offer and he said:

Thy money perish with thee, because thou hast thought that the gift of God may be purchased with money.

Thou has neither part nor lot in this matter: for thy heart is not right in the sight of God.

Repent therefore of this thy wickedness, and pray God, if perhaps the thought of thine heart may be forgiven thee. (Acts 8:20-22)

SIMONY IN THE CHURCH

The church became a part of the state at the time of Constantine's conversion. Simony was already practiced but it increased in the buying of ecclesiastical office and benefits. A bishop's office could be bought for so much money. The same was true of an archbishop's office, a cardinal's hat, an ecclesiastical living in parishes and in monasteries. Simony finally gave rise to the Reformation when all over Europe indulgences were sold in order to get money to build St. Peter's Cathedral in Rome. Finally, Martin Luther and the rest of those reformers inveighed against it so that out of it came the great Protestant Reformation. Simony, trafficking in spiritual things for money, is a curse.

Is this still being practiced today? I see it on every side. I do not know of a sin that is more common in the house of God than simony, that is, doing what one does because of what he gets out of it. "I am here because I am hired. I am here because I am a member of the staff. I am doing God's work for pay and money, and if I were not paid, I would not be here. If I did not have to, I would not be present." Universally, simony is a sin of the ministry, a sin of the whole Christian world—doing what we do for money.

I was preaching in West Africa and attending a mission. Mission in this case, is a word used to apply to all of the people who work in a nation. We were having a meeting of the mission in one of the cities in West Africa and I was seated by the secretary of our Foreign Mission Board, Dr. Theron Rankin. As I sat by Dr. Rankin, a fine-looking young doctor stood up to give his report for the year. As he gave his report, Dr. Rankin said to me: "I want you to take a good look at that young man. I want to tell you about him."

After the service was over, Dr. Rankin said, "Do you remember that doctor?" I said, "Yes." Dr. Rankin continued, "He was reared in one of the finest families in the eastern United States and he was trained to be a doctor. As he was finishing his medical degree, he was invited to be a member of a clinic in one of the great cities of the eastern seaboard at many thousands of dollars a year, but in the days of his medical training, he felt called of God to be a missionary. He came before me and the board and we appointed him, and you have just heard his report." At that time the salary of a foreign missionary was $1,000 a year. That brilliant young fellow, the son of one of the finest families in America, trained in his medical work, invited at a fabulous salary to become a part of a world-famous clinic, was in West Africa giving his report, and he was receiving a salary of $1,000 a year!

As the days passed, he came to America on his furlough and came to Dallas to see me. I presented him to the church, and when I did I closed with this word, "Dear people, I do not feel worthy to stand in his presence."

God's people are never to be controlled by "What do I get out of it; what is in it for me?" whether it is recognition, accolade, election, preferment, fame, notice, notoriety, advancement, or money. When we work for God it is a work of love and devotion. "I am doing what I am doing because Jesus called me to do it, and if I am not noticed, that will be all right because I am not doing it to be noticed. If I am not elected, I am not serving Jesus for election. If I am not preferred and advanced, I am not serving Jesus for preferment or advancement. I am serving Him for the love of God in my soul."

What wonderful things could happen to Christ's church if everyone in it —pastor, people, and staff—were working for the love of Jesus and would leave the rest to God.

He will not let you down. He will give you twice as much as you ever thought possible. God does not forget us. Trust Him, give your life to Him, work for Him, and He will see you through, lift you up, bless you abundantly. That is God!

40

The Message of Salvation

And the angel of the Lord spake unto Philip, saying, Arise, and go toward the south unto the way that goeth down from Jerusalem unto Gaza, which is desert.

And he arose and went: and, behold, a man of Ethiopia, an eunuch of great authority under Candace queen of the Ethiopians, who had the charge of all her treasure, and had come to Jerusalem for to worship,

Was returning, and sitting in his chariot read Esaias the prophet.

Then the Spirit said unto Philip, Go near, and join thyself to this chariot.

And Philip ran thither to him, and heard him read the prophet Esaias, and said, Understandest thou what thou readest?

And he said, How can I, except some man should guide me? And he desired Philip that he would come up and sit with him.

The place of the scripture which he read was this, He was led as a sheep to the slaughter; and like a lamb dumb before his shearer, so opened he not his mouth:

In his humiliation his judgment was taken away: and who shall declare his generation? for his life is taken from the earth.

And the eunuch answered Philip, and said, I pray thee, of whom speaketh the prophet this? of himself, or of some other man?

Then Philip opened his mouth, and began at the same scripture, and preached unto him Jesus.

And as they went on their way, they came unto a certain water: and the eunuch said, See, here is water: what doth hinder me to be baptized?

And Philip said, If thou believest with all thine heart, thou mayest, And he answered and said, I believe that Jesus Christ is the Son of God.

And he commanded the chariot to stand still: and they went down both into the water, both Philip and the eunuch; and he baptized him.

And when they were come up out of the water, the Spirit of the Lord caught away Philip, that the eunuch saw him no more: and he went on his way rejoicing. (Acts 8:26-39)

We have a marvelous story before us. It is the beginning of the Ethiopian church called the Coptic church. In the story, a sad and pitiful man is introduced. This Ethiopian was a victim of the terrible institution of the Oriental harem with its ever-present eunuch. He was an emasculated man. He was a dry root. He was a withered branch with no hope forever of family, issue, or posterity.

He must have been quite a gifted man, for he had charge of all the treasury of the nation. In England he would have been called the Chancellor of the Exchequer. In the United States we would call him the Secretary of the Treasury. He was a man of great importance and influence.

He must also have been a man with spiritual hunger in his heart. In some way that we do not know, he had been won to the truth of the Scriptures. He had made his way to Jerusalem, there to call upon the name of the true God. He also came into the possession of a precious scroll, the scroll of the prophet Isaiah. Returning to his native land, seated in his chariot, he was reading out loud the Book of Isaiah, and had come to chapter 53.

The Lord in pity extended compassionate grace toward that eunuch. He commanded Philip, a deacon-evangelist, to stand by the road in the desert, knowing that the eunuch would be passing by. Philip walked alongside the chariot and listened to the eunuch read Isaiah. He said, "Do you understand what you are reading?" The eunuch said, "I do not, nor can I, unless someone help me." He invited Philip to sit with him in the chariot. As the driver drove along with the Ethiopian looking at the scroll, he turned to the fifty-third chapter of Isaiah and asked, "Of whom speaketh the prophet this?" It was then that Philip began with the same Scripture and preached Jesus to him. He preached the gospel, the Good News to that lost man. What is the Good News?

The Gospel Message Is Jesus

First, the inspired record says that the Good News of the gospel is Jesus. When we send out a missionary to preach the gospel, what does he preach? When a man stands in the pulpit and preaches the gospel, what does he preach? We have an inspired answer in 1 Corinthians 15 as Paul begins the resurrection chapter like this:

Moreover, brethren, I declare unto you the gospel which I preached unto you. . . .
By which also ye are saved . . . how that Christ died for our sins according to the scriptures;
And that he was buried, and that he rose again the third day according to the scriptures. (vv. 1-4)

The gospel message is Jesus and Jesus only.

The gospel message is Jesus born of a virgin, Jesus ministering to the people, Jesus dying on the cross, Jesus buried in the tomb, Jesus raised from the dead, Jesus ascended into heaven, Jesus at the right hand of God, our mighty Mediator and Intercessor, and Jesus coming again some day for His own. The gospel message is Jesus.

One of the most moving stories I ever heard about Dr. Truett came from a man who had been with him in India. Dr. Truett had been sent on a preaching mission around the world and finally came to the vastly populated subcontinent of India. There he was invited to preach to a state university.

Before he came to the school, he was warned of the reception he would most certainly receive in that hostile environment because of the Brahman influence. The school officials warned: "When you are through preaching, people in the audience will accost you in the message that you have delivered. They will ask you questions that are difficult to answer. They will contradict and interdict everything that you said. Do not be upset or surprised at the reception that you will receive."

Dr. Truett prayed. The time came when he stood before the university to deliver God's message about Jesus. When he had delivered the sermon, he sat down. The president of the school stood behind the platform desk waiting for the vicious contradictions. He waited and there was nothing but a long silence. Finally a Brahman stood up and said to the president, "Sir, we have nothing against the Christ this man has preached."

How much we can say against the church and the people in it. How much criticism, and much of it justly said, against the way we live and do Christ's work in the earth. But it is difficult to find fault with the Son of God. The gospel message is Jesus the Christ.

JESUS IS THE WAY TO BE SAVED

Second, the great plan of salvation is Jesus. Always, and without variation, in the Bible, wherever God tells a man how to be saved, He points to the Lord Jesus. There is no other word, no other Scripture, no other way. The Scriptures are always pointing to Jesus.

A man described for me one time an unusual cathedral he had visited in Europe. He said that at the front of the cathedral was a statue of our Lord Jesus Christ. Then all the way around the great sanctuary there were statues of the patriarchs, prophets, and apostles. He said: "They were arranged like this. Over here would be a statue of Jacob whom God named 'Israel,' pointing to Christ. On the base of the statue would be a word from the Scriptures saying, 'The sceptre shall not depart from Judah, nor a lawgiver from between his feet, until Shiloh come; and to him shall the gathering of the people be' (Gen. 49:10). Then next to him would be a statue of Job pointing to Christ. On the base was the Scripture written, 'I know that my redeemer liveth, and that he shall stand at the latter day upon the earth' (Job 19:25). Next to him the prophet Isaiah, pointing to Christ. 'All we like sheep have gone astray; we have turned every one to his own way; and the LORD hath laid on him the iniquity of us all' (Isa. 53:6-7). Next to him would be the statue of John the Baptist pointing to Christ. 'Behold the Lamb of God, which taketh away the sin of the world' (John 1:29). Next to him, a statue of Simon Peter pointing to Christ. 'To him give all the prophets witness, that through his name we should receive remission of sins' (Acts 10:43). Next to him the apostle Paul pointing to Christ. '[God] hath made him to be sin for us, who knew no sin; that we might be made the righteousness of God in him' (2 Cor. 5:21). Next to him the sainted apostle John pointing to Christ. 'Unto him that loved us, and washed us from our sins in his own blood . . . to him be glory and dominion for ever and ever. Amen' (Rev. 1:5-6)."

What an effective and beautiful portrayal! The whole Word of God points to Jesus. There is no place in the Bible where God tells a man how to be saved but that He points to Jesus.

He came unto his own, and his own received him not.

But as many as received him, to them gave he power to become the sons of God, even to them that believe on his name. (John 1:11-12)

And as Moses lifted up the serpent in the wilderness, even so must the Son of man be lifted up,

That whosoever believeth in him should not perish, but have eternal life. (John 3:14-15)

Believe on the Lord Jesus Christ, and thou shalt be saved. (Acts 16:31)

If thou shalt confess with thy mouth the Lord Jesus, and shalt believe in thine heart that God hath raised him from the dead, thou shalt be saved. (Rom. 10:9)

The great message of the Gospel is always Jesus.

CONVERSION IS THE COMMITMENT OF YOUR LIFE TO JESUS

Third, the great soul-determining act of conversion is the simple response of committing your life and destiny to Jesus.

One time I bowed my head before the Lord and asked Him: "Lord, what is saving faith?" James says the devils believe and tremble. What is it to believe? The Lord answered that prayer with a Scripture in 2 Timothy 1:12: ". . . for I know whom I have believed, and am persuaded that he is able to keep that which I have committed unto him against that day." Believing faith, saving faith, is the committal of your life to Him.

We are to remember that all of life is just like that, a committal of faith. We drive down the highway across one bridge after another. We never get out to look at the support of the bridge because we have faith in the highway department that built it. We drive over the bridge not thinking, just trusting.

A pharmacist gives a man a vial of medicine but he does not know actually what is in the bottle. He trusts the pharmacist, and by faith takes the prescription.

When you ride an airplane, you don't know all the gadgets on the panel of the aircraft. You just sit there, trusting the pilot by faith.

When I was a little boy living on a farm I developed a large abscess on my body. My mother took me, thin, emaciated, and unable to walk, to the nearest large town, which was Trinidad, Colorado. There she placed me in the hospital. My doctor was a Dr. Friedenthal, a Jewish physician. Mother told him all about me and placed me in his hands. That doctor, taking me to the operating room, put me to sleep, and operated. I did not know him, nor did my mother, but seeking someone who could help me be well, she carried me in her arms and trusted that physician.

It was that same mother who, in a revival meeting, turned to me and said with tears, "Son, will you trust Jesus as your Savior today?" That day I trusted Jesus as my Savior. That is what it is to be a Christian. It is the committal of your life to Him. When I die, that same committal will bring peace and assurance to my soul. "Lord Jesus, into Thy hands I commit my soul. Take care of me, Lord, save me." And He will. The great act of conversion is this simple committal of your life in His care and His keeping.

The Entrance Into the Church
Is Through Obedience to the Lord Jesus

The entrance into the church is in obedience to a great commandment of our Lord Jesus. He said, "Go and make disciples of all the people, baptizing them in the name of the triune God, Father, Son, and Holy Spirit." In keeping with that commandment of the blessed Lord, Philip, preaching to the eunuch about Jesus, preached to him about the church, the body of our Lord, and the ordinance of baptism. "For by one Spirit are we all baptized into one body" (1 Cor. 12:13). By that same commandment are we all baptized into the fellowship of the church; baptized by that same Spirit and made a member of the body of Christ.

As they went on their way, the eunuch said: "Look. Here is water. I want to be baptized." Philip said: "If you believe in Jesus as Lord and Savior; if you commit your heart to Him; if you trust the Lord as your only hope in the forgiveness of sins, you may." That is what Philip meant when he replied, "If you believe with all your heart, you may." The Ethiopian replied: "I have trusted Him. I do take the Lord as my Savior. I do commit my life to Him. I want to be baptized." So both of them went down into the water, and Philip buried the eunuch in the likeness of the death of our Savior and raised him in the likeness of the glorious resurrection of our Lord. He was baptized into the fellowship of the church.

We cannot do much for God, but what we can do, let us do. He asked me to be baptized. I can be baptized as the eunuch was baptized, buried and raised, added to the body of our Lord, baptized into the fellowship of His people.

Notice how the beautiful story ends: "The Spirit of the Lord caught away Philip, that the eunuch saw him no more: and he went on his way rejoicing" (Acts 8:39b). The abundant life is always the Christian life. The happy life, the life of assurance, rest, and peace, is always the Christian life. "He went on his way rejoicing."

Oh, bless His name! That is the abundant life, the happy life, the beautiful life, the God-blessed life. Jesus is ours!

41

Philip and the Eunuch

And the angel of the Lord spake unto Philip, saying, Arise, and go toward the south unto the way that goeth down from Jerusalem unto Gaza, which is desert.

And he arose and went: and, behold, a man of Ethiopia, an eunuch of great authority under Candace queen of the Ethiopians, who had the charge of all her treasure, and had come to Jerusalem for to worship,

Was returning, and sitting in his chariot read Esaias the prophet.

Then the Spirit said unto Philip, Go near, and join thyself to this chariot.

And Philip ran thither to him, and heard him read the prophet Esaias, and said, Understandest thou what thou readest?

And he said, How can I, except some man should guide me? And he desired Philip that he would come up and sit with him.

The place of the scripture which he read was this, He was led as a sheep to the slaughter: and like a lamb dumb before his shearer, so opened he not his mouth:

In his humiliation his judgment was taken away: and who shall declare his generation? for his life is taken from the earth.

And the eunuch answered Philip, and said, I pray thee, of whom speaketh the prophet this? of himself, or of some other man?

Then Philip opened his mouth, and began at the same scripture, and preached unto him Jesus.

And as they went on their way, they came unto a certain water: and the eunuch said, See, here is water; what doth hinder me to be baptized? (Acts 8:26-36)

As we have looked at the first eight chapters of the Book of Acts we have seen the ways of God at work. In chapter 8 we saw the tremendous revival that Philip led in a city in Samaria. In the midst of an outpouring of the Holy Spirit countless numbers were born into the kingdom of God. In the midst of the revival an angel of the Lord spoke to Philip and took him away. Not only did the angel take him away from the city and

279

from the revival, but the Spirit of God sent him into the loneliness, stillness, and solitude of the desert, to be alone with nothing but the endless, shifting sand. What a remarkable thought that a man could be on speaking terms with angels. It is also wonderful that Philip obeyed the voice of the messenger of God.

Philip went, not knowing why, as Abraham went out, not knowing where he was going, but obeyed the voice of God. The true servant of the Lord always walks by faith and not by sight.

THE MEETING IN THE DESERT

Philip left the city, left the revival, left the Samaritan believers, and is now standing alone in the midst of a desert waiting for the purpose of God to unfold. But God always has a reason. He has a purpose and a plan. In the center of that desert a statesman of Ethiopia, a eunuch drove by in his chariot with his cortege. God had sent Philip to stand by the side of the road in order to bring a message of salvation to that one man.

That is God's way. He not only cares for the masses and the throngs, but he cares for one person. Out of all the millions of people in the earth, he knows you, he knows your name, he knows all about you, and in compassion God wishes for you the finest and the best that only heaven can afford.

So the Lord sent this evangelist, deacon-layman Philip into the midst of the desert to meet one lone man. We can read about that rendezvous in the desert.

Our story begins with the word "Behold." I can just see the meaning of that exclamation. Philip, standing in the desert, sees an approaching chariot which suddenly appears on the horizon. As Philip looks at the oncoming chariot, he sees that riding in it is evidently a man of great stature and authority. Who is he? What is his name? What is he? What does he do?

In verse 27 we are introduced to that great statesman. He was a eunuch from Ethiopia. One of the attendant evils of the Oriental harem was the ever-present eunuch. This Ethiopian was a victim of that terrible institution, without hope of posterity or family.

He was a eunuch, yet he was a gifted man. He is described as one of great authority under Candace, queen of the Ethiopians. He had charge of all her treasure. He was the most trusted man in that ancient Ethiopian kingdom.

But there was something else about the Ethiopian eunuch that is glorious. He had a heart-hunger for God. Meroë, the capital of ancient Ethiopia in the upper part of the Nile where he lived, was miles away from Jerusalem, but somehow, somewhere, in some way, this man had been won to the true faith of Jehovah God and had come to Jerusalem, as the King James version beautifully states, "for to worship." He was a proselyte of the temple, not of the gate like Cornelius of Caesarea, who was still a Gentile. A proselyte of the gate was someone who embraced the moral codes of Moses, had renounced his heathen gods, and had accepted the moral legislation of Moses but remained a Gentile, a heathen. Not so, this man. He had become a proselyte of the temple. He had renounced his gods, he had embraced the true God Jehovah, and had gone to Jerusalem to call upon His name. Maybe this is one instance of many when he had made that pilgrimage to the holy and heavenly city to worship the Lord God.

Even though he had given his heart to the Lord there was still a searching in his soul, a hunger in his heart. He still was seeking the grace of God in his life. This tells us that religion in its manifestations may, in so many instances, be beautiful, expressive, and inspirational, but it leaves a life desolate, empty, and powerless. The whole world is filled with religion.

One time I was the guest of a wealthy family in Mexico City. They belonged to the state church, but they found it so empty that they were seeking some other avenue to serve God. They attended church only for funerals and weddings.

A long time ago I stood in front of Notre Dame in Paris trying to think through the long history of that marvelous cathedral and house of God. I could think no thoughts at all, because I was pressed on every side by a throng of people who were selling pornographic pictures and literature. However I tried to escape, the sellers followed me around.

On another occasion I stood before one of the most magnificent architectural structures in the world, the Kali Temple in Calcutta, India. Above the main entrance into the temple was a large sign. Did it say, "This Is the House of God"? No. Did it say, "This Is the Gate to Heaven"? No. Did it say, "Enter His Courts With Holiness"? No. Did it say, "Come Unto Me, All Ye That Labor and Are Heavy-Laden"? No. The sign said, "Beware Of Pickpockets"; a den of thieves.

The world today, with all of its manifestations of religions, does not provide an answer for a soul thirsty after God. This eunuch, in the city of

Jerusalem with all of its accouterments of worship, had turned his chariot back home with his heart still hungry, still seeking and searching after God.

In the city of Jerusalem he had found a scroll of the prophet Isaiah. He was sitting in the chariot reading the scroll aloud. The ancient rabbis taught their pupils to read the Bible aloud. As he read the fifty-third chapter of Isaiah, his heart was filled with bewilderment and perplexity. The passage that he read was this:

> All we like sheep have gone astray; we have turned every one to his own way; and the LORD hath laid on him the iniquity of us all.
>
> . . . he is brought as a lamb to the slaughter, and as a sheep before his shearers is dumb, so he openeth not his mouth.
>
> . . . for he was cut off out of the land of the living; for the transgression of my people was he stricken. (vv. 6, 7b, 8b)

Who could this be, and of what does the prophet speak? Is he talking of himself or of someone else?

The Ethiopian eunuch had a virtuous gift from heaven. He was teachable. He was seeking light in order that he might follow it.

There are people everywhere, world without end, who magnify their doubts. They exult in their agnosticism, magnifying their bewilderment. They look with self-proclaimed, judicial superiority on others, who with cheaper and weaker intellects are satisfied with solutions and answers, but not they. They remain unconvinced, agnostic, and unbelieving.

But not the eunuch. With the scroll of the prophet Isaiah of the Old Testament in his hand, he was seeking and searching for an answer from heaven.

There is no such thing as a man who searches for God but that God has an answer for him. If you want to know, God will teach you. "If any man will do his will, he shall know of the doctrine, whether it be of God, or whether I speak of myself" (John 7:17). Anytime a man opens his heart to heaven, God will answer that man with words from above.

And God did so here. As the eunuch read the scroll and his heart searched for an answer from God, the whispered Word from the Spirit of God through Philip spoke: "Join thyself to this chariot."

Is that not God's way? In the exact time, in the exact spot, when that man is searching for an answer from heaven, God has His messenger standing at his side. Somehow the statesman sensed the authority of the stranger and invited him to sit with him in the chariot. As they rode through the desert together, the eunuch turned to the stranger and asked, "Of whom speaketh the prophet this? of himself, or of some other man?" He was asking, Who is this One upon whom all our sins and iniquities are laid? Who is this One by whose stripes we are healed? Who is this Lamb who suffers without a word?

The Delivered Message: "He Preached Jesus"

What is the message? "Then Philip opened his mouth, and began at the same scripture, and preached unto him"—he preached "Jesus" (Acts 8:35). If there were consecrated men in the legislature, on the bench, in the governor's chair, in the cabinet, and in all of the offices of American society, we would have a new day and a new people. "And he preached unto him Jesus."

First, he would speak about sin, that black drop in the human heart. All have sinned and have come short of the glory and the expectation of God. All of us are fallen alike. Then he would speak about the judgment of God upon sin, which is death. God Himself has linked the chain of sin and death together, and no man can ever break it. "The wages of sin is death." "The soul that sins shall die."

Then we can hear Philip tell the Good News of the story of Jesus, the atoning blood of the Lamb of God; that He died for our sins according to the Scripture and was buried. Philip would speak of the glorious resurrection of our Savior, who was raised for our justification, and to those who look for Him the Lord shall come back some day apart from sin in order to take us without blemish, forgiven, and washed to heaven.

Next, we can hear Philip summarize the whole gospel message which is portrayed in the holy, initial ordinance of baptism. We are sinners and we are buried with our Lord in the likeness of His death. We have been saved and washed and now we are raised in the likeness of His resurrection. Philip describes what baptism means—putting on Christ, casting off the old man, raised to a new life in the blessed Jesus—and while Philip is talking to the eunuch, "they come to a certain water," a stream, an oasis, a pool, and the eunuch breaks into the message of Philip and says:

> See, here is water; what doth hinder me to be baptized?
>
> And Philip said, If thou believest with all thine heart, thou mayest, And he answered and said, I believe that Jesus Christ is the Son of God.
>
> And he commanded the chariot to stand still: and they went down both into the water, both Philip and the eunuch; and he baptized him. (Acts 8:36b-38)

One time I had an experience similar to that. There was a man who was so worldly and so far away from the Lord that praying, witnessing, and trying to win him to Jesus were next to impossible. But a great sorrow came into his heart and life that broke him.

One Sunday morning he came in to the service and sat down. After the service was over, and everyone had left, he and I were there alone. He sat down by my side and poured out his heart of the tragedy that overwhelmed him. I said, "Let us kneel down here, pray, and tell God all about it."

While I was praying for that man, he broke in, he took me by the knee, and he shook me. He said: "Preacher, wait a minute, wait a minute! Something has happened in my heart. I have been saved. Jesus has come into my heart!" I said, "Then let us thank God and glorify His name." I baptized him as soon as we filled the baptistry.

What a heavenly joy! A new Christian will rejoice and say: "I have found the Lord. He has forgiven my sins. Washed in the blood of the Lamb, I want to be baptized, raised, and lifted up to walk in newness of life with Him!"

And when they were come up out of the water, the eunuch turned to thank the preacher for what he had done for him, and when he turned, the preacher had disappeared. The Spirit of the Lord had taken Philip away and only Jesus remained.

Sometimes I think of the story of the Transfiguration, the marvel of the iridescense of the light and deity of Christ, shining through the face of Jesus. Then the voice out of the heaven announced, "This is my Son; hear Him!"

When that voice from God the Father sounded, Peter, James and John fell down as though they were dead. The Lord put His hand upon them and spoke to them. When they lifted up their faces, they saw no one but Jesus.

That is what happened to the Ethiopian eunuch. The Spirit of God took away the preacher Philip, and the only one remaining was Jesus. A few moments before, the eunuch had an indispensable need. He had need for a guide. Now he had no need at all. As he went his way in his chariot, he had God's Book in his hand, the Spirit of Jesus in his heart, and that was enough.

As I see him in his chariot going down the way, I figure there were three in the chariot—the eunuch, the driver, and the attendant. But as I look, I see four in the chariot, and the form of the fourth is like the Son of God! "And he went on his way rejoicing." I can see him coming into the gates of Meroë, the ancient capital of Ethiopia, singing and rejoicing in the Lord.

What could be sweeter? I have found the Lord. I have found Him of whom Moses and the prophets spoke. I have found the Savior of my soul. I have found God!

DATE DUE